NEGOTIATING SURVIVAL

ASHLEY JACKSON

Negotiating Survival

*Civilian–Insurgent Relations
in Afghanistan*

OXFORD
UNIVERSITY PRESS

Oxford University Press is a department of the
University of Oxford. It furthers the University's objective
of excellence in research, scholarship, and education
by publishing worldwide.

Oxford New York

Auckland Cape Town Dar es Salaam Hong Kong Karachi
Kuala Lumpur Madrid Melbourne Mexico City Nairobi
New Delhi Shanghai Taipei Toronto

With offices in

Argentina Austria Brazil Chile Czech Republic France Greece
Guatemala Hungary Italy Japan Poland Portugal Singapore
South Korea Switzerland Thailand Turkey Ukraine Vietnam

Oxford is a registered trade mark of Oxford University Press
in the UK and certain other countries.

Published in the United States of America by
Oxford University Press
198 Madison Avenue, New York, NY 10016

Library of Congress Cataloging-in-Publication Data is available

Ashley Jackson.

Negotiating Survival

Civilian Insurgent Relations in Afghanistan

ISBN: 9780197606179

Printed in the United Kingdom by Bell and Bain Ltd, Glasgow

CONTENTS

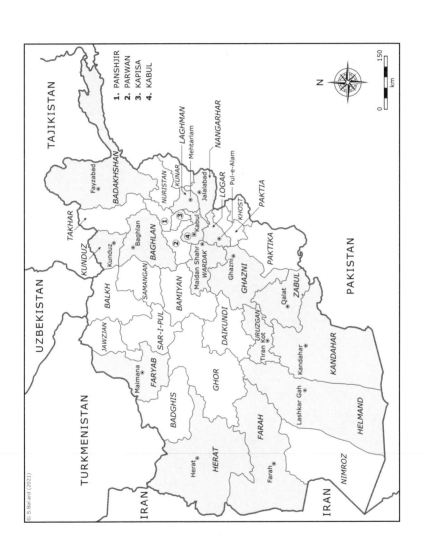

TURKMENISTAN

UZBEKISTAN

TAJIKISTAN

IRAN

IRAN

PAKISTAN

1. PANSHJIR
2. PARWAN
3. KAPISA
4. KABUL

N

0 ————— 150
km

© S.Ballard (2021)

Fayzabad ⊛

BADAKHSHAN

TAKHAR

KUNDUZ

Kunduz ⊛

Baghlan ⊛

BAGHLAN

NURISTAN

KUNAR

LAGHMAN

Mehtarlam

NANGARHAR

Jalalabad ⊛

LOGAR

Pul-e-Alam

KHOST

PAKTIA

① ③
② ④

Kabul ■

Maidan Shahr ⊛

WARDAK

SAMANGAN

SAMANGAN

BAMIYAN

BALKH

JAWZJAN

Maimana ⊛

FARYAB

SAR-I-PUL

GHOR

BADGHIS

HERAT

Herat ⊛

Ghazni ⊛

GHAZNI

PAKTIKA

Qalat ⊛

ZABUL

DAIKUNDI

URUZGAN

Tiran Kot ⊛

Kandahar ⊛

KANDAHAR

Lashkar Gah ⊛

FARAH

Farah ⊛

HELMAND

NIMROZ

ACKNOWLEDGEMENTS

I am deeply indebted to the individuals who agreed to be interviewed and share their experiences, their fears and their hopes for the future. None of this work would have been possible without their willingness to sit with me and talk about their lives. Nor would it have been possible without the expertise and support of my trusted intermediaries, translators and partners in crime, most of whom requested not to be named, due to safety concerns. But among those whom it is all right to credit, Aziz Tassal was a trusted guide and companion in the project. He is one of the bravest, sharpest journalists working in Afghanistan, and I am incredibly grateful that he agreed to help on this journey. His advice, insights and connections were invaluable, and he taught me much about Afghanistan and the war.

I would like to thank a great many other people for their help along the way. Rahmatullah Amiri has been an invaluable friend and research partner, and he has been instrumental in shaping my views on how the Taliban works. Alex Strick van Linschoten's insights and advice were essential from the outset, and his work with Felix Kuehn was an important resource in researching and writing this book. The late Waheed Muzhda talked me through his experiences with the Taliban with nuance, humour and generosity. Bette Dam's Taliban research, advice and viewpoint have been immensely valuable. Adam Pain's consistent encouragement—and the magic of Juby's Farm—convinced me to write this.

My thanks also to Ermina Strutinschi, Maarten Konert, Tomas Muzik, Nic Lee and others at the International NGO Safety Organisation for offering shelter in far-flung places and sound analysis over the years, both of which kept me safe and enriched this work; Kieran Mitton and Mats Berdal for supporting me and my ideas, and providing invaluable input throughout this process; the Danish and Norwegian governments for funding portions of my fieldwork; Sara

ACKNOWLEDGEMENTS

Pantuliano and the Overseas Development Institute for championing my ideas and publishing much of the research underpinning this book; Orzala Ashraf and the Afghanistan Research and Evaluation Unit for supporting the ideas and research that led up to this; and Michael Dwyer and Farhaana Arefin at Hurst, for bringing this book into being.

I also must thank Emilie Cavendish, for slogging through an earlier version and providing sound feedback; Lianne Gutcher, who was there from the beginning, and played Diana Athill at the end; Andrew Quilty and Florian Weigand, for their insights and willingness to share some (mis)adventures; Jessica Donati and Craig Nelson, for providing me with a home, writing advice and a great deal more in Kabul; and Tamar Zalk and Claire Anderson, for providing sanctuary (and, again, much more) in Istanbul.

For all of their advice, support and time, I thank: Lotti Douglas; Jerome Starkey; Jeremy Kelly; Lenny Linke; Zachary Constantino; Natalia Leigh; Sarah Craggs; Annika Schmeding; Adam Pain; Giulia Minoia; Najim Rahim; Tom Peter; Ed Hadley; Per Ilsaas; the brave and charming men of AIP and the Lashkar Gah Press Club; Terje Watterdal, Ian Kaplan, and many others at the Norwegian Afghanistan Committee; Lally Snow; Amita Gill; Shani Harris; Lauren Dawson and family; Amie Ferris-Rotman; Heather Barr; Jim Huylebroek; Johnny Walsh and others at the US Institute of Peace; Jamila Ephron; Ros Boatman; Isabelle Coche and Guillaume de Kleijn; and Tamara Leigh.

And, finally, thank you to Al and Deborah Jackson for giving me space to think and write, and for their unconditional encouragement; Rachel Jackson, for encouraging this book in so many ways; and Magnus Lorentzen for everything, ever since Kunduz.

ABBREVIATIONS AND ACRONYMS

AIHRC	Afghanistan Independent Human Rights Commission
ANSF	Afghan National Security Forces
BPHS	Basic Package of Health Services
DRC	Democratic Republic of Congo
GAM	Gerakan Aceh Merdeka
GIROA	Government of the Islamic Republic of Afghanistan
GDP	Gross Domestic Product
HIG	Hezb-i-Islami Gulbuddin
HIK	Hezb-i-Islami Khalis
IED	Improvised Explosive Device
ISAF	International Security Assistance Force
LTTE	Liberation Tigers of Tamil Eelam
LRA	Lord's Resistance Army
MSF	Médecins Sans Frontières
NLF	Front National de Libération
NATO	North Atlantic Treaty Organisation
PDPA	People's Democratic Party of Afghanistan
PRT	Provincial Reconstruction Team
RS	Operation Resolute Support
SIGAR	Special Inspector General for Afghanistan Reconstruction
UNAMA	UN Assistance Mission in Afghanistan

GLOSSARY

andiwali	camaraderie
hujra	village meeting hall, often used as a school or community gathering place
jihad	striving in the path of Allah
layha	policy; typically translated as 'code of conduct' specifically in reference to the Taliban
madrassa	Islamic school
mahaz	local fighting group
mujahedeen	in general terms, this denotes someone who is or was engaged in jihad; in the Afghan context, it can also specifically refer to Afghans who fought in the 1980s against the Afghan government and the Soviet occupying forces
qawm	network
sharia	Islamic canonical law based on the teachings of the Quran and the Prophet
shura	council
tirana	melodic chants or unaccompanied songs

INTRODUCTION

Haji Aman's village had been the site of a years-long tug of war between pro-government forces and the insurgency. He could not recall precisely how many people had fled or been killed, nor could he recount the precise number of homes or harvests destroyed. There had been moments of calm, but then the violence would begin again. I met Haji Aman during one of these lulls, in the summer of 2017. The Taliban had recently driven out most of the Afghan forces and government officials. Although there was still sporadic violence in the form of the occasional airstrike or raid, the Taliban were now effectively in control. Aman, like many others, was relieved by the relative quiet. 'It doesn't matter who is in control anymore, as long as one side has control and there is no fighting then we are happy,' he told me.

'Happy' was not quite accurate. There was less everyday violence and uncertainty than there had been before, but Taliban control created new problems. Many people were upset about the Taliban's rules and behaviour, and they came to Aman to complain. He had heard a veritable laundry list of objections to the insurgency's conduct: that the Taliban's intelligence officials were both sadistic and corrupt, arresting and beating people who had done nothing wrong; that the insurgents forced poor families to feed them, despite the fact that these families had barely enough food for themselves; that the Taliban had rejected an NGO proposal for a hydroelectric project that would have brought cheap power to the village; that the Taliban had closed all of the schools; and so on.

People complained to Aman because they expected him, as an elder, to do something about the situation. This put Aman in a difficult position. The Taliban had relied on fear and coercion to keep people in line, and they gave no indication they would be receptive to people's demands. Nonetheless, Haji Aman knew he was expected to at least try to speak up for the village. Plus, if he met with the Taliban, he could then go back to the community with their response, and he could at least say he had done his best. And, Aman hoped, the villagers would just maybe complain to him a little less.

Aman arranged, through a village mullah and other connections, to meet several times with local Taliban commanders to discuss the community's concerns. The Taliban were, according to Aman, unsympathetic. They insisted that it was the people's Islamic duty to feed the Taliban fighters. They rejected the NGO hydropower project, claiming that it was an elaborate enemy operation orchestrated by foreigners to infiltrate the village and spy on the Taliban. Haji Aman dropped these issues. Challenging the Taliban's idea of Islamic duty would win him no points, and defending the NGO might create suspicion that he too was allied with the Taliban's enemies. The one issue where he sensed a bit of leeway was the re-opening of schools. When Aman had first raised the issue with local Taliban, they had said the area was too insecure for the schools to re-open. When fighting initially broke out, the Taliban had shut all of the schools in the village and, indeed, in most of the rest of the district. But the situation had since changed. Now that Afghan security forces had abandoned most of their positions and the Taliban controlled much of the area, Aman felt that the Taliban's rationale for keeping schools closed was no longer valid. The Taliban repeatedly claimed they had brought security to the area. If that was true, he argued, why couldn't they open the schools?

Still, it was a complicated issue. Changing the Taliban's mind would only be the first step in a longer process. Aman would first have to find teachers, most of whom had fled the violence. Their replacements would have to be people from the area who were both educated enough to teach and, more importantly, approved by the Taliban. The Taliban would insist on vetting their backgrounds to ensure they could be trusted. Aman would then have to get government support. He would have to travel to the provincial capital, with Taliban approval, to meet the government education ministry. He would need to convince them that the schools could re-open, and he would have to obtain their approval for the replacement teachers. Moreover, he would have to secure their promise that the state would pay for the replacement teachers, as the Taliban surely would not do it. Aman would also need new textbooks and supplies, as the abandoned schools had been looted, some of them down to the windowpanes. What's more, considerable damage had been done to the schools. Some schools had been used as firing positions by either the Taliban or government forces, and would need serious repairs. Even if all of these problems could be solved, Haji Aman feared that many people would be afraid to send their children back to school. They would need not only Taliban permission, but their encouragement to do so.

When Haji Aman met the Taliban again, he presented his plan. The Taliban were initially annoyed that Aman was raising this issue after they'd refused him once before. Haji Aman persisted, albeit carefully. 'I explained that the situation had changed in important ways. Now that they were in control, they would have to provide something for the people,' Haji Aman later told me. 'I told them that the situation was not good. People were angry, and I warned them that I could not predict what those people might do if the situation continued like this. Perhaps it would become unsafe for them if they did not show the people a kinder face.'

The Taliban would have interpreted Haji Aman's suggestion that 'perhaps it would become unsafe' as a subtle threat. In Afghanistan, threats are rarely levelled directly in negotiation. While use of the passive voice and qualifiers like 'perhaps' mute the delivery of one's words, they amplify the underlying sentiment. When I asked Haji Aman whether it was wise to have taken this tack with the Taliban, he replied, 'We do not threaten the Taliban, we only discuss things with them as brothers.' He had a sly grin on his face as he said this, and at this point in the recording of our interview, I caught my translator laughing. This seemed like an incredibly high-risk strategy to me at the time, and I wondered how Haji Aman had overcome the mountain of logistical and resource issues, convinced the Taliban to re-open schools and persuaded the government to go along with all of it.

By the time I met Aman, the Taliban controlled large swathes of the country and had built a parallel bureaucracy replete with governors, courts, tax collectors and even school monitors. Thousands of foreign forces remained in the country, but the Afghan government continued to lose ground. When I first arrived in Afghanistan, nearly a decade earlier, few would have imagined such a scenario was even remotely possible. And yet, the far reach of the Taliban's shadow state was receiving remarkably little attention in the global media. The Afghan War made few appearances on the front pages of Western newspapers, the number of foreign correspondents in the country had dropped dramatically since the drawdown in 2014 and few independent foreign researchers were seriously looking at the Taliban on the ground. Worsening security left the vast majority of diplomats and foreign aid workers largely confined either to their compounds or to Kabul, with less and less understanding of what was happening beyond the capital. Scattered reports in the Afghan media and from local research organisations were the most reliable insights into various aspects of Taliban rule I could find.

Aman's experiences were hardly unique. Civilian bargaining with the insurgency gradually became a fact of life as the conflict worsened. As a former aid worker, I knew first-hand that nearly all of the aid agencies operating in Taliban-controlled areas of Afghanistan relied on elders like Haji Aman to negotiate on their behalf with the Taliban. Telecommunications companies, trucking firms and anyone else who wanted to do business in, or transit through, these areas all engaged in negotiations with the Taliban. These arrangements were rarely talked about openly and were typically referred to euphemistically, given the legal and other consequences of being seen 'talking to the Taliban'. Phrases like 'community support' or 'acceptance' typically served as industry shorthand for when elders like Aman cut deals with the Taliban to run schools, deliver humanitarian relief, pave roads and so on.

Despite an alliance of the world's most powerful militaries and billions of dollars in aid sent to the government of Afghanistan, the Taliban regained control of much of the country. An essential part of understanding the Taliban's once-improbable resurrection and ascent lay in their relationship with civilians. What became clear in my conversations with people like Aman, as well as with members of the insurgency, is that civilians played a critical role in influencing the Taliban's tactical calculus and overarching strategy. Yet I could find little in what has been written about Afghanistan, or in a broader study of its civil war, that captured and explained these dynamics. This book attempts to fill that gap, offering a framework for understanding the civilian–insurgent relationship and how it shaped the course of the Afghan War.

Negotiating for survival

Both civilians and insurgents have been forced to negotiate with each other in order to survive. The Taliban bargains with civilians because they need a nominal level of compliance from the population. At the very least, they must ensure that civilians will not oppose, obstruct or threaten the insurgency. As the Taliban exert influence over a given territory, they must ensure that civilians will follow their rules. While the Taliban can, and often does, use violence and coercion, this is not sufficient in itself. They typically combine that coercion with incentives like the provision of security or protection of goods, services and economic opportunities.

Civilians have considerably less power to wield in these negotiations than insurgents. Indeed, some try to avoid the Taliban for as long as they can, or they flee for government-controlled areas. Few who remain in areas of Taliban influence, however, can keep themselves entirely apart from the insurgency for long. In civil wars, people are, by definition, the prize. Neutrality is nigh on impossible, but it's more complicated than simply picking sides. For civilians, survival is often a question of simultaneously navigating the demands of both the government and insurgency. As the government and insurgency vied for dominance, large swathes of territory flip-flopped repeatedly between pro-government forces and the Taliban. Picking one side invites retaliation from the opposing side, and the conflict has been so long running and so deeply entrenched that few living through it believe there is an end in sight.

Commonly used terms and concepts in the study of civil wars, such as 'collaboration', 'support' or 'taking sides', betray a fundamental misunderstanding of the civilian–insurgent relationship. Listening to civilians themselves describe the situation, the disconnect is impossible to ignore. I remember interviewing a teacher who refused to express an opinion about Taliban rule, despite my best attempts to get him to do so. He kept insisting there were 'no problems' with the Taliban and that he merely did what was needed to keep the school running. Khairullah, a translator and research assistant helping me that day, was clearly amused by my ineffectual prodding. 'You think people have a choice to take sides. He's telling you that the Taliban does not allow there to be any "civilians,"' he said. 'Even if you do not fight with them, you must be on their side.' I was not only asking a dangerous question in pushing the teacher to express a preference, but—worse yet—I had implied that he had much of a choice at all. Once we had all of this out in the open, the teacher was (perhaps unsurprisingly) less reticent to talk about just how complicated it was to run a government school under Taliban control.

The best (or perhaps least bad) course of action is for civilians to leverage what they can—compliance, social connections and so on—to their advantage in bargaining with insurgents. For this to work, they must be deliberate, strategic and creative. They must also be keen conflict analysts because their fate in part depends on how well they can understand and predict what combatants want, what the risks of engaging with them are and the overall dynamics of the war. As in Haji Aman's case, civilians may leverage the promise of their collective compliance or issue subtle threats. They may craft persuasive arguments, which invoke the insurgency's political objectives or ideals, or offer a quid pro quo. This could be intelligence in exchange for access to opportunities, or collective compliance in exchange for a greater degree of community protection.

Civilian–insurgent bargains might have been routine by the time I started my research for this book, but they varied enormously across space and time. Haji Aman was able to secure a deal with the Taliban on schools, but unable to do so on a number of other issues. Why did bargaining dynamics differ so significantly over time? And why have they varied so much across areas of Taliban influence or control, sometimes even differing in neighbouring villages or districts? The answer to this question does not point to a single factor or a straightforward explanation. The short answer is that civilian–insurgent bargaining— like any negotiation—is dynamic, bound by definition to vary according to a range of endogenous and exogenous factors. Negotiations are complex social processes, rooted in the specific context in which they occur and shaped by interpersonal dynamics. Broader conflict dynamics are equally important. Civil war is nothing if not volatile and fluid, and insurgent strategies and behaviour evolve in response to these shifting dynamics. The Taliban (much like any other insurgency) has behaved differently towards civilians when it is under intense military pressure than when it has had the battlefield advantage. Haji Aman raised his requests many times with the Taliban, but his success was partly down to timing: the Taliban had by then assumed firm control of the area, and thus felt obligated to re-open schools (or, at the very least, they probably felt that it was in their interest to do so, now that they were the de facto governing authority).

Alongside this, the character of the insurgency and the ideology it espouses shape the conduct of fighters and their interactions with civilians. The nature and terrain of bargaining with an Islamist nationalist insurgency like the Taliban will likely be different to that of a Marxist or socialist insurgency. Here, understanding the degree to which an insurgency is coherent—meaning that it has relatively clear objectives shared up, down and across the movement, and its adherents are mostly able to act in a unified way to achieve those objectives—is essential. Coherence is often a by-product of maturity, so older insurgencies are more likely than very young ones to be able to bargain consistently and reliably with civilians. In Afghanistan, the Taliban's interests, leverage and range of viable options have dramatically transformed since it emerged as an insurgency in 2002. But even across the terrain they influenced and controlled, the ways in which the Taliban bargains with civilians have varied.

One of the single most important factors influencing this variability is social capital. Those who write about or analyse conflict often talk about combatants and civilians as though they are completely distinct categories. This does not match the lived reality of civil war. Civilians and the Taliban are enmeshed in the same cultural, social and kinship fabric. That civilians are agents within the broader landscape of the conflict gives them leverage. Most people I interviewed knew the Taliban somehow. Some were related to an insurgent by blood or marriage, while some had gone to school with someone who later joined the insurgency. Many used these links, or other forms of common ground, to bargain.

Khairullah was a case in point. He was a university student by the time I met him, but he had acted as a lookout for the Taliban when he was younger and had many friends on both sides of the conflict. His brother was still with the Taliban, and he had many acquaintances on the Taliban side. Khairullah was a born networker, cultivating as many links as he could and using them to protect himself, to help friends and relatives negotiate with the Taliban and, indeed, to help me with the interviews for this book. After four decades of near-continuous armed conflict, many felt that relationships, perhaps above all else, were integral to their survival.

Another problem with the way we talk about civilians is that we tend to lump them all together by default. We define the term 'civilian' as essentially anyone who isn't bearing arms or actively fighting on one side or another, and we disregard the fact that many of them may actually have very little in common beyond this. Instead of talking about civilians as one undifferentiated mass, this book seeks to break them down into three ideal categories, defined by the interests that drive them to engage with the insurgency, and by the power they possess. This way of breaking them down is purely functional, and admittedly imperfect, but it helps to illuminate different patterns of civilian behaviour vis-à-vis the Taliban.

This is elaborated further in Chapter 3, but of the three civilian 'types' this book examines, the first is customary authorities, comprising elders like Aman, as well as village leaders and religious officials. They typically negotiate group interests, meaning that their greatest leverage with the Taliban is that they can deliver—or withhold—the collective compliance of the communities they represent. The second is private organisations, denoting any organised entity, from NGOs and charities to farming associations to international companies. They tend to negotiate in pursuit of their organisational interests, and their greatest leverage is the incentives they can offer (i.e., aid projects, financial payments, services, jobs or other economic opportunities). The final category is the most unwieldy: individuals, or those negotiating with the Taliban on their own behalf, usually in pursuit of survival or other interests. Social position and social capital, which may endow one person with enormous power by virtue of the family or tribe they are born into, are again critical. But so too are less tangible, more individualised (and incidentally less theorisable) qualities like appetite for risk and networking skills.

Objectives and outline

As is likely already evident, I had overlapping objectives in writing this book. The neglect of civilian perspectives and behaviour, in Afghanistan as well as beyond, dangerously impairs our understanding of modern conflict. That combatant behaviour is privileged in the study of war is unsurprising, but the weight of the current imbalance is both intellectually and ethically questionable. More attention to civilian perspectives can help us better understand how and why wars are fought, and they should be better integrated into the study of wars and counterinsurgency theory writ large. My hope is that this work can contribute to a move towards a more productive understanding of how civilian agency influences the conduct and outcome of civil wars.

To that end, Chapter 1 introduces a theoretical framework for understanding civilian–insurgent negotiation. It draws on insights into bargaining dynamics from behavioural economics and sociology to help us better understand how civilians and insurgents interact, and what might drive certain behaviours. This framework was developed specifically to apply to the post-2001 war in Afghanistan, and the basic structure of this theory is adapted to organise analysis on the Taliban and civilians in the later chapters. The idea that parts of this theory might be relevant to other civil war contexts beyond Afghanistan is explored in the Conclusion.

At its heart, this is a book about understanding the war in Afghanistan. The voices of civilians living under the Taliban (and, to some extent, voices from the Taliban as well) are all-too-often absent from contemporary narratives on the Afghan conflict. They have lived through the war, they have witnessed it and they have shaped it. I hope that the empirical work here will be of use to those seeking to understand the Afghanistan war—or, at the very least, that it will stir curiosity and debate. False claims and misunderstandings persist in commonly accepted 'expert' narratives of Afghanistan. These have led to farcical policy decisions with catastrophic consequences, many lives lost on all sides and a war in which the Taliban regained control (as of this writing) of the majority of the country.

I lay little claim to the 'facts' or what 'really went wrong'. Yet, as an outsider who has worked on Afghanistan for the past decade, I have often felt like I'm waiting for a perpetually delayed reckoning with the international community's self-delusion that led to so much seemingly pointless violence. As I write this, the Taliban's return to power looks all but unstoppable. The least any of us can do now is strive for a clearer-eyed understanding of how that came to be. I hope this book modestly contributes to that aim.

Chapter 2 explores the broader social, cultural and political history of Afghanistan. It is by no means a complete overview, but provides enough backstory for readers not well versed on Afghanistan to understand the historical and social context relevant to civilian–insurgent relations. The chapter begins by investigating social relations and the nature of social capital in Afghanistan. It then provides a brief summary of Afghanistan's political conflicts since 1978, with particular focus on the ascent of the post-2001 Taliban insurgency.

Chapters 3 and 4 are the empirical foundation of this book. Chapter 3 explores Taliban attitudes towards and tactics in bargaining with civilians, while Chapter 4 looks at civilian experiences of negotiating with the Taliban. The picture of civilian–insurgent relations that emerges from Chapters 2, 3 and 4 is explored more deeply in Chapter 5. This chapter nuances and integrates the preceding discussion, tackling the questions of why some civilians have been more successful in negotiating with the Taliban than others, and why the Taliban's strategy has varied according to time and place.

Chapter 5 necessarily complicates the more linear and generalised narratives and theories put forth in Chapters 3 and 4, and digs into localised experiences of conflict. The war in the southern province of Helmand, for example, was a different war in many ways from the war in the eastern province of Logar, and so on. These differences tell us a great deal about what drove specific Taliban behaviours and tactics, and consequently what circumstances and attributes gave civilians more or less leverage in dealing with them.

INTRODUCTION

I wrote and structured this book with a mind to making it accessible to different readers. Some might be familiar with Afghanistan and others will not. Some will be more interested in the theoretical grounding, or in interrogating the methodological approach, and they should read directly on from the Introduction. Those explicitly interested in the post-2001 Afghan conflict and the more original aspects of this book might want to skip the methods and theory, and start reading at Chapter 2 on Afghanistan. Or, if they are already familiar with Afghanistan, then they may wish to begin with Chapter 3 on the Taliban.

Methodology and approach

The insights in this book are based on 418 interviews with members of the Taliban and civilians from fifteen of Afghanistan's thirty-four provinces, primarily between July 2017 and February 2019. The people I interviewed included Taliban fighters, commanders, leaders, interlocutors and ex-members; government officials, employees (including teachers and doctors) and aid workers; and civilians who have lived or are currently living under Taliban rule. The lines between combatants and civilians are slippery in real life, so these categories sometimes overlapped: an aid worker could at one point have been a Taliban fighter; a government worker, likely to be seen by the Taliban as a combatant, would be a civilian in my view. Some ex-Taliban acted as interlocutors or helpers, introducing me to civilians and Taliban alike. Some civilians were seen as Taliban 'in their hearts' even if they did not take an active role in the conflict.

Interviewing Taliban fighters and commanders and the civilians living under their control was, to put it mildly, exceedingly difficult. Getting access to Taliban areas and the people who lived in them was a deeply uncertain endeavour, and took up most of my resources and time. Afghanistan is one of the most researched contemporary war contexts, and analysis of the Taliban has been central to recent academic debates over insurgency, terrorism and counterinsurgency. Yet much of this discourse has not been based on direct fieldwork, and it is often difficult to tell how researchers working at a distance have derived and verified the information that substantiates their claims. In academia more broadly, direct engagement with violent armed groups—particularly after

9/11—has typically been discouraged in favour of safer, more easily controllable research designs. These approaches are complementary pieces of the puzzle (and, indeed, I draw on a number of insightful quantitative studies and theoretical works), but working at an arm's length would not have been sufficient to understand life under the Taliban.

Going to see what was happening—or as much of it as I could—was essential. I would have otherwise missed critical details about how life actually worked under the Taliban and the constraints people faced, and I don't think I would have understood the role of fear, anger and pure exhaustion in quite the same way. Exposure, however limited, to the kind of terror and violence people lived with forced me to conceptualise their motives and behaviours differently than I might have done otherwise. I also have a feeling that my physically showing up encouraged certain people to be more open and forthcoming when speaking with me. Of course, some of the people I interviewed with thought I was crazy to have shown up at all, given the risks. But, even then, there was often a bemused curiosity which I suspect worked to my advantage.

This is not to romanticise the research process. Much of it consisted of waiting around for the phone to ring, sweating profusely under my burqa, cursing traffic, revising and re-revising methods and plans, bumping along on unpaved roads, making embarrassing miscalculations and interpersonal faux pas of all sorts, and just generally struggling to talk to the right people and get them to talk to me. Sometimes I could not stay in these areas for more than a night or, as was more often the case, a few hours. Some people travelled to meet me in nearby areas, away from their homes and often in areas of government control, for our mutual protection. Some interviews occurred in fairly anonymous buildings (clinics, private homes, journalist offices) or inside the back of a Corolla as the driver looped around in circles. At times, it simply was not possible to speak directly with those I wished to interview. Twenty-three interviews were conducted remotely (via phone or messaging apps) or by intermediaries, where I was not present.

As I started this research in mid-2017, the most comprehensive, reliable reporting on the Taliban came from Afghan media. Afghan journalists working on these issues were extraordinarily generous with their time and advice, and I ended up working with several across the country. Aziz Tassal became a good friend and guide, whose insights, companionship and introductions were invaluable, and his patience and kindness helped me keep my faith in this project even when it looked impossible. I worked with a number of other reporters throughout the country, as well as teachers, aid workers and others who helped me in their spare time. If I do not properly credit them by name it is out of concern for their own security, or for related reasons. One journalist I worked with in Helmand, Aliyas Dayee, was killed in a targeted assassination while I was finishing the edits for this book. The Taliban denied responsibility, and as of this writing it is not clear who killed him or why. It is unlikely anyone will ever be held accountable for his death, or the deaths of so many others reporting on the war or working on the frontlines.

Given the difficulty of interviewing Taliban fighters and officials, as well as of safely accessing civilians who had negotiated with them, personal networks and connections were essential. One interviewee would often recommend others, who would in turn recommend others. Aid workers might refer me to members of the community who had helped them to negotiate, or Taliban fighters might refer me to fellow fighters. In the very loosest methodological terms, this might be referred to as a snowballing, or chain sampling, technique. I went into these interviews with a list of questions in mind, but rarely stuck to them. I might have detailed questions about how the schools were run, or want to double check something someone else had said, but I typically learned much more when I gave people space to tell the story on their own terms. Usually I would ask them about when the Taliban first came to their village and what happened next, or when they first interacted with the insurgency, and the conversation would flow from there.

The research was subject to changing circumstances, and what I'd initially planned to do bears little resemblance to what I actually ended up doing. (Those uninterested in the deeply nitpicky methodological details may wish to skip ahead at this point.) The plan at the outset was to conduct a case study approach comparing three districts: Charkh district in the eastern province of Logar, Nad Ali district in the southern province of Helmand and Chardara district in the northern province of Kunduz. This design would allow me to explore how dynamics varied across different places and in the same places at different times, in what I thought would be considered a methodologically rigorous way (at least according to prevailing political science standards).

I began to realise, however, that a focus on three districts (in a country with nearly 400 districts) was far too limiting to sustain. Interview subjects and acquaintances regularly challenged my methodological choices in subtle and obvious ways. A man I interviewed from Charkh pointed out that negotiations with the Taliban in neighbouring Baraki Barak district were far more difficult on certain issues. A know-it-all dinner guest at my home in Kabul challenged my observations about the Taliban, rattling off anecdotes from provinces I had not covered. How might my conclusions differ if I widened my scope, and what would that diversity reveal? The benefits of an iterative approach ultimately trumped any desire I had for methodological neatness.

Ultimately, I attempted to have the best of both worlds: I took a comprehensive approach in the three core districts and a lighter, more flexible approach in thirty-two other districts (see Figure I.1). I began interviewing individuals from elsewhere in Helmand, Kunduz and Logar provinces, making sure that I did interviews in as many neighbouring districts as possible. This helped demonstrate how and why things might vary between districts, even between areas that were just a twenty-minute drive away from each other. I ultimately branched out into twelve other provinces. In some districts and provinces, the number and nature of interviews were fairly light, but allowed me to create a basis for comparison on basic conditions, Taliban structures and policies, and civilian–insurgent dynamics.

Other districts involved more in-depth research and repeated engagement, drawing on my previous work in Afghanistan. I had lived in the eastern province of Nangarhar in 2011 while working for the UN, and had travelled to neighbouring Laghman, so I drew on previous knowledge and relationships in these areas. I had travelled back to the east to do research multiple times in the intervening years. My past analysis and pre-existing contacts were invaluable. The western provinces of Faryab and Herat offered a similar opportunity, as I had originally done research in these provinces in 2009–11 and I had returned in early 2019 to look at the Taliban courts. In some ways, this book is the result of thousands of interviews and discussions in various places across Afghanistan over the years.

INTRODUCTION

Figure I.1. Level of coverage by district

Level of Coverage	District and Province
Light Touch Approach, Anecdotal Interviews	Alishang, Laghman; Aqtash, Kunduz; Arghandab, Kandahar; Dahan-i-Ghori, Baghlan; Garmsir, Helmand; Ghoryan, Herat; Gul Tepa, Kunduz; Gulran, Herat; Gurziwan, Faryab; Herat City, Herat; Ishkashim, Badakhshan; Jalalabad, Nangarhar; Kabul, Kabul; Khas Uruzgan, Uruzgan; Kohestan, Faryab; Marja, Helmand; Mohammad Agha, Logar; Pashtun Kot, Faryab; Qalat, Zabul; Rodat, Nangarhar; Sangin, Helmand; Shindand, Herat; Shinkay, Zabul; Shirintagab, Faryab
Substantial Interviews, Field Study and/or Historical Research	Almar, Faryab; Baraki Barak, Logar; Chak, Wardak; Khushk Robat Sangi, Herat; Kwajasabzposh, Faryab; Musa Qala, Helmand; Nawa, Helmand; Saydabad, Wardak; Tala wa Barfak, Baghlan
In-Depth Study	Chardara, Kunduz; Charkh, Logar; Nad Ali, Helmand

I spoke with some people multiple times and tried as much as possible to triangulate information. This was important, albeit time-consuming, as accounts of the same event by different individuals were often contradictory, sometimes in minor ways and sometimes with major discrepancies. On rare occasions, I got lucky and was able to talk to a number of civilians who had all experienced the same event, as well as more than one of the Taliban involved, to hear their side of the story. Often Taliban interlocutors, or someone else giving second-hand accounts of Taliban decision-making, would have to count as a second or third source. But even then, trying to get to the precise 'truth' of what happened and why in a certain incident was often laborious or downright futile.

I'm not sure these dynamics would have differed much even with perfect access to all players involved. People have compelling reasons to express false preferences or give inaccurate accounts in wartime, whether for their own security and protection or out of mercenary self-interest. Some lapses seemed incidental; people misremembered, or mistook widely circulated rumours for fact and recounted them as such. At times, it was only through probing them and my interlocutors that I realised my interviewees had given me inaccurate information. A thornier problem lay in the fact that people simply experience events in different ways, and they interpret those events through a prism of their own experiences, fears and biases. One example relates to a school in Nad Ali, allegedly burnt down by the Taliban. Two other researchers, independently of me and of each other, had previously tried to figure out exactly what had happened: was it the Taliban? And if so, why did they do it? Was it down to jealousy and feuds in the community? Or something else? All three of us talked to many of the same people. Some of them told all three of us the same story and some did not. All three of us walked away with completely different conclusions on what the 'facts' were as to who had set the fire and why.

Figuring out what 'really' happened and why wasn't necessarily as important as understanding why people were telling me a certain story and why they crafted a specific narrative out of the events they had experienced. It helped that we usually had one or more mutual connections who could crosscheck 'facts' and provide background which might explain why they might be saying (or withholding) certain things. There were instances where my translator, frustrated with a key point I was missing or a fact I couldn't have known about, interrupted the interview to make sure I understood what was really going on. There were times where someone concealed an aspect of their identity or lied about something early on in the interview until they felt they could trust me. There were elders who initially concealed links to the Taliban or government, aid workers who at first insisted they did not interact with the insurgency and others who exaggerated and bragged about their closeness to the Taliban. On one occasion, I found myself halfway through an interview with a man introduced as a teacher only for him to tell me that he was actually the school's Taliban education monitor. He lied because he'd heard that I wanted to talk only to teachers, and he thought he'd 'do a better job' explaining the Taliban system because he had 'the whole overview'.[1] While I initially suspected he was trying to slant things in the Taliban's favour, it turned out he was deeply critical of the insurgency's approach. He had ideas about what they should improve, and, knowing that I was then working towards a doctorate, he was eager to talk pedagogy.

Out of these conversations, I slowly began to piece together a bigger picture of life under the Taliban. Chapter 1, which articulates a theory of civilian–insurgent bargaining and frames the subsequent chapters on Afghanistan, is the result. Trying to trace causality led me beyond political science and the study of war, and into negotiation theory. The study of negotiation is a diverse field, encompassing a range of methods and insights from behavioural economics, social psychology, anthropology and social science. I borrowed widely, piecing together something that explained what I saw on the ground. Integrative negotiation theory, pioneered by William Fisher and Roger Ury, was particularly influential (Fisher and Ury, 1991). Beyond this, empirical insights into reciprocity in negotiation, risk tolerance and the role of emotion (so often neglected in the study of war) from a range of works on negotiation were essential to explaining specific dynamics in Afghanistan.

Ethics and security

This work was predictably fraught with ethical dilemmas. The primary concern was keeping everyone—the people I interviewed, the people helping me and myself—safe. The escalating violence across Afghanistan made access consistently unpredictable and required a dynamic understanding of the risks. Much of this was in my case derived from listening to the wisdom and guidance of others. I devoted a great deal of time to building relationships and networking, and on seeking advice. I developed relationships with Afghans with extraordinary connections, and with Afghan and foreign analysts at the UN and NGOs, to better understand the security situation. In particular, I owe a deep debt of gratitude to the International NGO Safety Organisation, a humanitarian NGO focused on understanding security dynamics, for their insights and advice and for hosting me in their field offices, as well as to various people at the UN Assistance Mission to Afghanistan

(UNAMA). I owe an even larger debt of gratitude to the numerous Afghans who shared their own advice, experiences and homes.

Even with access to solid data and reasonable safety precautions, there was typically no one purely 'safe' course of action. My research assistants, interlocutors and I continually discussed ethical and safety concerns, in the context of the research I was doing and why. Above all, I followed their lead on what risks were manageable. I count many of these individuals as friends; at the same time, I was compensating most of them for their help in one way or another, and that created a certain power dynamic. I was keenly aware that, no matter what I said or did, some might still feel some obligation—emotional, financial or otherwise—to help me. I paid attention to physical and non-verbal cues, as well as indirect signalling, which I took as seriously as verbal communication. That said, I probably would not have known what to look for, or pay attention to, had I not spent many years previously living and working in Afghanistan. The implications of offhand remarks, bad dreams and other omens were considered and discussed. In some instances, a nightmare or gut instinct was enough to postpone or cancel a trip or interview. We had a mutual responsibility to respect and look after one another, which tempered any urge I might have had to push for certain things to happen.

It was equally important that the people I interviewed understood who I was and what I wanted, so that they could make an informed choice about whether they wanted to speak with me, under what conditions and what they wanted to share. This was more difficult than it might sound. A foreigner asking questions about the Taliban is bound to raise questions and pose perceived risks. Research of this sort is an abstract idea in rural Afghanistan, and it tends to look a lot like spying. My interlocutors, translators and I explained the purpose of the research in the ways that we believed would make the most sense to the interviewees. We stressed that the interviews could be stopped at any time and issued all of the usual ethical disclaimers. But what seemed more important was to watch for non-verbal cues, make small talk, leave room for silences and create space for the interviewees to direct or redirect my questions in ways that both made them feel safer and kept them engaged.

INTRODUCTION

I promised the people I interviewed, and some of the people and interlocutors I worked with, that I would not reveal their names or any biographical details that could render them identifiable, whether verbally, in conversation with others or in writing. Where I refer to a person interviewed by their first name, it is not their real name. I have given people pseudonyms for the sake of narrative coherence (i.e., it is easier to tell someone's story, or refer back to their comments later, if they have a pseudonym). Well-known or 'public' figures that were directly interviewed are referred to by their first and last name, but only in the very few instances where doing so does not threaten their well-being, reputation or security.

Most people were remarkably magnanimous with their time, open and good humoured in the face of my numerous questions. That wasn't always true, of course. Outsiders, let alone Americans, asking questions about the conflict might reasonably spur any number of reactions. Some people—including men who told me they had been tortured by Americans in Guantanamo or Bagram, and a man whose child had recently been killed in a US airstrike—understandably confronted me, as an American, about my government's policies. This was, however, rarer than I had anticipated.

Much as my nationality might have raised a few people's hackles, my gender often seemed to do the opposite. I acknowledge this begrudgingly, because I cannot recall how many times I was asked by (predominantly male) Western analysts, diplomats and others about how being a woman might have hindered my ability to do this work. This is a question I resent, simply because men are rarely asked to account for how their gender, or how intersectional aspects of their identity, affects their work in the same way. My being female mostly seemed to elicit a greater degree of openness and vulnerability from those I interviewed. Additionally, given Afghanistan's conservative gender norms, a male interviewer would not have been able talk to women to the extent that I did, or about the subjects I did.

There is a long legacy of foreigners misunderstanding Afghanistan (often regardless of what Afghans have tried to tell them), and I fear what I might have gotten wrong or failed to comprehend. A vigilant interrogation of positionality, both mine and that of those I interviewed, and the power dynamics at work in these interactions nonetheless deepened this work in unexpected and important ways. The unfortunate and awkward by-product is that I was necessarily a factor in my own analysis, and so I hope to be forgiven for making a few appearances in what follows, via my use of the first-person voice.

Terminology and concepts

An **insurgency** is an armed movement which uses violence to contest the authority of an established government. In general, insurgencies examined or referenced here seek political legitimacy, in that they (a) desire political recognition and (b) espouse some form of radical political change. Typically, they either aim to overthrow, replace or significantly reform the national governments they are at war with. A common goal is control of territory and the civilian population within that territory.

Civilians are individuals who are not actively, voluntarily or directly participating in wartime acts of violence. 'Civilian' is intentionally defined as broadly as possible. Standard and more formal conceptualisations of civilians, rooted in the laws of war, are limiting in that they often impart the notion of civilians as a neutral and distinct category from combatants. It is hardly ever that simple in reality.

Negotiations are defined as a social process of combining conflicting positions into a non-conflicting one, which is achieved through some form of exchange (Nikolaev, 2007; Zartman, 1989). The idea of negotiations as a *process* is integral to the dynamics explored in this book. In other words, they are not a one-off deal but a socially embedded dynamic of interaction and exchange. **Bargaining** is slightly more tactical in nature, while negotiation is generally used to describe the broader process (and the dynamics therein) of one side attempting to influence the other.

Violence and coercion, persuasion and incentives are treated as forms of leverage within negotiations. Some might argue that the violent nature of an insurgency vis-à-vis the corresponding civilian population negates the possibility of bargaining. Indeed, much negotiation theory defines negotiations as inherently non-violent and non-coercive, with parties entering into negotiation of their own free will (see Lewicki et al., 2010). This book instead argues that violence and coercion do not preclude opportunities for bargaining, they are instead but one strand of leverage among many within civilian–insurgent bargaining dynamics. This is not to underplay the horrific nature of civil war violence, and the deeply asymmetrical nature of wartime bargaining. The idea of **violence-as-leverage** seeks to balance the complexity and the intense pressures civilians must navigate on the one hand, with an analysis of how they exercise their agency within these dynamics on the other. Violence-as-leverage only makes sense if we see insurgent violence as strategic and rational (Arendt, 1970). Insurgents must use violence and coercion tactically vis-à-vis civilians for it to have a strategic impact. This assumption is grounded in various works that have explored how insurgencies use violence to send signals to civilians in order to compel certain behaviours (Boyle, 2009; Hirose et al., 2017; Hoffmann and Verweijen, 2018; Hultman, 2007).

Violence and coercion are often combined with other forms of leverage, such as incentives or persuasion, to pressure or convince civilians to comply with insurgent needs and objectives (and vice versa). In other words, the threat of violence doesn't necessarily stop civilians from negotiating; in fact, the desire to keep oneself safe may actually spur them to try to find ways to influence the insurgency. Additionally, while insurgents have a far greater power to coerce and levy violence than civilians, the power of coercion is also available to civilians, albeit considerably less so (Arjona, 2017; Kalyvas, 2006). Finally, allowing violence and coercion into the negotiation dynamic creates the possibility that civilians can influence the use of insurgent violence and coercion.

Persuasion is a process through which (a) one side attempts to influence the other side's attitudes, beliefs and behaviours, and (b) the other side's attitudes, beliefs and behaviours are formed, modified or recalcitrant in the face of such attempts (Ledgerwood et al., 2006). Because it is so diffuse, persuasion can be difficult to separate from other forms of interaction when applied to real-world examples. On the insurgent side, it can be difficult to delineate from propaganda or psy-ops. Given the intentionally threatening nature of much insurgent communication, it can thus also be difficult to separate persuasion from coercion. If it is too loosely defined, persuasion can bleed together with other forms of leverage so as to be indistinguishable.

Herein, **persuasion-as-leverage** is defined as the arguments, narratives and emotional cues that one side uses to get the other side to agree with its demands. Elements of persuasion can include styles of argumentation, thematic repertoires, rhetorical sequencing and the particular choice of evidence used to support one's claim. It is relational and targeted. Propaganda, for instance can be entirely one-sided, with no reference to whether its intended audience was convinced or took desired action. Persuasion really only constitutes leverage where it has some potential or actual power (i.e., its targets find it credible or convincing, and take action). It may include propaganda or coercion, but it isn't synonymous with either. Persuasion entails the intentional choice of specific discursive and emotional tactics—with a particular objective and rooted in context—geared at getting the other side to do something specific (see Weiss, 2015).

In addition to violence and persuasion, the negotiations framework sets out two further types of leverage. **Incentives** are assets or concessions that are deployed by one side to get the other to change their position. **Incentives-as-leverage** must also be relational and targeted in order to work. **Social capital** is the options and abilities that arise from shared values and social frameworks. Social capital is not just relationships and shared values and cultural context, but rather the new options and abilities that arise from them (Coleman, 1988). **Social capital-as-leverage** could be, for example, gathering information via one's relationships, or the cultural or contextual understanding required to navigate successful negotiations provided by one's upbringing and family ties. Social capital can also facilitate certain strategic action, such as collective bargaining.

1.

NEGOTIATED REBELLION

A THEORY OF CIVILIAN–INSURGENT BARGAINING

Insurgents and counterinsurgents alike have long agreed that the outcome of the wars they wage are heavily influenced by their relationships with the civilian population. Mao Tse-Tung compared guerrillas to fish, and the people to the water in which they swim (Mao, 2011). Che Guevara wrote that guerrilla warfare 'draws its great force from the mass of the people themselves' (Guevara, 2018: 59–61). Pick up nearly any counterinsurgency tome, or a core text on modern civil wars, and you will find that they all agree that an insurgency's relationship with the civilian population is determinative to its success or failure (see, for example, Thompson, 1966; Nagl, 2006; Kalyvas, 2006). Yet there is a paradox here: civilians are rarely constructed as full-fledged or meaningful actors within a conflict. Combatants are actors, and noncombatants are 'acted upon'. Civilians are understood to be mostly passive victims, even where it is argued civilian obedience or support is essential to insurgent survival and victory.

It's a curious contradiction, and part of the problem lies in how we study and write about civil war. The spotlight is almost always cast on those fighting the war, and civilian perspectives have been comparatively neglected. Civilians are stripped of agency both rhetorically and theoretically, and silenced empirically. Civilians come to the fore of analysis when belligerents need them in some way, but even here use of the passive voice is endemic. Civilian loyalty is 'secured' by combatants, their 'hearts and minds' won by one side or the other. Civilians never tip the balance of the contest, and their behaviour is fairly one-dimensional, driven by either survival concerns or naked self-interest (see Kalyvas, 2006; Metelits, 2009). The insurgent–civilian relationship is often constructed as a by-product of insurgent needs or choices (i.e., material endowments, power maximisation strategies, survival concerns) (Christia, 2012; Hovil and Werker, 2005; Lidow, 2011; Salehyan et al., 2014; Weinstein, 2006). Consequently, little on-the-ground, rigorous research has been done to understand what drives civilian behaviour in wartime.[1] After all, it makes little sense for political scientists to study civilians if civilians do not substantially impact combatant conduct or war outcomes.

The neglect of civilian agency is, however, particularly perplexing in the context of post-2001 Afghanistan, where counterinsurgency and stabilisation approaches have sought to win over civilians as a means of undermining the Taliban. To be sure, reams of research have been devoted to understanding the Taliban–civilian relationship, and into developing metrics meant to measure civilian 'support' for the Taliban. But, again, civilians aren't seen as meaningfully influencing the Taliban. They appear passive and one-dimensional, their motives and behaviours curiously uncomplicated. Their loyalty might be secured with aid or compelled through coercion. Despite some recognition of the importance of 'winning Afghan hearts and minds', it appears to have been taken for granted in mainstream policy thinking that civilians have little influence over the Taliban's conduct and strategy.

This chapter seeks to correct that neglect of civilian influence, and outlines an alternative framework for viewing civilian–insurgent relations. The core premise is that civilians and insurgents bargain with one another, and that process of negotiation affects the behaviour of both sides. As in any negotiation, there are three main elements of the civilian–insurgent bargaining process: the interests of each side (why they bargain), the types of leverage they have at their disposal (what they bargain with) and the options and strategies they pursue (how they do it).

NEGOTIATED REBELLION

Towards a theory of civilian–insurgent bargaining

Civilians and insurgents are best thought of as locked in an interdependent relationship. Insurgents need civilians to comply with their demands, in order to achieve their political and military objectives. Civilians, at minimum, need insurgents not to kill them or otherwise make their lives impossible. This drives them to bargain with one another (see Figure 1.1). Most negotiations follow a similar pattern. There is a back and forth in which each party takes a series of successive positions. They do this to assess their leverage over the other side and gauge how the other party will react to their next move. This process allows each side to gather information and evaluate their options. Even if the sides reach some kind of deal, the bargaining process doesn't necessarily have a defined end point. Agreements break down, or one side's interests may change, or their leverage may increase—all of which spurs renegotiation.

Unlike most negotiations, interactions between insurgents and civilians are underpinned by coercion, violence and fear. Insurgents live with the constant threat that civilians might betray or rebel against them, and civilians that insurgents might harm or kill them. Pervasive fear and uncertainty mean that there is a higher barrier to negotiating in wartime, which means that not all insurgents nor all civilians negotiate all of the time. Each side must trust the other enough to be able to interact, bargain and, ultimately, reach an agreement that both parties believe the other will uphold.

A corollary is that because wars are volatile, socially transformative processes, we can expect negotiations to be equally unstable. That said, certain patterns typically emerge. Civilian–insurgent bargaining is unlikely to be prevalent early on in the conflict. Insurgencies are typically weakest and most disorganised at their inception. They have little leverage over civilians (other than ad hoc or only semi-selective violence) and little organised capacity to bargain. As insurgents develop internal control and greater information-gathering capacities, violence becomes more selective. It can be used as a bargaining chip. As they gain strength, insurgents will likely be more receptive to civilian interests and may more actively seek to provide incentives to compel compliance. They duly use this information to inform their bargaining strategies, calculating risk versus reward. This process, however, is unlikely to be terribly linear, as military pressure and territorial control fluctuate. Armed groups typically show remarkably different capacities, attitudes and behaviours towards civilians as they gain or lose territory, have greater or lesser ability to devote resources to engaging with civilians and face greater or lesser military pressure from their adversaries (Kasfir, 2015; Wood, 2010).

All the while, civilians monitor the balance of the conflict, assessing the coherence of the insurgency and measuring their power vis-à-vis the incumbent state or other armed groups. Civilians carefully calculate the risks of engaging with the insurgency, and whether those risks are worth taking in light of prospective success. They might initially keep their distance from the insurgency, but when state abuses become intolerable or insurgent victory seems more likely they might change tack. Some civilians are savvier than others, calibrating their behaviour in ways that maximise their protection and enhance their status or gains. All of this depends on the power they possess over the insurgency and the quality of information they can access.

The problem, however, with gathering and analysing information in wartime is that rumour, misinformation and misperception are rife, distorted by coercion and fear (Kalyvas, 2006; Kalyvas and Kocher, 2007). Insurgents need strong intelligence-gathering systems. That means earning the trust of—or at least infiltrating—the civilian population, which takes time. For civilians, violence sends the loudest signal about what insurgents want, but they aren't always able to accurately interpret the meaning. Insurgent targeting of civilians may be erroneous or unhelpfully broad, or it may suddenly shift. Any negotiation can be compromised by emotion and pressure, but wartime contexts are extreme in this respect. High stakes and intense pressure influence each side's perception of their choices and risk tolerance.

Unlike most models of negotiation, which assume each party is on relatively equal footing, insurgent–civilian bargaining is deeply lopsided, myopic, unpredictable and high risk. Civilians are generally coerced into bargaining, and parties negotiate amidst a volatile and violent environment. Given the vast asymmetry of power between civilians and insurgents, civilians make enormous concessions and insurgencies relatively few. In general, civilians are faced with a choice between bad and worse. The insurgency will punish those that they believe support the government, and the government will punish those that they think support the insurgency. As such, civilians try to assess which option is least bad and weigh that against which punishment is more likely.

Models of interpersonal negotiation also generally assume that either party can walk away from negotiations at any time, for any reason. The entanglement between insurgents and civilians is more complicated. Most civilians would not freely choose to engage with the insurgency, had they much of a choice in the first place. Where insurgencies are locally embedded phenomena, civilians and insurgents are enmeshed in the same social fabric: they are family members, old schoolmates, acquaintances and so on. They are all but unavoidable. Civilians might prefer to opt out of interacting entirely, and do so by fleeing or taking up arms against the insurgency. If they stay, however, civilians typically have little choice but to negotiate. They also have few good options if negotiations fail, as insurgents typically mete out harmful (if not fatal) consequences for non-compliance.

A few further caveats, more of an academic nature: at the risk of stating the obvious, this is not a general theory that applies to all insurgents and all civilians in all civil wars; at best, it attempts to explain behaviour in the post-2001 Afghanistan War and might well apply, in whole or in part, to other wars. Moreover, it's exceptionally important to emphasise (at the risk of repetition) that there are those who choose not to negotiate. Some civilians simply obey rather than risk negotiating, while others flee. Some choose to fight against the insurgency and some join the insurgency, with a subset of those seeing the choice of joining the insurgency as the only safe or desirable option. Not all insurgencies negotiate, and this varies according to their goals, ideologies and other factors. Genocidaires or those with no concrete political objectives, for example, may not feel they need or want civilian compliance. A core assumption here is that insurgencies aspiring to political legitimacy—like the Taliban—are more likely to negotiate with civilians to compel compliance than those who do not seek political legitimacy or external recognition.

Figure 1.1. Civilian–insurgent bargaining dynamics

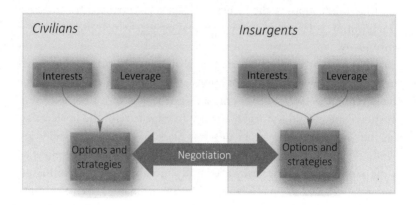

Interests

Interests are the concerns, needs and fears of each party engaged in negotiation. Some interests may be shared by both parties while others may be at odds, but shared interests are what necessitate negotiation. More broadly, interests are what motivate each actor to bargain in the first place, and they are what drives their behaviour afterwards (Fisher and Ury, 1991). The tricky thing about interests is that they are not always apparent. Parties typically tend to hide their interests for fear that expressing them openly will weaken their leverage or otherwise expose their vulnerabilities (Lewicki et al., 2010). The bargaining position encompasses the demands expressed in negotiations (reflecting what both parties think they can get or how they want to be perceived), while interests are the needs that drive negotiation (what they actually want).

In negotiating with insurgents, this framework assumes that civilians' primary interest is survival. Nathan Leites and Charles Wolf, referring to this as damage limitation, argue that the desire to limit damage to oneself, family or community is likely to take precedence over any innate preference or strongly held ideals (Leites and Wolf, 1970). Civilians do not want to be targeted by the insurgency and they do not want to be collateral damage. They may try to convince the insurgency to suspend fighting in civilian areas, or to give fair warning when villages are likely to come under attack. They may not want insurgents to plan attacks in or on areas that civilians frequent or that they consider to be 'civilian' in nature (i.e., the bazaar or town marketplace, frequently travelled roads, schools, clinics). Many protection interests are collective, but individuals also face unique problems which require negotiation. Some cases may be extreme or life-and-death scenarios (i.e., the insurgency may detain a relative) while others may be more routine (i.e., a civilian might be caught at a checkpoint and have to negotiate with the commanders manning it for safe passage).

Damage limitation may be combined with efforts to maximise the benefits that one can accrue from complying with insurgent rule (Leites and Wolf, 1970; Mason, 1996). The insurgency has the power to bestow advantages to civilians, either collectively or individually, as it sees fit—and civilians are well aware of this. In practice, the line between damage limitation and well-being can be permeable and subjective. Someone might inform upon someone else so that they can seize that person's property after they are rounded up by the rebels. One community may leverage its relationship with the insurgency in a dispute with a neighbouring community, or one business may draw on insurgent support to seek a competitive advantage. Not all civilians have the same interests, and pre-existing tensions, divisions, and forms of social organisation must be considered.

This framework assumes that organisational survival is the insurgency's most immediate and primary interest. The insurgency seeks to control the population so that civilians (a) do not inform on the insurgency to their adversaries and (b) comply with insurgent demands (safe passage, shelter, food, recruiting pools, concealment and so on). Controlling the civilian population is essential to the insurgency achieving their longer-term goal of territorial control, the expansion and consolidation of which is what ultimately leads to victory. The insurgency's interests are often veiled behind comparatively benevolent rhetoric, and many insurgencies present their interests as being aligned with the interests of civilians. Insurgents may frame their fight as a struggle for collective well-being. They may argue that they are seeking to rid the area of tyrannical interlopers or occupiers, or to establish a better form of government or a more just society. Regardless of whether civilians buy into these narratives, few among them would

29

doubt that the insurgency seeks to control their behaviour and keep them onside. Alongside this, insurgencies bargain with civilians because they want to increase their political power or recognition (i.e., taking part in government or replacing the incumbent government entirely). Of course, some insurgencies may be motivated by social or economic inequalities, or they might simply not seek legitimacy in this way (see Keen, 2012; Reno, 2015). Those that disregard legitimacy concerns may have little interest in bargaining.

That said, we cannot consider just group interests; we must also look at the interests of individual insurgents. The weight of individual interests may depend on the insurgency's structure and coherence: the tighter the structure, the less individuals can act on motives that conflict with group objectives (Hoover Green, 2016; Lidow, 2011; Staniland, 2014). Nevertheless, negotiations are interpersonal affairs, even where individuals are negotiating on behalf of group interests. One caveat is that in some cases individual insurgents may not, in fact, prioritise their own survival. Where martyrdom is a prominent part of the insurgency's ideology, for example, some fighters may actively seek opportunities to sacrifice themselves for the collective cause. Other fighters, however, may actually want to survive and want civilians to mostly survive too. Social relations and histories come into play. Insurgents from the community may be more interested in ensuring that civilians—including their family and loved ones—are protected and have access to things like schools and jobs.

Borrowing from Steven Metz's typology of insurgent motives, insurgents can be roughly divided into six non-mutually exclusive groups: the socially obligated, the survivors, the lost, the aggrieved, the thugs and the ambitious (Metz, 2012). For the socially obligated, ties and norms shape their behaviour. Metz argues that this may be particularly prevalent where tribal or traditional structures are strong, or as important as the individual's tie to the overall insurgency. Others may join an insurgency primarily to survive, particularly where joining the insurgency is perceived as less costly than not, or where membership bestows access to valuable resources. This is also likely to be more pronounced where the insurgency engages in forced conscription or where they are likely to retaliate against non-joiners (i.e., the Lord's

Resistance Army (LRA) in Uganda, the Maoists in Nepal, the Liberians United for Reconciliation and Democracy (LURD) (Gates, 2017).

People who feel lost or disconnected from society may find a sense of belonging in joining an armed group. Some may be driven by personal grievances or a broader sense of injustice, or by boredom or unemployment (Stern, 2003). Some may join an insurgency because they already have a propensity for aggression and violence, and the war gives them a chance to enact these tendencies. Others may join because they have a particular ambition the insurgency will help them fulfil. The ambitious may be more common in contexts where upward mobility is otherwise blocked for specific segments of the population. The ambitious might also more generally be found among insurgencies easily able to generate or exploit resources (Weinstein, 2006; Collier and Hoeffler, 2004; Keen, 2000). Here the line between the ambitious and the thugs gets blurry; Metz describes those motivated by personal profit as 'thugs', arguing that they 'seldom create or lead insurgencies, but they do provide many of its foot soldiers' (Metz, 2012). Yet even the greedy may be driven by multiple factors.

To be clear, insurgent motives are not uniform up and down, or across, a movement. The ambitious might fight alongside the lost and the aggrieved. We know that an affiliation with the Taliban or Al Shabaab might be little more than a means to an end for those seeking to profit from the drugs trade or the black market in Afghanistan or Somalia (Gopal, 2015; Harper, 2019; Joseph and Maruf, 2018). Yet there are also those who see themselves as true believers filling the Taliban and Al Shabaab ranks (Strick van Linschoten, 2016; Giustozzi, 2008; Ladbury, 2009; Hansen, 2013). A given fighter might be lost as well as aggrieved, while also seeking advancement and enrichment. Even in groups seen as heavily ideological, more mixed motives might be found among individuals. In groups most often described as Islamists or jihadis, there may be those motivated primarily by injustice and grievance, and secondarily religion (see Ratelle and Souleimanov, 2017).

What, then, does this mean for civilians seeking to bargain with insurgents? Civilians must understand both group interests as well as the interests of the specific individuals they encounter: where they come from, why they are fighting and what their pressure points might be. Insurgents with strong ties to the community, for example, can be more sympathetic to civilian survival and well-being concerns, and perhaps easier to bargain with. Thugs and the ambitious might be ruthless and cutthroat with the population, and best avoided. But not all individuals' motives will be straightforward or static. The lost might turn out to be unyielding zealots, or see themselves as compassionate saviours, and even those who see themselves as saviours can be abusive or dictatorial.

Leverage

An individual's power in a given negotiation typically either derives from that individual's unique attributes, or it derives from context (Dahl, 1957; Kotter, 1979; Deutsch, 1973). This makes it both relational and subjective (i.e., the way each person might gauge their own leverage varies), and inherently unstable and hard to predict with certainty. Those (somewhat substantial) caveats aside, this framework breaks down various forms of wartime leverage and how they are commonly used into four interlinked categories: violence and coercion; persuasion; incentives; and social capital.

Violence and coercion

Violence and coercion constitute leverage only where they are strategically and intentionally deployed to elicit civilian compliance. Random-seeming and ad hoc violence and coercion do not necessarily constitute leverage. As Frantz Fanon observed, 'unmixed and total brutality, if not immediately combatted, invariably leads to the defeat of the movement within a few weeks' (Fanon, 1967: 147). Brutality may stun the population into submission initially, but prolonged mass violence ultimately risks turning civilians against the insurgency and undermining insurgent legitimacy (Abrahms, 2012; Thompson, 1966; Schlichte and Schneckener, 2015; Valentino et al., 2004). If those complying with the insurgency and those at odds with it are equally likely to suffer, there is little to recommend compliance.

For violence to be strategic, it must be selective, guided by a logic that civilians can identify and navigate (Kalyvas, 2006). 'Selective' is nonetheless a broad and contextually bound category, influenced by local norms and civilian perceptions of proportionality. Inflicting terror and widespread casualties can still be 'selective' so long as it is rational and calculated, and it furthers the insurgency's objectives. Nonetheless, attacks aimed at inspiring fear are still a costly form of signalling, with a heightened risk of backfiring if they are seen as wildly disproportionate (Thompson, 1966; Kydd and Walter, 2002; Arjona, 2015; Revkin and Ahram, 2017).

Deploying violence as leverage requires an insurgency to demonstrably control fighter conduct. It also requires intelligence-gathering capacity, allowing insurgents to differentiate targets more precisely. The more targeted the violence, the higher the level of difficulty. Unsurprisingly, the degree of selectivity an insurgency possesses typically depends on the maturity of the movement. Indiscriminate violence should decrease over time as insurgent leaders recognise its counterproductive effects, and as the insurgency matures and develops tighter command and control (Kalyvas, 2006). Indiscriminate violence can broadly be understood as a weapon of the weak, because it is more common when an insurgency is just beginning, or when they are on the back foot. However, insurgents may be less selective when they are losing militarily or are in intense, violent competition with other insurgent groups (Hultman, 2007; Raleigh, 2012). Within this context, insurgent control is rarely uniform: indiscriminate violence may also be a tactic of a relatively strong insurgency in specific geographic areas where it is weak (de la Calle, 2017; Wood, 2010). When or where an insurgency lacks control and thus the ability to be selective, their capacity to bargain and deliver on their end of any deal is compromised. Civilians may consequently calculate that they cannot meet their basic interests through engaging with the insurgency.

So how do insurgencies identify the targets of their violence, and how does this shape civilian bargaining? Selective violence can be seen as having primary and secondary targets. Primary targets are those whose actions merit punishment, or who present such a grave threat that they must be eliminated. Some actions, such as forming a self-defence militia, may be public and definitive in their interpretation, practically inviting punishment from the insurgency. Other actions, such as secretly informing upon the insurgency, require more effort to uncover. Secondary targets are the wider civilian population, who are the audience for the violence effected. Punishment of primary targets must be so severe that it outweighs the benefits of betrayal, and it must be communicated to civilians so it can function as a deterrent. When insurgents deliberately target civilians in this way, they aim not only to punish the individual but to create atmospheric coercion that conveys the costs of resistance and sways civilian calculations (Leites and Wolf, 1970; Hultman, 2007).

Civilians can also employ coercion via the threat of betrayal or rebellion. However, they are—quite literally—outgunned, so trying to coerce an insurgency is a risky move. Typically, individuals faced with threats more generally in negotiations will consider two factors: the severity of the punishment and the likelihood of follow-through based on past performance (Horai and Tedeschi, 1969; Lindskold et al., 1969). They also tend to weigh the social power of the party levying the threat, in order to estimate the wider fallout (Faley and Tedeschi, 1971). This suggests that threats issued by civilians must be both grave and credible to have a meaningful impact. Moreover, they must weigh the costs of carrying out the threat (i.e., openly opposing the insurgency). In some instances, this would put individuals or the entire community at risk of retaliation. Not following through, however, would almost certainly entail a loss of face and diminish their leverage in future negotiations (Horai and Tedeschi, 1969).

Persuasion

Insurgent persuasion tends to overlap with violence and the movement's larger communication efforts. Contemporary insurgent groups typically use a sophisticated mix of traditional and newer methods, from word-of-mouth to social media, to get their message across to specific audiences (i.e., battlefield adversaries, foreign patrons, potential recruits and undecided civilians). More sophisticated strategies may articulate specific narratives for different audiences, and a given method may transmit multiple narratives, each to different targets. Threats might co-mingle with impassioned appeals for support, or with different formulas for different audiences. What then is coercion, what is persuasion and what do we consider a mixture of both?

Persuasion, as it is conceived of here, is relational. After all, persuasion isn't particularly powerful if its targets remain unconvinced. Insurgent persuasion is defined here as the arguments, stories and narratives that insurgents communicate to civilians to convince them to comply with their demands. It encompasses the day-in and day-out interactions between civilians and insurgents or their supporters and proxies. Context is critical: insurgents play on specific (and often localised) civilian beliefs, values and fears to make their case (Bolt, 2012). It is these narratives and tactics that we are primarily concerned with, alongside a consideration of how they resonate (or not) with civilians.

Insurgents typically rely on a combination of positive and negative storylines. They seek to persuade civilians that their cause is righteous, justifying their fight with religious, political or moral arguments. They are most likely to gain ground when their arguments are tailored to pre-existing values and beliefs. Through affirming civilian values and aspirations, they create a sense of common ground with civilians. By contrast, negative storylines often focus on delegitimising and demonising their adversaries. To do this effectively, the insurgents often seize upon abusive state practices and injustices. The added advantage of this is that it creates a Catch-22 for the state: the more the state cracks down on the insurgency (i.e., the more raids it conducts, the more people it detains, the more battles it wages, the more repression it enacts), the more it plays into the insurgency's hands. This effectively reinforces the cognitive plausibility and moral justifiability of co-operating with or supporting an insurgency (Goodwin, 2001). That said, a balance between negative and positive narratives is critical; work from Afghanistan, as well as from El Salvador and southern Thailand, suggests that narratives mirroring civilian beliefs and values, and conveying the sense of being under attack, tend to resonate most powerfully (Johnson, 2018; Wood, 2003; Askew and Helbardt, 2012).

Much of this is true of civilians as well. In negotiating, they typically use each interaction as a chance to shape insurgent perceptions, as well as locate, affirm and strategically manipulate insurgent values and beliefs. Effective persuasion for both sides is interactional, iterative and dynamic, and indelibly rooted in local social, historical and political context. One key difference between insurgent persuasion and civilian persuasion is that insurgents are usually actively communicating a repertoire of storylines, symbols, arguments and imagery that serves to justify their actions before any direct engagement. Civilians must then argue their case to insurgents reactively, in a rhetorical space constrained and shaped by insurgent discourses. Consequently, how civilians argue their case—in terms of both style and content—matters a great deal. Referring to specific ideological tenets or cultural obligations can be powerful. Civilians in Afghanistan, for example, often framed their arguments to the Taliban for the re-opening of schools in Islamic terms (Jackson and Amiri, 2019).

Argumentation and persuasion can reveal information which can influence the other side's position (Kipnis et al., 1980). The nature and presentation of an argument conveys the importance of a request which the insurgency may have neglected, forgotten or simply not understood. The insurgency may not, for example, realise that their tactics are harming civilians or inadvertently undermining their own interests. In southern Afghanistan, civilians recalled how insurgent violence had obstructed farmers from harvesting crops and bringing them to market. They explained to a local Taliban fighter that not only did this create economic hardship for farmers and their families, but those farmers would have nothing to feed the insurgents when they demanded food and no money to pay when they demanded taxes. Understanding the full weight of negative repercussions convinced the Taliban to temporarily halt violence so that farmers could collect their crops.

Who bargains with the insurgency also matters. In his study of persuasion, Joshua Weiss emphasises the importance of two distinct relational qualities: ethos, or credibility, and pathos, or emotional connection (Weiss, 2015). The legitimacy and credibility of the negotiator, which is shaped by the perceptions and values of the opposing party, impacts their power of persuasion. This helps explain why, from Aceh and Afghanistan to Somalia and Côte d'Ivoire, customary authorities and religious figures act as negotiators with the rebels on behalf of the community. In contexts where the insurgency sees such structures as oppressive or illegitimate, or where they have been wholly co-opted by the insurgency, this is unlikely to work out well. In some instances, pathos may be more effective. Those with direct links to the insurgency, such as relatives of insurgent commanders, can often leverage those ties most effectively in negotiations. Some insurgents might,

NEGOTIATED REBELLION

however, be immune to both ethos and pathos. A hard-bargaining rebel might thus deny even the most persuasive, impassioned requests, particularly if they saw no real benefit likely to come of it.

Incentives

While the threat of violence is always in the background, most insurgencies eventually recognise that incentives are required to sustain civilian compliance. These can be as meagre as protection from violence the insurgency would otherwise inflict, or they can be more substantial. Some incentives are collective (i.e., allowing schools and clinics to operate, specific prohibitions on the use of violence that protect the whole population and so on). Other benefits are selective and require individual action. If the insurgency enlists an individual to provide information, for example, the advantages that individual gets are usually specific to them and non-transferable.

Insurgencies that create systems of governance have more developed mechanisms for offering incentives, particularly collective ones. Building systems to maintain order or enable access to services and opportunities allows the insurgency to both (a) present predictable benefits for civilian compliance and (b) dissuade the population from collaborating with the government. Where territorial control is consolidated, and insurgent governance is firmly established, the insurgency is often effectively offering the civilian population a social contract of sorts (Podder, 2017; Revkin and Ahram, 2017). Under this social contract, the insurgency grants security and protection in exchange for civilian compliance. Insurgent governance systems also enhance the insurgency's ability to collect intelligence and punish non-compliance in a more predictable and precise manner. Insurgent-run courts can provide order and security, as well as a more 'civilianised' mechanism of coercion (Ledwidge, 2017). Ultimately, governance systems allow the insurgency greater leverage and the means to regulate civilian life. Further, the state-like provision of incentives allows the insurgency to better embarrass the incumbent state (Asal et al., 2020).

The most significant incentive that civilians can provide is compliance, and withholding it can be a powerful bargaining chip. If that is not enough, civilians may increase the attractiveness of their offer with material support. Civilians can, for example, volunteer to aid in insurgent recruitment efforts—particularly in scenarios where persuasion and argumentation alone are not enough—or they can provide information, or food and shelter. Offering costly incentives like these, which inherently put civilians at risk, shows that they are willing to make sacrifices in order to meet the interests of the other side. Sociologist Robert Cialdini's work suggests that we feel an urge to make concessions to someone who has made concessions or offered incentives to us, even where these are meagre (Cialdini, 1993). Various sociology and behavioural economics studies indicate that parties engaged in negotiation often reciprocate the acts of the other side, even when it is against their self-interest (Gouldner, 1960; Ortmann et al., 2000; Pillutla et al., 2003). It isn't always the value of the incentive, but the *act* of offering it which triggers the other side to make concessions. The principle of reciprocity also works for insurgents. Revolutionary leaders from Lenin to Castro and insurgencies from the NLF to the Irish Republican Army (IRA) used reciprocity to generate and shore up civilian compliance (Hagan, 2009).

Social capital

Drawing on sociologist James Coleman's work, social capital is defined here as an asset linked to 'some aspect of a social structure' that facilitates 'certain actions of individuals who are within the structure ... making possible the achievement of certain ends that in its absence would not be possible' (Coleman, 1988: 96). Social capital is not relationships and shared norms alone but the new options and abilities that arise from them. For example, it enhances the ability to gather information and the understanding required to navigate complex social interactions. Social capital also creates a safety net of trust and protection that enables an individual to take risks. It can be amplified when combined with other attributes and assets (i.e., individual skill, social status, wealth) and can accentuate other forms of leverage. For example, social capital may enhance the incentives one can provide or inform strategies for persuasion (i.e., the wealthy have more money to offer, the strategically minded have more persuasive arguments, the well-connected have more networks to draw upon).

We can expect that communities with tighter horizontal linkages and more resilient institutions have a greater stock of social capital than those with deep internal divisions, vast inequality or weaker institutions (Putnam, 2001). Some individuals have greater access to social capital by virtue of the family they were born into, who they went to school with, what they do to earn a living, their gender or ethnicity and so on. Civilians with a wealth of social capital can better draw on personal relationships with individual insurgents, or use those relationships to gain insight into how the insurgency thinks and what they want. Social capital can also enable a civilian to mobilise allies with greater leverage over the insurgency to act on their behalf.

A collective advantage of social capital comes in the form of unity and cohesion. The greater the community's stock of social capital, the more likely they are to co-operate effectively and efficiently. Tight-knit coalitions or collectives will also agree more quickly on their shared interests and the best way to negotiate for them. If they can do this, they can bargain collectively with the insurgency; bargaining collectively multiplies their bargaining power. When one side creates a coalition or mobilises allies, it heightens the cost incurred by the other side if an agreement is not reached (Sebenius and Lax, 1991). Instead of facing just one aggrieved civilian, the insurgency must now contend with a unified front of them.

Insurgents also need social capital. One means through which they can access this is ideology. Ideology might be rooted in religion or a revolutionary political agenda, centred around the restoration of shared values or identity, or anchored in economic grievances. Regardless of the content, insurgents draw on shared beliefs and symbols to persuade civilians that the insurgents' cause is valid and righteous. As hinted at in the discussion of persuasion, insurgent ideology is often both radical and familiar, with insurgencies tending to frame their political agenda—at least partly—in terms of common values and symbols. This co-option and distortion of shared meanings is a powerful tool to compel civilian compliance. Insurgent symbolic repertoires impose new rules and meanings, whilst erasing others in a coercive ideological and social reordering (Mampilly, 2015).

Within this ideological and social reordering, insurgents may co-opt or collaborate with customary institutions. Arjona refers to those insurgencies that lightly co-opt existing institutions as 'aliocracies', and more interventionist insurgencies as 'rebelocracies', which seek to disrupt or fully subordinate the existing social order (Arjona, 2016). Arguably, however, the wide variety of insurgent approaches is more accurately reflected by a spectrum (instead of Arjona's binary). Pre-war relationships matter, but they are typically transformed in unexpected ways by the conflict, with new modes of interaction, networks and relationship developing (Parkinson, 2013; Förster, 2015; Kendall, 2016; Hansen, 2013). Because social capital is rooted in a perpetually fluid context, attempts to generalise are bound to be undermined by exceptions. We have to leave open the possibility that, in some cases, various forms of social capital have little discernable influence on insurgent–civilian relations.[2]

In sum, social capital intersects with all of the other forms of leverage discussed so far. The conflict itself will also produce new relationships and forms of leverage, but we should expect that insurgents from the community will, all other things being equal, have greater social capital than those from outside. Insurgencies that draw their fighters from the local population have a clear advantage in that they know the local dynamics and have ties. But, again, they may be more vulnerable in other ways, particularly when civilians attempt to use their ties to insurgents as leverage.

Options and strategies

Figure 1.2. Spectrum of civilian options

We can assume that both civilians and insurgents have a range of options in any given situation (as illustrated in Figure 1.2). Where compliance with the insurgency is intolerable or negotiation likely to be fruitless, for example, civilians may flee the area while others take sides. In between, compliance and negotiation imply a range of possible behaviours. Civilians can proactively engage with the insurgency, seeking out opportunities to cultivate links and support for the group. For those who already know insurgents or count them among their kin and clan, this might be done with relative ease. Allying oneself too closely to the insurgency, however, creates other risks; civilians seeking to mitigate risks from both sides may opt to submit quietly while maintaining a safe distance. The problem is that few can keep themselves entirely separate from an insurgency for long. Insurgents want to establish themselves as the ruling authority and are consequently inherently intrusive. Most civilians will eventually face a choice of whether, or how, to negotiate their compliance.

We can expect civilians to weigh their options and assess the risks of a given action. To gauge risk, civilians gather information about the insurgency's likely reaction to specific demands and tactics based on past performance. Risk assessment relies on solid information and analysis. Understanding the risks may ultimately be a matter of trial and error, or learning from someone else's trials and errors. Friends or relatives may have direct experiences to share, or they may know others who have some valuable insight into dealing with the insurgency. Social capital helps here because it improves information gathering and tactical insights, and can broaden risk-management options. Being able to draw on strong networks and allies increases the potential costs faced by the insurgency. There are, nonetheless, instances where information is so obviously imperfect that no amount of social capital can help. Where an insurgency is young and less established, civilians may not have enough information to know whether it is advisable to negotiate with them, or if they can be trusted to keep their word. Until they have a better understanding of the situation, civilians may avoid engagement.

Once the risks are clear, civilians weigh them against potential benefits. Civilians gather information to understand the incentives the insurgency is offering and gauge whether they can be induced to provide more. Like risks, not all potential gains will be weighted equally. Further, we know that people generally weigh potential losses more heavily than the prospect of new benefits (Kahneman and Tversky, 1979). We can then reasonably expect that most civilians will risk more to protect themselves and hold onto what they have than they will to

41

accrue new benefits. An individual may assume great personal risk to get a relative released from insurgent custody, but be unwilling to take a similar risk in pursuit of self-interest or advancement.

Making generalised assumptions about risk tolerance is, however, difficult because the nature of risk tolerance is something of a mystery (Carmil and Breznitz, 1991; Tedeschi and Calhoun, 2004). Economists have traditionally seen risk tolerance as exogenous and fixed, although this view may be changing. Several recent studies suggest that the outbreak of conflict *should* impact risk tolerance (Cameron and Shah, 2015; Kim and Lee, 2014; Moya, 2018). Unfortunately, there is little consensus on this: some studies suggest that violent conflict spurs risk-seeking behaviour and negatively impacts patience; other studies find that war-related trauma leads to greater risk aversion; and still other studies suggest risk tolerance varies dramatically across individuals, depending on their gender, age, education, income, childhood and a variety of other factors (Voors et al., 2012; Callen et al., 2014; Moya, 2018; Dohmen et al., 2011; Eckel and Grossman, 2002). What all of this tells us is that civilians in wartime will likely display different risk-tolerance levels based on an array of individualised and common factors that include, but are not limited to, the conflict. Some civilians, numbed by the daily exposure to brutality and life-or-death choices, may have heightened risk tolerance. Others, ridden by anxiety and pervasive uncertainty, may become more risk averse.

Incorporating their assessment and tolerance of risk, civilians evaluate which options are most likely to be successful. To do this, they must predict whether the insurgency will be receptive to one approach over another. This requires understanding the insurgency's objectives and values to ascertain if they share common ground. This shouldn't be difficult to figure out, as insurgencies tend to advertise their beliefs. Civilians will also try to understand the insurgency's negotiating style. If negotiations work best when relatively formalised, they will try to learn the established rules and procedures. They will try to analyse how the insurgency has reacted to various tactics in similar cases. They will also presumably do a bit of power analysis to identify exactly who they should be negotiating with to obtain a definitive agreement. This is no small feat when dealing with a shadowy or fragmented insurgency, where the command structure may not be obvious. By contrast, this will be easier to discern where an insurgency is coherent and has stable territorial presence.

In this tactical evaluation, they will talk and trade information with those who have experience negotiating with the insurgency. The resulting information narrows the field of options. For example, a civilian may hear that levying threats leads to punishment and moral arguments are useless, but offering to provide information to the insurgency leads to a favourable outcome. That civilian will then likely abandon any ideas he or she had about using threats or persuasion; instead, he or she will likely set about obtaining valuable intelligence to bargain with. If the civilian learns that informal negotiations work better than the formal processes, he or she will try to find a personal link to the insurgency. Perhaps they went to school with someone who joined the insurgency, or maybe a close relative knows an influential commander. The civilian might then use these connections to bypass formal processes and make a personal appeal.

In addition, civilians attempt to predict the future. Much of the existing literature on civilian behaviour in war indicates that civilians try to predict long-term, end-of-war outcomes in assessing their options (Kalyvas, 2006; Leites and Wolf, 1970). Understanding the overall balance of the conflict influences their strategies. No one wants to be associated with the losing side, or a side that is losing ground, if they can avoid it. Protection and benefits will falter, and there may be reprisals against those seen as 'collaborators'. To figure this out, various scholars suggest that civilians try to gauge insurgent resource flows, territorial gains or losses, fighting strength and fighter morale. My own research with anthropologist Giulia Minoia on civilian behaviour in Afghanistan suggests something slightly different. We found that civilians working with a high level of risk, volatility and incomplete information tended to adopt short time horizons (Jackson and Minoia, 2019). This does not necessarily mean that civilians entirely discount end-of-war predictions, but it strongly suggests that shorter-term events take precedence in their negotiations.

One obstacle to predicting the future is the lack of accurate information in wartime. Social capital cannot entirely mitigate the challenges of the wartime rumour mill. Discounting the future may be a more common phenomenon in conflicts with entrenched insurgencies, where territory changes hands multiple times over several years. Where the insurgency loses control to the government, local fighters may melt back into the population, keeping an eye on how the community behaves and plotting their return. If, as T.E. Lawrence recommended, the insurgency operates like 'an influence, a thing invulnerable, intangible, without front or back, drifting about like gas', it becomes impossible for civilians to evade entirely (Lawrence, 1920). Civilians may feel that, with no end in sight, they cannot predict the future accurately. In these kinds of situations, we should expect civilians to sacrifice long-term interests to fulfil short-term ones. They may then discount longer-term negative repercussions and concern themselves more with the short-term fallout.

An important caveat here is that emotion influences the kinds of options civilians and insurgents see as desirable, as well as their decisions. Just as emotion colours risk tolerance, it affects other aspects of analysis and decision-making. While we know that emotions shape wartime behaviour, theorising about the precise impact of emotion is a fraught endeavour (Halperin and Schwartz, 2010; Lindner, 2006; Petersen, 2002). There is, however, no scientific consensus on precisely what emotion even is in physiological terms (Cacioppo and Gardner, 1999; Schacter et al., 2011). In the absence of an agreed definition, emotion has often been synonymous with irrationality and seen as incompatible with rational choice models. Rational actor assumptions tend to predominate more generally in analyses of behaviour in civil wars, despite well-established arguments highlighting their blind spots and limitations (Keen, 2000; McDoom, 2012; Mitton, 2015).

Emotion has similarly been constructed as a 'problem' in the study of negotiation. It has been seen as an obstacle to effective negotiation, 'becoming emotional' as something to be avoided (Fisher and Ury, 1991; Neale and Bazerman, 1992). Recently, however, there has been a shift towards accepting that emotions are an integral part of negotiating behaviour, and of the human condition writ large. Various scholars have begun to explore the ways in which respect, identity, acknowledgement and personal ties shape interests, positions and actions (Leary et al., 2013). By considering emotion, for example, we can begin to more clearly see what shapes an individual's risk tolerance. We can also more readily explore why individuals sometimes make choices that appear contradictory to their needs and interests.

In situations where one so often feels like a victim of circumstance, the desire simply to take action, to whatever end, can exert a strong pull. Some people may even weight such action as heavily as their own physical survival. They may have a stronger interest in enacting their own agency in a precarious situation than they do in protecting themselves. They might value dignity restored through defiance above the safety they gain through compliance. Taking a moral stand might allow someone to escape the nihilism that so often pervades the violence and uncertainty of civil war. An act of defiance can restore one's dignity amidst degrading and demoralising conditions. Emotion, in other words, reveals another dimension to an individual's interests, and they co-mingle with more 'rational' drivers of behaviour.

Figure 1.3. Spectrum of insurgent options

In bargaining around compliance, insurgents too face a range of options (as illustrated in Figure 1.3). The insurgency can reject civilians' demands wholesale, but this presents risks. Rejecting civilian demands may entail a heavier reliance on using violence to quell discontent, which could spur resistance and dissatisfaction, leading civilians to inform on or otherwise obstruct the insurgency. At the other end of the spectrum, the insurgency may accept civilian demands. Where insurgents feel relatively secure and trust civilians to deliver on the deal, they may do so relatively quickly. These kinds of win–win negotiations are likely to be rare, particularly if the insurgency is motivated to maximise civilian compliance. We can assume that civilians, keenly aware of the risks of being seen to support the insurgency, are likely to offer the bare minimum required to get what they want. This, in turn, results in insurgents pressing for more.

Both sides engage in a back-and-forth: insurgents may not accept civilian demands in full, but they are willing to talk about what concessions might be feasible and satisfactory for both sides. Within this, insurgents assess the strength of civilians and the consequences of refusing their request. If the insurgency is, for example, confident it can divide and rule civilians, they may use pre-existing internal strife to diminish civilian leverage. Micro-level conflicts can end up playing out in new ways within the broader macro-level conflict.

Like civilians, insurgents will analyse risk, make tactical evaluations and attempt to predict the future. Two interrelated factors shape insurgent behaviour in assessing options: internal control and relative strength. A weak and immature insurgency will thus behave differently to a strong insurgency with a significant degree of territorial control. Where the insurgency is just starting out, lack of trust between insurgents and civilians may undermine negotiations. Even if they have sufficient information and a workable basis for trust, insurgents may not have the internal coherence or territorial control to deliver on agreements reliably. Non-delivery renders any agreement useless and results in the insurgency losing face with the civilian population.

In bargaining with civilians, insurgencies weigh the risk to their survival. Civilian demands may conflict with the insurgency's military objectives or pose a perceived threat to the security of fighters on the ground. Insurgents gauge risk using information about the civilian population, their own internal coherence and their relative strength vis-à-vis their adversaries. All other things being equal, a robust, coherent insurgency will likely assume more risk than a weak insurgency. However, we can assume that insurgencies will (a) strive to protect themselves and achieve their core military objectives first, and (b) prioritise the prevention of losses over any new benefits.

Civilians might request that insurgents do more to protect them, by, for example, suspending fighting in civilian spaces or being more precise in their targeting. The insurgency, however, may perceive these requests as impeding its ability to protect itself or achieve its objectives. They are most likely to agree to tighten internal restrictions on the use of force only if (a) they feel that not doing so will result in them losing civilian compliance and (b) they have enough internal control to mitigate all other risks. Or civilians might request that the insurgency grant permission for an aid agency to initiate a project in the village. Insurgents may fear that the aid workers are spies, secretly there to inform on them. They might only grant permission if they feel the risks of denying permission are higher than granting it, and if they are confident they can reduce the likelihood of threats being realised. With greater internal and territorial control, for example, they can develop systems for surveilling and monitoring the aid agency to detect and neutralise any threats they pose.

There may be ideological limits on what the insurgency grants civilians, particularly if civilian requests conflict with insurgent ideology. If the insurgency says one thing and does another, it may lose face with its rank and file, benefactors or constituents. Granting the request may be too much to bear. They could, however, agree if (a) they feel that not doing so poses a serious risk of losing civilian compliance and (b) they have enough ideological control to create a plausible justification. The purpose of insurgent ideologies is to further military and political objectives, not the other way around, so they are typically adaptable to the political needs of the insurgency. Even the most seemingly rigid ideologies have some degree of pragmatic mutability. This provides space for processes of 'framing and learning', which allow them to shift their ideology to the practicalities of waging war (Gutiérrez Sanín and Wood, 2014: 222).

At the organisational level, risk tolerance for insurgents is shaped by the maturity and experience of the group, which provides the knowledge, capacity and confidence to understand and handle risks. We can also assume that greater internal coherence and control increases risk tolerance. Coherence and control add to confidence, create the ability to generate and share best practices, and enable risk sharing. Finally, a relatively strong insurgency, with a significant degree of consolidated territorial control, will be expected to show greater risk tolerance. The trouble is that insurgencies, even the most unified ones, still comprise individuals whose risk tolerance varies according to factors related and unrelated to the conflict. Relatively young or inexperienced insurgents, for example, may have little reason to assume additional risk; conversely, they may be more prone to seeking out risks, unconstrained by much responsibility or the lessons learned by experience. More seasoned fighters may feel that they can better manage risks or that the risks are worth taking. Insurgents that come from the community may feel more confident that they can control civilians, and thus be more likely to engage in non-violent bargaining. Those who are deployed from outside the area may lean more heavily into coercion.

More sophisticated insurgencies will capitalise on civilians' links to develop intelligence-gathering networks, but even very young insurgencies will have some capacity to assess civilian positions. Communities that overtly side with the government are likely to be targeted for violent retribution, for example, while fence-sitting or neutral communities are likely to be exempted from the worst brutality. Within this, the insurgency may calculate that the atmospheric coercion created by violence against government supporters will induce neutral communities to comply (Hultman, 2007; Leites and Wolf, 1970). Insurgents may then be more likely to deploy direct coercion, persuasion or incentives in neutral communities. Individual betrayals are generally harder to identify than group betrayals, so the choice to target individuals will again depend on an insurgency's intelligence and tactical capacities. Typical insurgent standards of evidence are skewed towards minimising the risk of not detecting betrayal, rather than protecting the innocent (Joshi and Quinn, 2017).

Information about civilian coherence shapes insurgent tactical choices in other ways. The insurgency will deal with strong, united civilian entities differently to internally divided ones. Insurgents may seek to divide already fragmented communities further, pitting one side against the other and creating a system of allies and enemies. It is much easier to bargain with a weak opponent than a strong one. Fragmented communities can be more easily co-opted, broken down and reconstructed in ways that benefit the insurgency's objectives.

Information about civilian values, aspirations and beliefs will signal the potential effectiveness of various options. Persuasion has greater power where civilian ideologies are similar to that of the insurgency. Conversely, persuasion will likely be less effective where insurgent and civilian ideologies are opposed (Aydin and Emrence, 2015). In these instances, the insurgency might rely on other tactics. A religiously inspired insurgency may expend more energy on persuading fellow believers but use violence against those belonging to different sects or faiths. A Marxist insurgency, by contrast, may attempt to persuade poor farmers but assassinate rich landowners.

Where insurgents cannot see the long-term future, short-term objectives will take precedence. We can assume that an insurgency struggling to gain a foothold is focused on immediate survival first and expansion second. They weigh immediate risks most heavily and discount longer-term consequences. Brutality towards civilians is thus more attractive to insurgencies with little territory. Insurgencies with significant territorial control, seeking to enact a governance agenda, might weight more heavily the negative consequences of violence towards civilians. Further, stronger insurgencies develop punishment mechanisms that enable them to rationalise and systematise violence. Strong insurgencies are more likely than weak ones to think beyond the war. When they feel like victory is near, they tend to act more like governments, favouring persuasion and incentives alongside state-like mechanisms for surveillance and discipline. Additionally, their desire for international recognition and legitimacy increases. This 'political transformation' influences their interests and shifts the parameters of their bargaining tactics (Jo, 2015). Depending on their values and post-war vision, they may seek to demonstrate compliance with international norms or prove that they genuinely enjoy popular support.

2.

DANCING WITH WHOEVER IS THERE

SURVIVING THE AFGHANISTAN WARS

On a warm October afternoon, I had an unusual interview with a teacher from Logar. Things started out well enough. I thanked him for meeting me and began by explaining why I was eager to speak with him. I didn't get very far before he interrupted. He asked about where I had studied, quizzed me on the US constitution, and chided me for my poor Dari. I tried to regain control of the conversation by asking him how long he had been a teacher. His answer: since long before I was born. I asked what subjects he taught, and he recited some Macbeth ('life is but a walking shadow, a poor player, that struts and frets his hour upon the stage'). I could only imagine what he was like in the classroom.

When he eventually allowed us to begin talking about the Taliban, he turned neutral, almost evasive. He conceded that, yes, Taliban education monitors visited his school. He said this in a way that suggested it was unremarkable. And when I asked whether they had any objections to the way the school was run, he conceded that they blacked out a few pages in the state textbooks and made some other changes. But he emphasised that working under the Taliban was no problem. I told him I was surprised by that, and I asked him whether he thought they should have the right to take things out of the textbook or tell him how to do his job.

He smiled patiently and said it was no problem, that they could adapt. I didn't believe for a moment that someone of his character, or what I had seen of it so far, would have 'no problem' with anyone, let alone the Taliban, dictating the terms upon which he lived his life or did his job. I asked him whether he supported the Taliban and if he believed that what they were doing was right.

'It is not about who we can support, we do not have that luxury. I must dance with whoever is there. We must surrender to whoever is there,' he said. 'When the *mujahedeen* came, we surrendered. When the Karzai government came, we surrendered. If the Taliban come, we surrender. This is how we survive.'

Afghans have been forced to cope with armed groups on and off for most of their lives, from the *mujahedeen* factions at war with the government and Soviet forces during the 1980s and early 1990s, to the Taliban and other groups at war with the government and a coalition of international forces in more recent years. Continual war and upheaval have diminished the various organisations and institutions that might help Afghans to protect themselves (not least of all because various combatants have deliberately, repeatedly targeted these institutions and other forms of social organisation). And yet, dancing feels like a more apt description than surrendering. Civilians have been forced to develop different responses, tactics and strategies to survive. Chronic conflict, as destructive and devastating as it has been, has given rise to new capacities, new forms of organisation and collaboration, and new methods of subversion.

When the post-2001 insurgency emerged, few civilians initially wanted to engage with them. In the eyes of many, they were a shadowy group of armed men who threatened to upset the tentative peace. Even as the Taliban grew in influence, the diffuse nature of the insurgency in these early years limited the possibilities for bargaining. Yet as the insurgency became more coherent and more powerful, engaging with the Taliban became necessary for communities to survive. As in the past, customary institutions, relational ties and shared experience informed civilian engagement with the insurgency. By the time I began this research into the Taliban in 2017, they had established a shadow state in many parts of Afghanistan. Their influence was inescapable in these areas, and nearly everyone I encountered had a story about dealing with the Taliban.

This chapter introduces the social and cultural features most salient to understanding civilian–insurgent bargaining in Afghanistan. It does not provide a comprehensive history of modern Afghanistan's conflicts or social geography, but it does provide enough context for those not familiar with Afghanistan to understand the unique factors that have shaped civilian survival strategies, the political and social order, and insurgent war fighting strategies. It begins by sketching out Afghan forms of identity and social organisation in order to contextualise bargaining experiences and dynamics. It then examines Afghan experiences of conflict since the outbreak of internal armed conflict in 1979, with an eye towards how these experiences have shaped civilian bargaining capacities and behaviours.

Social organisation in Afghanistan

Forms of identity and social organisation

Anthropologist Louis Dupree once described Afghanistan as 'a cultural, as well as physical, melting-pot', nearly as diverse in its landscape and environment as it is in its people, cultures and traditions (Dupree, 1980: 57). While the population of 37 million people[1] is nearly entirely Muslim (predominantly Sunni Hanafi, although there is a sizable Shia minority), Islam is one of few broad commonalities. There are fourteen officially recognised ethnic groups, yet some studies have put the number as high as fifty-five, with many more sub-groupings (see Glatzer, 1998). Ethnicity and tribe are defining features of Afghan identity, yet data on Afghanistan's ethno-demography is limited by the fact that, as of this writing, no census has ever been completed.

Pashtuns are typically portrayed as the largest ethnic group, comprising 42 per cent of the population by one estimate, although that majority status is subject to debate.[2] Pashtun social organisation centres around tribal structures based on an egalitarian model (Rubin, 2002), comprising an intricate array of sub-groupings which descend from tribal confederations, to tribes, to clans, to lineages. Tajiks comprise the second-largest grouping, estimated to be around 27 per cent of the population. Tajiks are distinguished from Pashtuns both by language (they typically speak Persian and not Pashtu) and in that they are organised according to local lineages and geographic ties rather than tribe (Rubin, 2002; Dupree, 1980). Hazaras and Uzbeks are each believed to comprise around 9 per cent of the population. Uzbek generally refers to Turkic speakers organised along Central Turkic tribal lines. Many are believed to have emigrated to Afghanistan in the early twentieth century, although some have lived in Afghanistan for centuries (Dupree, 1980; Glatzer, 1998). Hazaras are Shia Muslims, also likely Turkic in origin, believed to have arrived in Afghanistan far earlier than Uzbeks, sometime between 1229 and 1447 (Bacon, 1951). The remainder of the population consists of smaller groups such as the Aimaq, Turkmen and Baluch, among others. Ethno-geographic distinctions—that Pashtuns predominate in the south and east, Tajiks in the north/northeast, Uzbeks in the north/northwest, Hazaras in the central region—are broadly resonant but deeply fluid. Ethnic groups have mixed, married, traded and relocated into new territory for centuries (Dupree, 1980).

The implications of ethnic and tribal identity are complex and have often been misunderstood. Scholar Christian Bleuer describes much of what has been written as 'ethnic stereotyping of behaviour or assumed behaviour based on lack of knowledge' (Bleuer, 2014). To support his case, Bleuer recalls that conventional wisdom in Western policy circles before 2010 was that Pashtuns in the north would never join the Taliban—until they did, along with Uzbeks and Tajiks, who many also believed would never be drawn to the Taliban for reasons of identity politics. Because identity is unpredictably fluid, attempts to claim knowledge on the determinative nature of ethnic and tribal dynamics can easily, and often do, overstep the mark. These forms of identity matter, but their meanings have been politically manipulated, reshaped by conflict and, at times, militarised over decades of conflict (Barfield, 2010).

The key distinction to bear in mind is that while Afghanistan's twentieth-century conflicts have often been organised along ethnic lines, these conflicts were rooted in ideology, not identity (Rubin, 2002; Barfield, 2011). While there might be little political cohesiveness among ethnic groups, the accounts of those I interviewed underscored that ethnic and tribal identity does indeed play an operational (if not always straightforward) role in political and economic life. At the same time, Afghans often display closer links to the people they live with—their kin and neighbours (or *qawm*)—than they might with any broader national level co-ethnic grouping (Barfield, 2010; Rubin, 2002). *Qawm* is, in essence, one's personal network. What this suggests is that Afghan forms of identity are functional and situational, and that Afghans mobilise various elements of their identity to suit the circumstances at hand. Crucially, forms of identity and social organisation—whether *qawm* or tribe or ethnic group—are shored up by reciprocal relationships. These kinds of connections are often necessary for gaining access to nearly everything of importance: getting a place at university, obtaining employment, securing a development project for one's village, getting elected to political office, getting a relative released from jail and so on.

There are, of course, those who see ethnic and tribal identity as more stable and determinative of behaviour and political dynamics in Afghanistan (Christia, 2012; Martin, 2014). This book takes a more nuanced stand: ethnicity and tribe are not the only forms of identity that matter, and in many instances they may not even be the most important ones. Further, one form of identity is not necessarily useful in and of itself; utility derives from its potential to unlock resources and other advantages. Complex and diverse processes of reciprocity and exchange underpin and sustain identity-based linkages. Another way of understanding these dynamics is to define identity and networks as forms of social capital. Social capital, as discussed in the previous chapter, enhances the ability to gather information and the understanding required to navigate complex social interactions. It also creates a safety net of trust and protection that enables an individual to take risks. Particularly in the context of a weak state and institutions, one's social capital—and ability to use it strategically—heavily influences one's access to opportunities and protection (Rubin, 2002; Sharan, 2013).

The Taliban, like Afghanistan itself, is ethnically and geographically diverse. While the movement's philosophy and core tenets are rooted in rural Pashtun values, and it is commonly assumed that the Ghilzai Pashtuns play a dominant role within the Taliban, the movement today extends far beyond this base. The Taliban's resilience partly derives from its ability to adapt to local dynamics and appeal to different audiences. The Taliban's post-2001 insurgency first penetrated predominantly Pashtun areas of the south, southeast and east, but as they expanded they inevitably had to contend with Afghanistan's diversity. As the Taliban spread through the north, they had to contend with ethnically mixed, and often consequently internally divided, communities in the north and west. In Herat and Faryab in the northwest and Kunduz in the north, for example, the Taliban exerted significant influence even in predominantly Tajik and Uzbek communities. Even within heavily Pashtun areas of the south and east, the Taliban comprised a relatively diverse mix of tribal identities. The post-2001 Taliban typically downplayed ethnicity or tribe, presenting themselves as a movement representing all Afghans (Johnson, 2018; Peterson, 2017; Ruttig, 2010). The Taliban has become increasingly multiethnic in their rhetoric, composition and the territory they seek to control. They have recruited locally and widened ethnic representation at the senior level by appointing more Tajiks and Uzbeks, including to the Taliban's leadership council (Jackson, 2018b).

In the 1990s, part of the Taliban's success lay in the fact that they emphasised, validated and elevated a specific, purist version of Afghan village culture and Islam (Edwards, 2002; see also Gopal and Strick van Linschoten, 2017). The deep divide between Afghanistan's urban and rural populations can be traced to the government's modernising efforts in the early mid-twentieth century. The divide was then widened under the People's Democratic Party of Afghanistan (PDPA) government, which sought to remake rural society as part of a modernisation agenda. The PDPA effectively attacked rural values, traditions and modes of organisation, while privileging more liberal and progressive urban values. While admittedly more complex than we have time to explore here,[3] the current conflict has tracked along this fault line. The majority of Afghans live in rural areas, but they have seen fewer post-2001 benefits than those living in urban areas (i.e., standard of living improvements, access to opportunities) (Pain, 2012). Afghans in largely government-controlled urban areas, by contrast, tend to be more educated, wealthier (thanks in part to the aid economy) and more connected, through media and internet, to the outside world (Asey, 2019).

By 2019, the Taliban had crept closer to urban areas but did not control major cities, and even the district centres it controlled can be considered rural (i.e., typically no or few paved roads, little electricity, an economy primarily reliant on agriculture and related trades and businesses). The Taliban remains an insurgency rooted in the mentality and beliefs of Afghanistan's more conservative countryside, which has given them leverage with rural populations. While it has de-emphasised tribal and ethnic links, it still draws on various forms of identity and feelings of marginalisation to gain traction. As an insurgency, the Taliban has reflected, affirmed and elevated specific rural values, beliefs, biases and practices (Giustozzi, 2008; Gopal and Strick van Linschoten, 2017). It has drawn on these beliefs and practices to wage its war, using social capital to attract converts and compel civilian compliance.

The impact of conflict on identity and social organisation

One tie that binds Afghans together is the experience of conflict. The majority of Afghans alive today were born after Afghanistan descended into conflict in 1979. One woman I met talked about wanting to see peace simply because she could not imagine what it might be like, explaining that she was 'now twenty-one years old and my whole life has been spent in war'.[4] Most Afghans have fled fighting at least once in their lives. Nearly half have lost family members to war, and almost half of all Afghan men have been wounded as a result of the violence (International Committee of the Red Cross, 2009). The toll of the violence has, however, varied over time and across the country. During the communist era, Afghan state and Russian forces waged a war against the *mujahedeen* in the countryside while the cities remained relatively untouched. During the civil war, violence tracked along cleavages among the *mujahedeen*. Kabul was wracked by fighting, the city divided by factional front lines. The countryside was largely lawless, with various *mujahedeen* factions battling one another for control. The Taliban swiftly seized control of 80 per cent of the country between 1994 and 1996, but remained at war with the Northern Alliance.

After the fall of the Taliban in 2001, the country experienced peace, albeit briefly, for the first time in decades. The Taliban began regrouping in 2002 and the insurgency spread into the south and east by 2006. By 2017, few areas of the country were immune from the violence. Major cities remained under government control but were periodically subject to Taliban and other insurgent attacks. In some areas of the countryside, the conflict resembled a tug of war between pro-government forces and the Taliban. Some people interviewed in Helmand, for example, referred to several different wars since 2001 because their villages had changed hands multiple times between the government and the Taliban. Narratives of the current conflict consistently portrayed a relentless sense of fear and uncertainty, marked by repeated surges of violence. One man told of how his house had been raided and damaged by pro-government forces four times since 2009. Another had his farm mined by the Taliban, his property ransacked and destroyed by pro-government forces and family members killed by both Taliban and pro-government forces. These stories were typical rather than exceptional.

There are two important implications here. The first is that Afghans have had to negotiate their survival with a rotating cast of armed groups since 1979. In the beginning, they learned how to negotiate their survival with both the PDPA and Russian forces on the one side, and with the *mujahedeen* on the other. One man interviewed explained that 'it was just like now: you needed to have friends who are communists and friends who are *mujahedeen*, and now you need friends that are government and friends that are Taliban'.[5]

Even if they fled to refugee camps in Pakistan, their survival still hinged on these kinds of links. Afghans were required to affiliate themselves, directly or through a refugee *malik*, with a *mujahedeen* group in order to receive aid, and several camps were known to be under the control of *mujahedeen* commanders or their proxies (Rubin, 2002). After the Taliban rose to prominence in the 1990s, people had to deal with the group's notorious Vice and Virtue Police or negotiate with other Taliban authorities. One friend, then a teenager, negotiated with the Taliban to run a girls' school in Kabul. The Taliban granted their permission, so long as she agreed to operate discreetly, and also to admit a local Taliban official's daughters. To be clear, civilians had amassed formidable collective capacity to negotiate with armed groups by the time the Taliban returned after 2001.

The second implication lies in understanding how conflict has affected forms of identity, organisation and social cohesion. Prolonged violence, mass migration and dislocation have profoundly reshaped local power dynamics and practices. Further, the fact that Afghanistan's wars have been predominantly ideologically driven has meant that they have often been fought through, and over, social practices and modes of organisation. Combatants have repeatedly targeted the very relations, organisations and institutions that might help civilians to cope and negotiate their survival. The most important of these, particularly in rural areas, are customary authorities, which pre-date the establishment of the Afghan state and have endured successive regimes that have sought to either co-opt or disempower them. Customary authorities are defined here as formal or informal institutions based on custom, religion and tradition, and which are broadly recognised and accepted by the people.

Customary authorities are generally comprised of three core entities in a given community. First, there is the village leader, usually a *malik* or *arbab*, who acts as a liaison with state authorities. Then there are the religious figures, mullahs and *ulema*, who provide guidance based on their knowledge of sharia, spread information and political messages via their preaching and preside over the mosques that are central to village social and spiritual life. Finally, a council, or *shura*, comprised of elders maintains community cohesion, settles disputes and enforces rules governing communal resources. The village leader or religious figures may also be part of the *shura* or be called upon to advise and support it. The degree to which state structures have penetrated rural life has varied over time, but formal government presence has generally been limited and intermittent (Brick Murtazashvili, 2016).

Community leaders and mullahs were targeted throughout the wars, as successive ruling factions sought to remake rural society. The PDPA enacted sweeping rural reforms, banned various traditional practices and disempowered customary authorities (Roy, 1990). At the same time, the war obliterated government presence in many areas. During and after the Russian withdrawal, Astri Suhrke writes, a 'virtual refeudalization' occurred in some places, with traditional structures reassuming responsibility for local defence and taxation (Suhrke, 1990: 243). *Mujahedeen* elsewhere sought to replace customary authorities with their own representatives, creating a new rural elite (Brick Murtazashvili, 2016). The Taliban subsequently elevated the role of mullahs and religious authorities over that of elders and *shuras*, and tried to replace customary norms with their interpretation of sharia. In the south, for example, many traditional elders and elites were banned from holding government positions, and their influence over state affairs was restricted (Gopal and Strick van Linschoten, 2017).

This complex picture of assault and resilience directly contradicts the post-2001 dominant narrative that by the time of the international intervention, customary authorities had been irrevocably damaged or destroyed by decades of conflict. In discourses about the post-2001 intervention, Western policymakers framed Afghanistan as a place in which the economy, institutions, social fabric and nearly everything else had been destroyed and therefore must be rebuilt from scratch.[6] The Taliban resurgence was seen as the consequence of this breakdown in traditional forms of authority and the absence of the state.

There are strong reasons to doubt these assumptions. In her study of informal governance in Afghanistan, Jennifer Brick Murtazashvili argues that, despite the damage inflicted by conflict, many customary institutions found a 'renewed sense of importance' in filling a gap between the government and the people (Brick Murtazashvili, 2016: xxxi). Customary institutions tried, to varying degrees, to maintain local order and ensure security, and they remained a conduit for collective resources and public goods. These structures may not have looked the same, and individuals may not have gone by the same honorifics as they had in the past, but customary authorities nonetheless regenerated to respond to the circumstances. And they remained deeply relevant to many Afghans: in a 2008 study, 82 per cent of Afghans said that, outside of their family, they would consult a customary authority if they had a problem (Brick, 2008).

The ability to regenerate, of course, varied according to local conflict histories and dynamics, and these were far from uniform across the country (Nojumi et al., 2008). At one end of the spectrum, some village leaders were able to bargain with groups that sought to rule while, at the other end, many were killed, abducted or forced to flee. Some authorities allowed themselves to be co-opted by ruling authorities, while others retained a higher degree of independence. Depending on the circumstances, any one of these choices might have diminished or enhanced their effectiveness, cohesiveness and legitimacy. The impact of the conflict might have been one factor, but only one factor among many.

There does, however, seem to be a link between the weakness of customary structures and the Taliban's post-2001 geographic expansion. Taliban presence was seen as roughly correlated, at least in the early years of the insurgency, to areas where tribal structures and authority was weak. Where customary authorities failed to keep social order and secure or provide public goods for their constituents, the Taliban appeared to have greater leverage. When customary dispute resolution was weak, for example, internal conflicts over resources or other issues often festered and escalated. This gave the insurgency traction, and the Taliban sharia courts subsequently responded to these needs. By contrast, the Taliban could offer little added value in this way (and likely found fewer internal grievances to exploit) in areas where customary authorities were functional and respected.

Additionally, the Taliban dealt with specific types of customary authorities differently. Because village leaders were often explicitly associated with the government, for instance, the insurgency generally saw them as having 'taken sides'. They also likely saw village leaders as rivals for authority. Consequently, the Taliban typically targeted or mistrusted village leaders. Where village leaders were not targeted, the Taliban either sought to co-opt them into existing structures or sideline them entirely. By contrast, the Taliban expected, and compelled, religious figures to support and enable them. The Taliban's narrow interpretation of Islam and their desire to elevate religious authority above all else appealed to some rural mullahs, who supported them voluntarily (Giustozzi, 2008). The notion of 'voluntary support' is, however, tenuous, given that in many cases it may have been suicidal to do otherwise. Many of the religious figures that opposed the Taliban were harassed, threatened and killed. The BBC estimates that the Taliban assassinated some 800 religious figures between 2003 and 2013 (Azami, 2013).

Like Afghan rulers before them, the Taliban relies on religious figures to legitimise their rule.[7] Village religious figures are often co-opted into Taliban structures and play an influential role in collecting information and acting on the Taliban's behalf. As one man from Uruzgan said, 'Taliban cultivate the mullahs because they can say anything, convince people of anything.'[8] Mosques have served as meeting places and shelter for the Taliban, as well as forums through which the Taliban can deliver messages. Several people interviewed described mullahs in

Taliban areas as 'loudspeakers' for the Taliban, broadcasting their rules and edicts during prayer times.

Elders, and the *shuras* they comprise, occupy a different kind of space. They are uniquely mandated to mediate and solve problems. They do not have the power of religion or the authority of a village leader per se, but their legitimacy derives from a kind of neutrality and benevolent wisdom. The *shura* is the de facto consultative body of the village and the core mechanism for solving disputes and making decisions. The *shura* is a particularly clever device for accommodating competing interests because it is relatively representative and democratic, and it prioritises consensus and accommodation (Newell, 1972). It is the most influential decision-making body at the local level because it derives its authority directly from, and is accountable to, the people. The legitimacy of the *shura*, and thus its power, rests on its ability to maintain community cohesion, harmony and well-being.

Both civilians and the Taliban have described elders as apolitical. Elders have traditionally played a useful intermediary function between ruling authorities and the population. When the Taliban returned, elders typically sought to deal with them as they had with other ruling authorities: by negotiating. Taliban attitudes towards elders were mixed. Where they could be ignored or undermined, the Taliban often tried to diminish their influence. Where they were strong, however, the Taliban had to work with them. In exchange, elders effectively delivered civilian compliance. This was not a one-off 'delivery' of obedience per se, but a process of managing the civilian population for the Taliban (and vice versa). Elders mediated problems between the people and the Taliban, and they provided the first line of response when trouble arose between the two.

Experiences of conflict

Afghanistan's modern era of political instability began with the overthrow of Daoud Khan in 1978 and subsequent invasion by Soviet forces in 1979. This section begins with a brief overview of Russian occupation and the war of *mujahedeen* resistance, civil war and Taliban rule, followed by a more comprehensive discussion of the conflict since

2001. During the nascent insurgency (2002–9), Taliban tactics were marked by a combination of persuasion and violence, reflecting the Taliban's own disorganisation and lack of internal control. The Taliban under military pressure (2009–14) describes the Taliban's response to the US troop surge and counterinsurgency strategy (December 2009 through September 2012). Territorial expansion (2014–19) covers the contraction of international forces and the subsequent expansion of Taliban influence across the country.

Russian occupation and civil war (1979–89)

After decades of relatively stable monarchic rule, King Zahir Shah was overthrown by his cousin, Mohammad Daoud Khan, in 1973. Daoud sought to remake Afghanistan into a modern republic, yet dissatisfaction with his reforms fuelled the growth of national communist parties, which began to receive significant support from the Soviet Union. In 1978, Daoud and his family were executed in a communist coup, referred to as the Saur Revolution, led by Nur Mohammad Taraki. Taraki, like his successors Hafizullah Amin and Babrak Karmal, employed suppression and violence—including mass arrests, torture and summary executions—to implement reforms. Many well-educated Afghans, landed elites and religious leaders (the primary targets of the regime's violence) fled the country (Maley, 2002). The brutality sparked resistance from Islamic factions, later known as the *mujahedeen*, and a series of violent uprisings in the spring of 1979. Amin, the leader of a rival communist faction, overthrew Taraki in October 1979 but was killed by Soviet-backed assassins in December of that year. He was replaced by Babrak Karmal, who resigned in 1986 and was in turn replaced by Najibullah Ahmadzai.

The Soviet Union invaded Afghanistan in late December 1979. As with the post-2001 conflict, the Afghan government and Soviet troops retained control of most cities while *mujahedeen* factions waged a guerrilla war in rural areas. The groups that comprised the *mujahedeen* were never a unified movement; they were diverse in terms of capability and often fragmented (although many factions were loosely aligned at various points). Most were grassroots in nature, shaped by ethnic, religious and tribal affiliations (Shahrani and Canfield, 1984). Typical *mujahedeen* military operations were small-scale and localised, focusing on things like hit-and-run tactics, shelling government targets, sabotaging infrastructure, assassinations and rocket attacks (Jalali and Grau, 1995).

Although initial Soviet troop presence was light, the *mujahedeen* effectively drew the Soviets further into the conflict. Soviet and Afghan government forces employed brutal counter-tactics that were not only direct violations of international law but arguably genocidal in nature (Fein, 1993). These tactics included launching airstrikes on civilian areas, laying mines in rural areas to cut off supply routes and conducting violent raids on villages alleged to be harbouring *mujahedeen* (Maley, 2002). Suspected 'collaborators' were detained and often tortured; many disappeared (Laber and Rubin, 1988). An estimated 870,000 Afghans were killed between 1978 and 1987, an average of 240 each day, 1.2 million Afghans disabled and 3 million wounded (Khalidi, 1991). More than 5 million people—nearly a fifth of the estimated population—fled to Pakistan and Iran, and 2 million more were internally displaced (UNHCR, 2005; Schmeidl and Maley, 2006).

The *mujahedeen* government and civil war (1989–94)

The withdrawal of Soviet forces began in 1989 and was completed by 1992. The Afghan government, led by President Najibullah, distanced itself from communism and pivoted towards nationalism, but these efforts never gained much traction. The government subsequently collapsed after Najibullah resigned in April 1992 (Tomsen, 2011). The UN brokered the Peshawar Accords, a shaky power-sharing deal among most of the major *mujahedeen* factions, the same month. Rather than creating a viable government, the Accords resulted in violent competition among the *mujahedeen* (several key factions had refused to take part in them) and intensified meddling by regional powers (Dorronsoro, 2005; Saikal, 1998). The *mujahedeen* government instituted sharia law, including severe restrictions on women, but its internal divisions and limited territorial control rendered it deeply ineffectual. Fighting with those *mujahedeen* factions not part of the deal continued in Kabul and the countryside. Sibghatullah Mojaddedi, who occupied the first term of the rotating presidency agreed in the Accords, refused to step down in December 1992. Factions previously allied with the government mutinied, and overt civil war erupted.

This was not an ideologically driven or identity-based conflict so much as a war for power and control (despite the fact that many *mujahedeen* mobilised ethnic divisions to garner support). Alliances and hostilities among factions were often tactical and short-lived. As agreements broke down and territory changed hands, civilians were subjected to retaliatory punishments by victorious forces (Amnesty International, 1995). An estimated 10,000 individuals were killed across the country in 1993 alone, and thousands of individuals were abducted and never heard from again (Amnesty International, 1995). Rape was condoned by some *mujahedeen* leaders as a means of punishing civilians and rewarding fighters (Amnesty International, 1999). '*Mujahedeen*' became synonymous with violence and predatory tactics such as 'taxes' levied at checkpoints, robbery and varying forms of organised, and often disorganised, crime (Dorronsoro, 2009). The *mujahedeen*, seen by many Afghans as heroes during the Soviet occupation, became feared and reviled for the chaos they wrought. By 1994, over a million Afghans had fled to Pakistan and just under a million to Iran (UNHCR, 1995).

Taliban rule (1994–2001)

In November 1994, a group of religious students and former *mujahedeen* who would later be known as the Taliban seized control of Kandahar, vowing to restore order. They harshly punished alleged criminals and eliminated predatory checkpoints. In the early days, the Taliban had little professed intent beyond ridding their districts of abusive commanders and restoring some form of law and order (Zaeef, 2010). A May 1995 letter attributed to the Taliban's then-leader, Mullah Omar, explains:

> We went to all these corrupt leaders and begged them to stop the intimidation of their people and put an end to the crisis in the country. We begged them to stop fighting ... Our wish was the implementation of the law of the Qur'an and it still is. We are fighting so that our countrymen can have a peaceful and prosperous life.[9]

There is a strong narrative that as the Taliban expanded they encountered little resistance from a war-weary population.[10] This may have been true in some places, but elsewhere Taliban soldiers executed prisoners, slaughtered civilians and enacted blockades that obstructed food and necessities from reaching civilians (Afghanistan Justice Project, 2005; Human Rights Watch, 1998; Maley, 2002). Their ascent was nonetheless swift. By September 1995, the Taliban controlled most of the eastern, western and southern provinces. They captured Kabul the following year, seizing former President Najibullah from a UN compound, where he had sheltered since shortly after his resignation in 1992. They tortured and executed him before stringing up his body at a traffic circle. By September 2001, the Taliban controlled nearly 80 per cent of Afghanistan but remained at war with *mujahedeen* factions in remote pockets of the country.

Once the Taliban gained territory, they were immediately confronted with a problem that they were ill-equipped to solve: governance (Strick van Linschoten, 2016: 128). Early Taliban commander Mohammad Akbar Agha writes that the Taliban government 'was an interim administration in a time of war, one without political knowledge' (Agha, 2014: 1452–3). It was also a government without many educated or trained civil servants and an almost non-existent budget.[11] While the Taliban could provide security—via coercion and fear—and justice—through their sharia courts— they faltered on most other fronts. Contrary to popular narratives, their system of governance was not revolutionary. It was, for the most part, patched together from what was left of state institutions. Reconstructing a state from the ruins of the Afghan civil war would have been a formidable task for any actor. For the Taliban, this was made all the more difficult by the fact that they lacked any experience of governing, received almost no external recognition or support and were further hamstrung by a 'conservative neo-fundamentalist mindset that regarded much of the new endeavours with great scepticism' (Strick van Linschoten, 2016: 131).

The West arguably saw only the latter part of that equation. The Taliban came to be defined by their religious extremism and brutality towards civilians. The Taliban Vice and Virtue Police enforced a strict set of rules, especially in the cities, based on an esoteric interpretation of Islam and sharia law. Educated and professional women in urban areas particularly suffered, with a strict dress code enforced through beatings, a near-total ban on female education, dire access to healthcare and prohibitions on women working outside the home (Hatch Dupree, 1998). The regime destroyed cultural artefacts and curtailed or banned activities that they deemed un-Islamic, including watching television and flying kites. The Taliban quickly became international pariahs. Aid was withheld by Western governments in response to their treatment of women and human rights violations, as well as their harbouring of Osama bin Laden and other Al Qaeda figures.

The Taliban's largest problem, at least until September 2001, appeared to be financial. The economy was in shambles. Afghans became heavily dependent on external support to meet even basic nutritional needs, a situation exacerbated by a severe drought—which the Taliban badly mismanaged—in 2000. At one point, half of Kabul's population was reliant on food delivered by humanitarian agencies (Rashid, 2001). The black-market economy became increasingly important to gaining access to food and other resources that enabled survival (Bhatia et al., 2003). In April 2000, the government cut 40 per cent of its staff because they no longer had the money to pay their salaries (Dorronsoro, 2005). The exodus of Afghan refugees continued, with nearly 1.5 million fleeing to Iran and 2 million to Pakistan by September 2001.[12]

International intervention and nascent insurgency (2001–9)

After the 9/11 attacks, the Taliban's continued refusal to hand over bin Laden and his Al Qaeda associates to US authorities became the pretext for war. On 7 October 2001, a coalition of international forces, led by the US, declared war on the Taliban government in Afghanistan. Anti-Taliban forces occupied Kabul by November 2001, and the Taliban surrendered their stronghold of Kandahar the following month. At the Bonn Conference in December 2001, an interim government was created, with Hamid Karzai named as its president and an international peacekeeping force, the NATO-led International Security Assistance Force (ISAF), mandated to maintain security in Kabul. In May 2003, the US announced an end to major combat operations. At that point, it appeared that the Taliban had been decisively defeated. Several key Taliban leaders, Mullah Omar reportedly among them, attempted to surrender to the US in late 2001, but they were largely rebuffed

(Knowlton, 2001). Some Taliban leaders were arrested, but the majority, including Omar, fled to Pakistan, while much of the Taliban rank and file dissolved back into the population. Few details are known about the early days of the insurgency, but, according to Taliban accounts, they began regrouping in Pakistan at some point during 2002, and started sending small teams across the border into southern and eastern Afghanistan to lay the groundwork for infiltration (Giustozzi, 2018; Farrell and Giustozzi, 2013).

Mohibullah, a Taliban fighter from Logar, described how this unfolded in his village. The first concrete sign of Taliban return was a Taliban night letter posted by the village mosque, warning that those collaborating with enemy forces would be punished. And then the attacks began. 'For the first three years, there was only the Karzai government, no Taliban,' he said.

> But then they were active from the night time, and we were scared. We did not know what they wanted or what would happen. We did not know the reality about America, we saw the American soldiers in the bazaar, patrolling, joking with us, giving candy to us, and toys. But the Taliban educated us about their true mission and their war against Islam.[13]

Mohibullah remembered his father being alarmed at the growing attacks, but he and some of his friends were curious. 'At first, they were difficult to find, but then I learned that they would be in mosques or houses at night time, so I would just go and listen to them,' he recalled.

> I was around 15 at the time, and I left school to help them. I was learning English and third in my class, but I dropped out. The Taliban was getting stronger, and I thought it would be shameful to keep going to school, to a government school. It was a Karzai school. It was shameful somehow. The Taliban was fighting for jihad, you see?[14]

Mohibullah and his friends would act as lookouts at first but eventually began planting improvised explosive devices (IEDs) on local roads. The Taliban had no weapons to supply, so he stole his father's Kalashnikov to bring on operations. His father, a former *mujahedeen* commander, was deeply opposed to his son joining Taliban ranks, and they had furious rows. His father pleaded for him to stay in school and told him that the Taliban were only going to cause trouble for the village. Mohibullah argued that he was obligated as a Muslim to wage jihad on the Americans, just as his father had done against the Russians. US forces began hunting the Taliban in the area. They orchestrated searches and raids, arresting young men from the village and bombing the houses of suspected Taliban fighters and commanders. A teacher from Mohibullah's village recounted how the increase in military operations against the Taliban created a backlash. 'It really allowed the Taliban to increase their support and recruitment because they killed civilians,' he said. 'People wanted revenge on the US and were convinced the only way to get that was to fight with the Taliban.'[15]

Patterns differed across the country, with social exclusion and government harassment elsewhere playing a more significant role in the Taliban's expansion. These divisions fell mainly along tribal and ethnic lines, between warlord patronage networks aligned with the Karzai government on the one hand and their marginalised adversaries on the other (Englehart, 2010; Farrell and Giustozzi, 2013; Gopal, 2015). A new political order was taking shape inside Afghanistan, but it was not the one premised on democracy and inclusion that the international community had promised. Of the first group of appointed governors, twenty of the thirty-two appointed were strongmen, former militia leaders or *mujahedeen*, or warlords (Giustozzi, 2008). A system of winners and losers; acts of revenge, retribution and reprisal by government allies against their adversaries; and broader social, political and economic exclusion sowed the seeds for the insurgency. The Taliban capitalised on these grievances to recruit new fighters and generate sympathy among civilians.

The Taliban initially focused on building networks to elicit information from civilians, to help them target Afghan and international forces, and the government. Their primary interest at this point was to gain a toehold in Afghan territory from which they could begin to wage a broader war. They also sought to gather recruits for their nascent force. Where they found sympathetic elders and mullahs, they would be given shelter in the village and allowed to preach in the mosque, outlining their grievances to the people (Giustozzi, 2008; Yousafzai, 2009). Where they encountered reticence or resistance, they relied more heavily on threats and violence. This strategy allowed the Taliban to gain footing in the south and east. In 2003, much of Paktia province in the southeast was under Taliban control, along with districts in nearby

Ghazni and Zabul. From there, they expanded into the south and further into the east (Giustozzi, 2008).

Early attacks focused on military targets, including the newly trained Afghan police and army as well as international forces, and anyone or anything affiliated with the government, including teachers, schools, clinics and aid workers. Data from this period is patchy, but it indicates that attacks were sporadic and contained within specific areas in the south, southeast and east (see Figure 2.1). Taliban violence inflicted scores of casualties on US forces in 2003, 2004 and 2005, but non-hostile causes of the conflict remained responsible for more deaths during this period (Semple and Lehren, 2008). Attacks on aid workers increased, with sixteen Afghan aid workers and at least one foreign aid worker killed between March 2003 and August 2004. Attacks on foreign civilians were also on the rise, with sixteen killed in the first six months of 2004 alone (Semple and Lehren, 2008). However, attribution for these attacks is unclear, and some may have been part of criminal or otherwise factional conflicts. The UN did not systematically record the number of Afghan civilians targeted by the Taliban until 2008. News reports indicate the Taliban killed 119 Afghans in the first half of 2003 and 179 during the same period in 2004, but these were mostly members of the newly created Afghan state security forces (Schmitt and Rohde, 2004). While documentation is scant, civilian accounts nonetheless suggest that intimidation and civilian harm were prevalent in areas of Taliban presence.[16]

2006 was a turning point. Scattered hit-and-run attacks and assassinations morphed into a more significant threat. Taliban violence increased by 200 per cent from 2005 levels. The Taliban targeted military installations and government buildings but also schools, clinics and aid projects (AIHRC, 2008; Human Rights Watch, 2007). In 2006, threats and attacks reportedly led to the closure of some 200 schools across southern Afghanistan (Gall, 2006). Suicide operations and incidents with IEDs dramatically increased. Between 2002 and 2005, there were twenty-nine suicide attacks; in 2006 alone, there were 139 (Human Rights Watch, 2007). IED attacks doubled between 2005 and 2007. Rudimentary IED use can be traced back to the *mujahedeen* days, when they were used against the Russians, but they—along with suicide attacks—were relatively rare until 2006. As Taliban intelligence improved and they got better at making and using explosives, their capacity to attack international forces increased.[17]

Figure 2.1. Growth of insecurity in Afghanistan, June 2003–June 2006

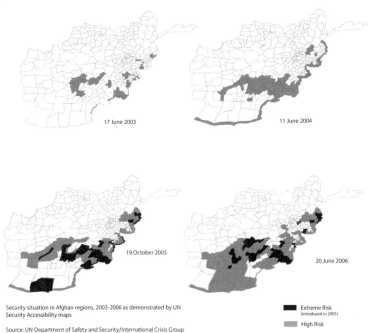

17 June 2003

11 June 2004

19 October 2005

20 June 2006

Security situation in Afghan regions, 2003-2006 as demonstrated by UN Security Accessibility maps

Source: UN Department of Safety and Security/International Crisis Group

Extreme Risk (introduced in 2005)

High Risk

A more fundamental factor in the Taliban's expansion is that, as Astri Suhrke argues, the international intervention unwittingly created a target-rich environment which played to the insurgency's strengths (Suhrke, 2008). The United States responded to growing Taliban presence by sending more troops to insecure areas and increasing patrols and operations.[18]

This gave the Taliban opportunities to strike. Additionally, international forces intensified their reconstruction and governance efforts, mostly through military-led Provincial Reconstruction Teams (PRTs). Funding for US PRT projects rose from around $40 million USD in 2004 to over $200 million in 2007 (SIGAR, 2012).[19] PRT projects like schools and roads were not as well defended, and far easier to attack, than purely military targets (i.e., bases and convoys).

Making matters worse, international forces, lacking sufficient resources or capacity, relied heavily on local power brokers for intelligence, support and security. That the United States and its allies were unable to establish responsive government institutions exacerbated this dependence. The Afghan state itself was reliant on a patchwork of alliances with warlord types to cultivate the appearance of control, thus creating a breeding ground for patronage and exclusion (Berdal, 2019; Coll, 2018; Jackson, 2016; Malejacq, 2019). These powerbrokers perpetrated widespread abuses against civilians while enjoying international protection and favour; this in turn undermined the legitimacy of both international forces and the government, and fuelled civilian fear and anger (Forsberg, 2009; Gopal, 2010; Dorronsoro, 2009). The Taliban exploited these grievances and offered civilians an opportunity to fight back.

The international strategy continued to inadvertently paint targets for the Taliban. In 2006, the ISAF mandate revision expanded NATO forces' presence through the country.[20] In response, the Taliban leaned more heavily on IEDs, suicide bombs, assassinations and attacks on soft targets like aid projects. The more troops NATO deployed and the more operations they conducted, the more they were targeted by the Taliban. The more PRTs tried to cultivate local support, the more the Taliban targeted civilians who co-operated with the PRTs. This is how the Taliban drew international forces further into the conflict, creating a vicious cycle that would persist for the next decade.[21]

While its military capacity had expanded, the Taliban was struggling to control its ranks. The Taliban military command was far from unified, comprised primarily of small, autonomous, localised armed groups. Fighters were loyal to their commanders rather than to the broader movement in any meaningful sense. A member of the Taliban leadership explained to me, almost apologetically, that 'that time was very different. Everyone was just coming to fight the war by themselves'. Individual commanders were operating their own fiefdoms and playing by their own rules. 'Every commander had his own government,' he recounted. 'If a person has ten fighters, he was thinking like, "I am the boss." He could do anything.'[22] This included beheadings and extreme acts of collective punishment, which spurred public outrage and concern among the Taliban leadership (Al Jazeera, 2007; Gebauer, 2007; Shah and Gall,

2007). Additionally, international forces routinely targeted insurgent commanders. Because these Taliban fighting groups were mostly autonomous and disconnected from one another at this point, these killings caused considerable disruption to Taliban operations.[23]

In response to the problems created by its decentralisation, the Taliban leadership sought to impose hierarchical control.[24] They did this in two main ways. The first was to impose ground rules on its ranks. The issuing of the *layha*, or code of conduct, in 2006 was the first apparent effort to set boundaries on fighter behaviour and communicate a clear organisational structure (even if it was not yet fully operational). The *layha*, initially consisting of thirty articles but later expanded, delineated rules for the kind of war the Taliban sought to wage. It was, in part, a war for legitimacy. A former Taliban official involved in drafting the *layha* explained that 'with the *layha*, we needed to show we could be accountable and could form an accountable government that everyone could accept'.[25]

The *layha* served practical as well as ideological objectives, framing the rules within a clear agenda and values-based framework. It underscored fighters' obligation to behave in line with Islam and in furtherance of the Taliban mission to restore 'true' Islamic values to Afghan society. Several articles aim to curb corruption and theft, reflecting the need to address the problematic behaviour of some commanders. The *layha* was accompanied by broader efforts to exert control from the top. The Taliban developed rudimentary systems to monitor fighter conduct. Phone numbers were distributed in Taliban areas so civilians could lodge complaints about Taliban conduct or operations (Strick van Linschoten and Kuehn, 2012a). These efforts were uneven and limited at best, but teams of Taliban investigators were deployed to some areas to investigate complaints. Reports emerged that several Taliban found to have committed abuses or failing to fulfil their duties were expelled, replaced and punished (Giustozzi, 2008; ISAF, 2012a; Jackson and Amiri, 2019).

Secondly, the Taliban sought to create a more hierarchical organisational structure. The leadership centralised military command under four main military fronts, or *mahaz*, which corresponded to geographic zones inside Afghanistan. They then unified this under one military commission, which reported to the senior leadership council. Reorganisation extended to provinces and districts. At the provincial level, shadow governors and military commissions were appointed to plan operations, manage logistics and resolve intra-Taliban disputes. At the district-level, military commissioners were selected to co-ordinate local *mahaz* and ensure commanders complied with orders from above. Experienced fighters were transferred to areas where the insurgency sought to expand. This allowed the Taliban to both capitalise on its growing expertise as well as disrupt personality-centric command structures.

The Taliban's desire to create a workable relationship with civilians was a driving factor of its centralisation efforts. Civilian compliance was necessary for the insurgency to survive, so the Taliban leadership undertook measures conducive to eliciting more sustainable compliance. Tighter command and control, however, also allowed the leadership to use violence more selectively to ensure that civilians would not inform upon them, and to alienate them from state and international forces.

By 2008–9, the Taliban had enough control and internal coherence to start implementing a system of governance. They began enforcing policies that reflected their ideological objectives: banning music, regulating beard length, meting out justice in accordance with their interpretation of sharia and so on. Governance systems allowed them to more effectively monitor and control the population and also enabled them to begin providing more predictable incentives to encourage civilian compliance. While the evolution of the Taliban's shadow government would be stop–start and patchy, it would ultimately grow to govern civilian life in over half of the country by 2019.

The surge and drawdown (2009–14)

In late 2009, US President Barack Obama ordered a revision to the military strategy which nearly tripled the number of US troops deployed to Afghanistan (as illustrated in Figure 2.2). The United States sent 33,000 more combat soldiers to Afghanistan, bringing the total US troop count to over 100,000 by mid-2011. The United States envisioned that this surge would be brief: international forces would steadily decrease from July 2011 onwards, the surge would end by October 2012 and Afghan forces would assume responsibility for security by 2014 (CNN, 2009; Agence France-Presse, 2010).[26] The United States and other countries that had contributed troops repeatedly asserted that this transition to Afghan responsibility for security would be con-ditions-based (i.e., premised on security improvements). In reality, political imperatives and mounting US domestic disenchantment with the war—rather than conditions on the ground—ultimately drove the transition timeline (Berdal, 2019).

Figure 2.2. US troop levels in Afghanistan, 2001–18

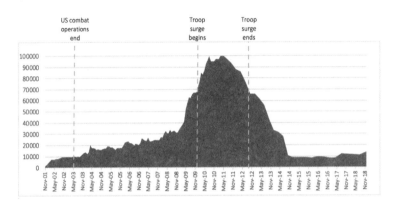

Source: Data until late 2017 comes from the US Department of Defense (DoD). In late 2017, the DoD stopped reporting the number of US military personnel deployed in support of operations in Afghanistan. The remainder of the figures for 2017 and 2018 come from Lubold and Youssef (2017), Cooper (2017), Gibbons-Neff and Mashal (2019), Lopez (2020), and Al Jazeera (2021).

The surge's objectives were never quite clear. How the United States and its allies would determine that Afghan forces were ready to assume control was never concretely defined. Rather, the goal of the surge was opportunistically defined and redefined at different times for different audiences. President Obama initially defined the surge's goal as 'disrupting, dismantling, and defeating al Qaeda and its extremist allies' in the region (CNN, 2009). This strained credulity. The Taliban regime may have refused to extradite Al Qaeda members, but the relationship between the two groups was fraught and Al Qaeda played little role in the Taliban resurgence (Strick van Linschoten and Kuehn, 2014). Plus, the degree to which Al Qaeda fighters were present in Afghanistan by 2009 was negligible and certainly not a driver of insecurity; the real cause of insecurity was a homegrown insurgency (albeit one that received significant safe haven and support from Pakistan). Framing the objective as counterterrorism was realpolitik: positioning Afghanistan's insecurity as a threat to US security helped justify an increased troop presence and funding to US citizens. More importantly, a counterterror objective inherently constrained US engagement and suggested that the insurgency would necessarily not have to be defeated in order for the United States and its allies to disengage. State-building objectives, by contrast, implied a more substantial and protracted involvement.

On the ground, a key US priority was to secure enough of the country so that elections could be held as planned in 2010 (Hoffman and Crowther, 2015). Over the longer term, the surge was designed to halt and reverse the Taliban's momentum—and to fortify the government and extend its control—yet it expected do so very quickly, in a predetermined timeframe. The surge was a combination of counterinsurgency and state-building-on-speed. State-building, in some form, was at least rhetorically required; it was illogical to expect that 'extremism' could be defeated without a stable national government in place. But the problem is that state-building is a slow process, and neither the United States nor its allies were willing to invest the time and resources that it would have required.

The troop surge indeed eroded Taliban control, inflicted heavy losses, disrupted their command structures, diminished their capacity to provide governance and forced the insurgency into a defensive posture; but it did not entirely halt Taliban momentum. The Taliban leaned back into guerrilla tactics, focusing their energy on violence and propaganda. They remained present in vast swathes of the south, southeast and east during this period and made new inroads into the north and west of the country. By the end of 2010, government officials could barely access one-third of the country (Jackson, 2010). In August 2009, the insurgency levelled 2,700 attacks on international forces; in August 2012, they lodged 3,000 attacks (ISAF, 2012b). Levels of violence were higher and Taliban presence more widespread in September 2012, after the surge ended, than they had been before the surge began.

Despite this enormous pressure, the Taliban underwent several significant forward-looking structural and policy shifts during the surge. The group's de facto leader (the then deputy of the movement), Mullah Mansour, was effectively positioning the Taliban to assume power. Interviews with current and former members of the Taliban leadership indicated that they began planning for the end of the surge and international withdrawal almost immediately after the strategy was announced in December 2009.[27] The Taliban played a long game, confident that they would be able to outlast foreign forces. They knew, however, that they would need to provide different means of controlling the population. Mansour focused on building command structures and internal coherence, aiming to transform the Taliban's disparate fighting forces into a unified political movement. Mansour understood that the Taliban would need international recognition to realise its ambitions. The Taliban regime of the 1990s was a pariah state, recognised only by Pakistan, Saudi Arabia and the United Arab Emirates. Few within the leadership wanted their future government to suffer the same fate. In an appeal for legitimacy, Mansour encouraged greater openness towards aid agencies and created a Taliban commission to investigate civilian casualties. This commission regularly met in Gulf States with UN human rights officials to discuss civilian harm.

More importantly, Mansour steered the group towards greater openness to diplomatic talks with the United States. Although there had been intermittent dialogue in previous years between the Taliban, the Afghan government and various Western governments, there had been no concrete progress on a political settlement to end the war. According to interviews with several people close to him, Mansour sensed that the drawdown of international forces planned for 2014 was an opportunity to reposition the Taliban on the international stage. Taliban representatives engaged in a series of informal peace talks, and the movement established an official presence in Qatar in 2013.

Taliban expansion and insurgent state-building (2014–19)

In 2015, ISAF was replaced by Operation Resolute Support (RS), a NATO non-combat mission to train, advise and assist Afghan forces, who would now assume responsibility for security. The presence of US forces further decreased from 34,000 in February 2014 to approximately 10,600 in January 2015 (USFOR-A Public Affairs, 2015). Afghan forces, at least in theory, would now take the lead on the battlefield. They were ill-prepared for the task, plagued by poor retention, corruption and a lack of adequate facilities such as medivac (SIGAR, 2017; Smith, 2015). US aid to the Afghan forces nonetheless dropped sharply as international troop levels decreased (Cordesman, 2017).

This shift in battlefield dynamics presented the Taliban with both risks and opportunities. They would now be fighting primarily Afghan forces, albeit still supported by RS. The Taliban's centralising reforms meant they now had the internal coherence needed to launch the kind of ambitious ground campaign required to engage Afghan forces directly. Combat became more symmetrical. As international troops decreased and air operations reduced, ground operations by Afghan forces became more frequent and more substantial (UNAMA Human Rights, 2014). From the end of the surge in 2012 up to 2016, civilian casualties from ground battles more than doubled, as can be seen in Figure 2.3 (UNAMA Human Rights, 2018). The Taliban often stood their ground, using heavy and light weapons, mortars and other explosives, and they were able to mount large-scale troop movements and strategic offensives. They seized district centres and cities, notably capturing Kunduz City in 2015 and attempting to do so again in 2016. In most cases, they could not hold cities or major towns for long in the face of international forces' airstrikes and ground counteroffensives. But, by 2017, large swathes of rural Afghanistan were effectively under Taliban control.

While levels of violence remained high during 2017–19, the nature of that violence started to change. The United States increased troop levels from 7,000 to 14,000. The UN reported that civilian casualties caused by airstrikes nearly doubled between 2016 and 2018, and the number of civilians killed in airstrikes in 2018 was equal to that of 2014, 2015 and 2016 combined.[28] Aerial operations appeared to target homes or compounds where Taliban were believed to be present, ostensibly to slow their momentum (Gibbons-Neff and Mashal, 2019). Airstrikes were rarely linked with attempts to establish or expand government control. Instead, the strategy increasingly focused on protecting cities rather than protecting vulnerable rural areas or re-asserting the government in rural areas already under significant Taliban influence or control (Gibbons-Neff and Cooper, 2018). Pro-government forces effectively ceded much of the countryside to the Taliban.

Figure 2.3. Civilian casualties caused by ground engagements, 2009–19

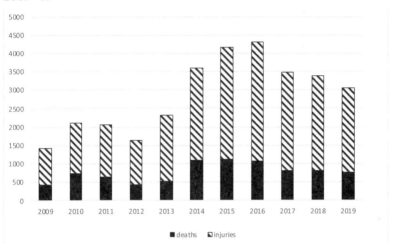

Estimates of how much territory the Taliban influenced or controlled are unreliable. In October 2018, the US government, using data provided by RS, estimated that the Taliban controlled or contested 46 per cent of the country's districts and the area where 37 per cent of the population resides (SIGAR, 2019). RS's data, perhaps unsurprisingly, has been challenged by many, and was later classified. By contrast, the Long War Journal claimed that the Taliban controlled, influenced or contested 65 per cent of the country's districts in 2019, while in 2018 the BBC estimated that the Taliban were 'openly active' in 70 per cent of the country's districts (Roggio and Gutowski, 2019; Sharifi and Adamou, 2018).

The picture on the ground was much more nuanced than any of these estimates imply. On visits to districts that RS classed as contested or government controlled, the district centre compound was often all that remained of government presence. Even there, control was tenuous. Taliban flags, for example, were often visible less than twenty feet away from Afghan police checkpoints. If an accurate map of Taliban influence existed, it might resemble Swiss cheese. Government influence outside major cities was permeable and increasingly encircled by the Taliban. District governors, judges and other state officials often resided elsewhere for their own safety; those who remained did so at the discretion of local Taliban. Some Afghan security forces struck tacit deals with the Taliban. Government checkpoints might be manned by Afghan police until around four in the afternoon, at which point they retreated and were replaced by Taliban checkpoints until the next morning.

More generally, the Taliban sought to directly compete with the Afghan government in areas they contested, and to replace it in areas they controlled. The Taliban implemented a sophisticated system of civilian governance, covering everything from regulating schools to levying taxes and adjudicating disputes. The Taliban sought to act like a state, and its relations with civilians reflected this in the areas they controlled. Taliban coercion of civilians, for example, took on a more predictable and state-like appearance. The Taliban's judges and governors issued and enforced rules. Taliban justice, in particular, became more systematic and widespread. Alleged spies were less likely to be executed on the spot and more likely to be given a Taliban trial. The Taliban also made concerted efforts to get government security forces and civil servants to switch sides (rather than threatening or attempting to kill them, as they had in the past). The Taliban promised Afghan soldiers and government workers who surrendered that they could live in peace. In other instances, they induced or coerced security forces or civil servants to spy for the Taliban (again, instead of killing them).

Nonetheless, tactics varied between areas where (a) the Taliban had relatively consolidated control, (b) it violently contested power and (c) it sought to establish influence. Inside its strongholds, Taliban coercion and violence was more formal and predictable. This greater predictability gave civilians a more explicit basis for decision-making. It even persuaded some that they might be able to secure some protection if they fully complied. Many people felt the Taliban, where it was unchallenged, was less likely to use war-like violence (i.e., IEDs, abductions, executions) against civilians. In more contested areas, by contrast, the opposite was true. As the Taliban expanded, violence increased: IEDs and suicide attacks accounted for 42 per cent of all civilian deaths in

2018 (UNAMA Human Rights, 2019). Insurgent attacks targeting civilians increased steadily between 2016 and 2018, in every region except the southeast.[29] In some areas where the Taliban had, theoretically, been routed and government control re-established, they nonetheless remained present, orchestrating attacks and exerting influence from the shadows. A farmer in Helmand, whose village was technically government controlled, said that 'the Taliban have never left us, and even when the government comes back, there are IEDs, attacks on checkpoints, and we know the Taliban are here'.[30]

The Taliban orchestrated a campaign of creeping influence in areas they sought to control. Coercion, coupled with the more popular aspects of Taliban governance, softened the ground. In major cities under government control, they often levied taxes and provided justice. They sought to regulate government service delivery in line with their ideology, visiting schools to inspect the curriculum and ensure boys and girls were educated separately. On a November 2017 visit to Kunduz City (then ostensibly under government control), I found that Taliban letters were pasted up in the central bazaar, shopkeepers and business owners provided receipts for Taliban tax payments and the results of the Taliban's regulation of private universities were evident (e.g., curtains placed across rooms to enforce gender segregation, objectionable pages excised from textbooks). These measures were not as strictly or uniformly enforced as in areas where the Taliban had consolidated control. Rather, the Taliban's coercive governance practices undermined state legitimacy and signalled to civilians that they should be preparing themselves to comply with Taliban rule.

3.

COERCION, CO-OPTION AND CO-OPERATION

TALIBAN TACTICS AND STRATEGY

In many civilian and Taliban accounts of the war, there were two versions of the Taliban: the Taliban as they existed at the beginning of the insurgency and the Taliban during its post-2014 ascent. In January 2019, I met a high-ranking Taliban official in the lobby of a four-star hotel in Dubai. He talked about many aspects of the movement's evolution, but what struck me most was how he described the early behaviour of the Taliban insurgency. When I asked him about the widespread assassinations of elders in the south, he described that time period as a 'fear government' and conceded, 'We made some mistakes in the past.'[1]

'These guys in some of these places, they were just taking revenge, doing what they could,' he explained. 'There were no rules, and okay, maybe they targeted people who should not have been targeted.' He insisted that now things were different, and the Taliban had a parallel government full of 'educated people' who knew how to run things and cared about the well-being of civilians.

The idea that their shadow state was full of 'educated people' who prioritised civilian well-being did not match what I had seen on the ground, but it was true enough that the Taliban had become far more organised. The official's dismissal of widespread assassinations as 'some mistakes' would have been laughable were it not so callous. But it was a clever narrative, and one which served the insurgency's long-term political objective of returning to power. The message was clear: the Taliban may have done horrifying things in the past, but they had changed. Not only did they see the error of their ways, they had built a government-in-waiting capable of acting responsibly.

It was undeniable that the Taliban's circumstances, if not the Taliban itself, had radically changed. The US Special Representative for Afghanistan Reconciliation, Zalmay Khalilzad, was holding talks with members of the Taliban's political commission in Qatar. The notion that the United States would negotiate with the Taliban had long been unthinkable to many, and few I spoke with at that point thought the talks had much chance of success. Two weeks after our meeting in Dubai, however, the United States announced that they had agreed on the outlines of a deal with the Taliban, whereby the United States would withdraw its forces from Afghanistan in exchange for counterterrorism guarantees from the Taliban. The Taliban were gaining international recognition and coming ever closer to achieving their goal of forcing a US withdrawal.

The story civilians told about the Taliban's evolution was predictably more nuanced. An elder I met in the northwestern province of Faryab in early 2019 said that local civilians had no influence with the Taliban in the beginning, but things changed when the Taliban came to control the area. (He estimated that they held '98 per cent of the district' when we spoke.) He felt that the Taliban now recognised that they had an obligation to 'help the people'.[2] To support his point, he said that elders had negotiated with the Taliban to ensure schools were running, roads were safe for civilians to travel and government employees and aid workers could work safely in the district. That mutually beneficial engagement would have been almost unthinkable during my last visit to the province in 2011.

This evolution varied throughout the country. In Helmand, for example, the Taliban seemed far less sympathetic to civilians than they were in Faryab or practically anywhere else I had been, almost wholly unconcerned with civilian welfare, suspicious of requests for aid or education and just generally difficult to deal with. The war at this point, circa 2019, was highly kinetic and particularly brutal in Helmand, with both sides showing a profound disregard for human life, even when meas-ured against the low bar set by the Afghanistan War in general. Yet even here, Taliban behaviour toward civilians had changed. A man from Helmand said that 'at first [the Taliban] had a cruel strategy', and described them as 'impossible' to engage with.[3] Now, under the right conditions, he felt 'they could be convinced to do something for the people'. While he still had plenty of negative things to say about the Taliban, what he was trying to convey was that the Taliban had realised they needed to make some concessions to civilians, and that meant that there was room—however slight—for manoeuvre. And, to him, that was a substantial and meaningful difference.

Still, the significance of this difference would have been hard to dis-cern from any available datasets or hard numbers. The UN reported at the time that the Taliban were responsible for record high numbers of civilian casualties countrywide and widespread human rights viola-tions. The data suggested that the Taliban had become more violent on the whole, presenting a graver risk to civilians than ever before. They had far greater capacity for violence and more territorial reach through which to enact that violence. But what most numbers don't convey is that during this time the Taliban also became more controlled, strate-gic and sophisticated in the ways they chose to exercise that violence.

This chapter traces the Taliban's evolution from a disparate insur-gency to a government in waiting. In the beginning, the Taliban had very little to offer civilians and no real overarching strategy. Violence was haphazard, and attempts to persuade civilians to their cause rested on appeals to their Islamic values and a vague sense of injustice. As the Taliban gained greater internal control and its ideology came to bear on its practices, violence was deployed more strategically to compel civilian compliance. Persuasion also became more sophisticated, geared at changing civilians' minds rather than simply terrifying them into submis-sion. As the Taliban began to hold territory and develop more capacity to govern, particularly after 2014, they increasingly sought to present themselves as a nationalist movement with civilian support. Violence towards civilians became more precise, and they started to mimic state-like behaviours. Their value proposition to civilians also became clearer, particularly as they developed governance structures, and there was a broader space for civilians to bargain with them.

While there was a discernible evolution in Taliban strategy, policies and norms, the Taliban's actual behaviour was not necessarily uniform across the country, nor was that evolution linear at the micro-level. Among other challenges, the Taliban encountered diverse conditions and an array of civilian attitudes on the ground. Consequently, there was persistent tension between leadership directives on the one hand and the pull of local exigencies on the other. This chapter attempts to explain what factors influenced the Taliban's evolving relationship with civilians, while also paying careful attention to the inherent messiness of Taliban–civilians interactions throughout the insurgency. This analysis is primarily based on interviews with the Taliban in various provinces, former Taliban members, Taliban interlocutors and senior members of the Taliban leadership, as well as civilians, with secondary sources used for history and context.

Violence and coercion

As mentioned in the Introduction, this book departs from broader thinking by positioning Taliban violence as a tactic within their negotiating strategy with civilians. Again, some might argue that violence and coercion hardly imply room for negotiation. That is, however, not how most Afghans interviewed saw it. Civilians were generally not cowed by Taliban violence, even in the many instances where it was unspeakably horrific. Many civilians instead engaged, either passively or actively, with Taliban violence. They intuitively analysed patterns and targets of Taliban violence. Not all violence is the same, nor does it produce the same behaviours. Granted, the haphazard violence of the early Taliban insurgency often felt too random for civilians to make sense of, and didn't leave much space for bargaining. But as the Taliban evolved and was able to use violence more selectively, that violence communicated specific 'asks' of the civilian population. This provided civilians with information they used to protect themselves, and to bargain with insurgents. Civilians used their analysis and insights to hone their tactics, appeals and arguments with which they approached the Taliban. They often sought to lessen the impact of violence on civilians, although this was typically the most difficult issue to negotiate. Even when faced with a high likelihood of failure, they nonetheless tried to find ways to convince the Taliban to extend greater protections to civilians.

Targeting civilians

At the outset of the insurgency, with limited means of waging war or eliciting support, the Taliban primarily relied on a combination of persuasion and violence. As they began travelling across the border from Pakistan in late 2002, they made ideological appeals. Some civilians gave the Taliban sanctuary and allowed them to preach at local mosques. This appears to have been more common in areas where (a) the Taliban had individual or familial/tribal links, and/or (b) individuals felt harassed by international forces and marginalised by the government (Strick van Linschoten and Kuehn, 2012a; Yousafzai, 2009). The Taliban, however, made few inroads through persuasion alone. For most civilians, there was little reason to support the Taliban at this point in time. Few, even among those sympathetic to the Taliban's grievances and appeals, wanted to undermine the first peace Afghanistan had experienced in decades. Plus, the risks of associating with the Taliban were high. Foreign forces might arrest those found to be feeding or sheltering insurgents or ex-Taliban. As many civilians interviewed saw it, the Taliban brought with them only violence, and they could not protect civilians from the risks incurred by supporting them.

Where persuasion alone failed, the Taliban used force. The objective was not only to eliminate opposition, but to send a message that dissuaded others from opposing or obstructing them. Mullahs and religious figures were often the first groups the Taliban targeted. The Taliban's initial approach was still typically persuasion, but if religious leaders were reluctant, or if they resisted Taliban appeals and requests, they were often threatened or killed. The Taliban also approached elders for permission to enter and stay in their villages. If the elders resisted, they too would be targets for intimidation: the Taliban would send threats via text message, over the phone or through night letters.

Civilians would already have been familiar with the meaning of night letters, as they had been a tactic commonly used by the *mujahedeen* (Johnson, 2007). David Kilcullen memorably describes night letters as 'armed propaganda', in that they not only levied threats but were also appeals to switch sides (Kilcullen, 2011: 59). They were often posted in public places, or their contents relayed onwards by word of mouth. Night letters softened the ground for Taliban influence, and the Taliban used them to communicate their agenda to civilians. Early Taliban night letters focused on US 'atrocities' and the corruption of the government in Kabul. As the group gained strength, the night letters increasingly sought to project Taliban power and highlight its military successes, using images of the bodies of international and Afghan troops and their destroyed equipment and vehicles.

Many people interviewed expressed having been afraid of Taliban retribution during this period, but in a way that was distinct from how they expressed their fears related to the Taliban later on. In the early years of the insurgency, they did not know who the Taliban were or what they wanted. They were a shadowy, disparate and unpredictable force. Civilians interviewed described early Taliban violence as random and not always easy to predict, even where we can discern patterns in retrospect. Similarly, one member of the Taliban leadership at the time described early Taliban violence as 'mushroom-like ... with a momentum of its own'.[4] The idea that anyone could be targeted created widespread terror. Uncertainty and anxiety magnified civilian perceptions of Taliban cruelty. Yet the Taliban's growing selectivity, and civilians' ability to gradually understand the logic behind this violence, appeared to lessen—or at least reframe—perceptions of cruelty associated with the Taliban over time.

Targeted threats and assassination

As the Taliban's initial internal consolidation (starting in roughly 2006) allowed them to use violence more selectively, their targeting of civilians gradually narrowed. At the strategic level, the violence was very much aimed at shaping civilian behaviour and eliciting compliance. This was part of a broader process of internal development. The leadership began to impose clearer rules on fighters through the *layha*, as well as a more centralised command. The 2006 *layha* stresses the importance of trying to turn, rather than eliminate, Afghans on the other side. The first two articles of the code state that 'any official can invite any Afghan who is in the infidels' ranks to accept true Islam' and that the Taliban would 'guarantee to any man who turns his back on the infidels, security for himself and his possessions' (Clark, 2011: 25). The *layha* also states that anyone working for the state 'must be given a warning. If he nevertheless refuses to give up his job, he must be beaten', and if insubordination continued, 'the district commander or group leader must kill him' (Clark, 2011: 26).

Did actual Taliban violence reflect these rules and objectives? The picture on the ground is mixed. As they began to operate more strategically, violence, threats and intimidation were more clearly oriented towards two core interlinked goals: eliminating those who posed a threat to the Taliban, and convincing other civilians to comply (AIHRC, 2008). Again, with its use of violence against civilians, the Taliban were not only neutralising individual threats but sending a broader message about the costs of defiance. Atmospheric coercion, generated by violence and threats, signalled these costs to civilians and aimed to compel compliance.

Additionally, the Taliban was still using an exceptionally wide net in their targeting. Nearly anyone who might be collaborating with the government or pro-government forces appeared to be a legitimate target in their view. A wide-ranging 2008 study of insurgent abuses against civilians by the Afghanistan Independent Human Rights Commission (AIHRC) catalogued the list of Taliban targets as including (and not limited to): doctors, teachers, students, government-aligned elders, *ulema* council members, civilian government employees, suppliers and day labourers engaged in reconstruction work and on military bases, former police and military personnel, and unassociated relatives of civil servants (AIHRC, 2008). More generally, the AIHRC report noted extensive intimidation and violence directed at schools, medical services, humanitarian aid and commercial supply lines. Similarly, the UN documented cases in 2008 in 'which victims were threatened or severely beaten for "cooperation" as inconsequential as having a foreigner's number saved in a mobile phone or accepting food aid from the World Food Program' (UNAMA Human Rights, 2009: 29).

In line with the *layha*, the Taliban might warn targets before enacting violence. The UN found that 'in most cases victims are first warned—often several times—by means of written or verbal threats'; if these warnings were not heeded, the Taliban employed 'violence ranging from beatings to abductions to mutilation and murder' (UNAMA Human Rights, 2009: 29). A night letter from Kandahar, translated and reproduced by AIHRC with identifying details redacted, reads:

> To X., as per previous announcements that have been give[n] to the people not to work for this puppet government and forbidding people and their relatives to work with any NGOs. If you do not obey and follow this, you will face the consequences and punishment based on the decree of the Ulema Council.
>
> Therefore you are requested to forbid your family members, such as your sister who is working for XXXX [withheld], from going to such offices. Otherwise the consequences would be the same as those faced by your friend Y in [location withheld], based on the decree of the Ulema Council.
>
> X! We have given you a lot of time, it is enough now. You with Y were having affairs with women and drinking alcohol as well, but you didn't learn your lesson after the shooting of Y.
>
> Now you are continuously doing the same work. You are going to the governor and to Americans every day. We have followed you and you are going and spying ... [5]

Even where executions were carried out without prior warning, they served as an example to others. The UN noted several cases in 2009 in which individuals killed by the Taliban were found with letters attached to their bodies as warnings to others (UNAMA Human Rights, 2010a).

With the US troop surge that began in late 2009, international forces intensified their operations: foot patrols, airstrikes, searches, detentions and ground operations markedly increased (UN General Assembly, 2010). Airstrikes alone rose from 2,644 in 2006 to 5,100 in 2010 and 5,411 in 2011 (see Figure 3.1).[6] ISAF explicitly targeted mid- and senior-level Taliban commanders in operations, through a strategy referred to as 'kill or capture'.

The toll of 'kill or capture' on the Taliban was significant, compounded by the effect of more general airstrikes and ground operations.[7] Analysis of ISAF public statements between 1 December 2009 and 30 September 2011 suggests that pro-government forces orchestrated an average of twenty-five 'kill or capture' raids each week (Strick van Linschoten and Kuehn, 2011). ISAF killed an average of nine Taliban a day between July 2010 and March 2011 (Commander of ISAF quoted in Jaffe, 2011). By eliminating the middle management of the Taliban, the kill or capture strategy sought to disrupt and destroy the command structures the Taliban had worked so hard to build.

Figure 3.1. US airstrikes in Afghanistan, 2006–18

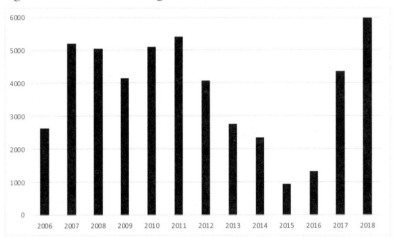

Source: Allied Forces Central Europe cited in Wellman (2018)

Surge-era military pressure, combined with growing Taliban presence, ultimately resulted in more widespread Taliban brutality towards civilians. Violence overall increased, and Taliban violence against civilians spiked. In 2010, 75 per cent of civilian deaths were attributed to the insurgency, a 28 per cent increase on 2009 (UNAMA Human Rights, 2011). Some civilian casualties were incidental or collateral damage from IEDs or suicide attacks, but much of the Taliban's violence towards civilians was intentional. In 2010, the UN noted that intimidation and assassination of civilians had become 'intensified, systematic and widespread' (see Figure 3.2), with Taliban assassinations of civilians up 105 per cent from 2009 with an average of eighteen per week in May and June alone (UNAMA Human Rights, 2010b: 11; UNAMA Human Rights, 2011).

Figure 3.2. Violence against civilians by anti-government elements

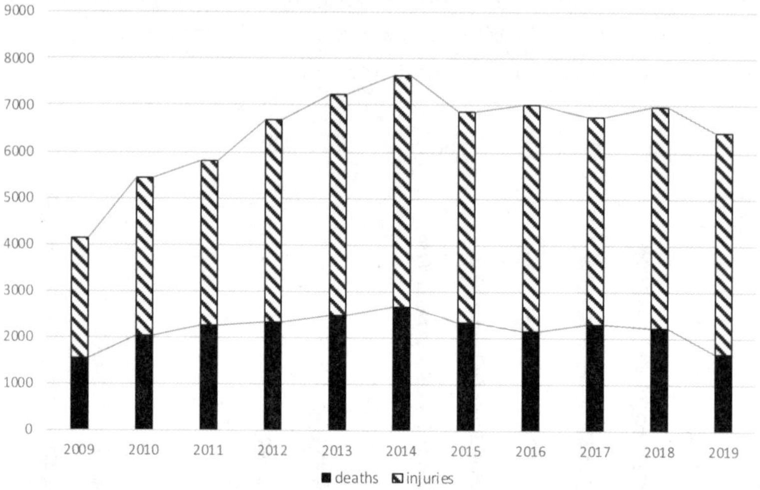

Source: UNAMA Human Rights

Insurgents, particularly those with an intense fear of betrayal, are likely to accept a wide margin of error (Joshi and Quinn, 2017). In the context of ISAF's intensified targeting, it is then unsurprising that the Taliban heghtened their targeting of potential informants and raised the repercussions for betrayal. The Taliban justified many extrajudicial kill-ings during this period on the basis that their targeted victims were spying for the enemy (UNAMA Human Rights, 2011; UNAMA Human Rights, 2012). How much ISAF relied on civilian tip-offs over other intelligence sources (i.e., monitoring Taliban communications, surveil-lance operations, extracting information from alleged Taliban detain-ees) is unclear given the secretive nature of ISAF operations. Regardless, the Taliban could implement various measures to protect themselves from some forms of intelligence gathering (i.e., moving only at night, using radios and cell phones sparingly), but the threat posed by civilians was nebulous and omnipresent. Further, the Taliban's growing footprint throughout the country increased its vulnerability.

Again, Taliban targeting appeared designed to send behavioural cues to civilians. In some instances, the Taliban took measures to make clear their logic to civilians. The UN, for example, documented a case in which the Taliban summarily executed two civilians in Kandahar in October 2010. The Taliban later explained to the community why they had had to kill these two individuals: one victim had allowed the government to dig a well for him, which led to suspicions that this was done in exchange for his spying on the Taliban, and the other had transported construction materials to Afghan police bases, making him a collaborator (UNAMA Human Rights, 2011). The Taliban communicated this not only to justify their actions but also to dissuade others from similar behaviour.

Targeted killings remained high in 2011 and 2012. Threats and violence explicitly targeting suspected informants could dramatically vary by region (see Figure 3.3), and the reasons for civilian targeting were not always clear or clearly recorded. Further, there is no corresponding public data on pro-government operations disaggregated precisely enough to draw meaningful conclusions from. Drawing direct correlations and providing causal explanations in general is thus difficult.

Those caveats aside, people interviewed suggested that civilian targeting became narrower or less frequent when or where the Taliban felt that: (a) they had been successful in silencing opposition, (b) they felt counterproductive effects or (c) they had gained a military advantage. By contrast, targeted killings seemed to be most intense where the Taliban felt acutely threatened. According to UN data, targeted killings decreased in the south in 2011, where they had been most intense in 2010, but they increased in the west and east, where the Taliban were expanding influence and consolidating control respectively (UNAMA Human Rights, 2012). In Helmand in 2010, then the site of extensive, highly publicised international military operations to rout the Taliban, there was a 588 per cent increase in targeted killings (UNAMA Human Rights, 2010a).

Figure 3.3. Insurgent attacks against suspected informers, 2011–18

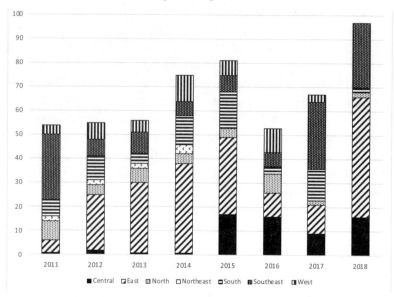

Source: Data was provided in May 2019 by an NGO that collects extensive data on conflict-related violence. The NGO requested not to be named, given the sensitive nature of its work.

While individual targeting is hard to trace in a rigorous way, village-level violence did appear to fit this pattern. A study of Taliban attacks overlaid with data from perception surveys of Afghan civilian preferences from 2011 finds that villages supporting the government experienced far more attacks on average than 'neutral' or pro-Taliban villages (Hirose et al., 2017). Prohibitions on the use of violence (i.e., those introduced with the *layha*) were relaxed in pro-government areas, with little distinction between military and civilian targets in these locales. While this analysis is based on data from 2011, qualitative human rights reporting suggests this patterning of attacks evolved far earlier (Human Rights Watch, 2007; UNAMA, 2008). The aim of this strategy was dual: to punish oppositional villages as well as to signal to neutral or pro-Taliban villages the costs of collaborating with the enemy or otherwise obstructing the insurgency.

An overall decline in military pressure (from roughly 2012 through mid to late 2017) likely influenced the Taliban to narrow its targeting of civilians. That said, Taliban fighters interviewed asserted that their targeting had already become more precise as the surge ended in 2012.[8] There is some evidence to support this. As the drawdown of international troops and the transition to Afghans taking the reins on the battlefield approached, the Taliban focused its assassinations and intimidations more clearly on those explicitly associated with the government and security forces (rather than, for example, teachers, doctors, construction workers and aid workers, who were no longer considered targets).[9] While targeted killings doubled between 2011 and 2012, assassinations of government workers increased by 700 per cent in 2012 (UNAMA Human Rights, 2013). Policies were created to support this shift; for example, the Taliban introduced a more systematic requirement that trials be held before executions occurred.[10] How closely were these policies followed on the ground? Again, the picture is mixed. UN public data does not indicate how many executions were carried out after a trial, but a UN official confirmed an increase in the proportion of Taliban punishments occurring after some kind of 'official' process.[11] The Taliban also made concerted efforts to 'demobilise' Afghan forces rather than simply kill them, although targeted killings continued alongside this. In 2016, the practice became an official policy whereby the Taliban offered amnesty to anyone associated with the government or international forces. For example, Afghan security forces were allowed to return to civilian life, provided they surrendered their arms, apologised for the harm done and had a trusted elder vouch for them.

An enduring caveat is that the Taliban's use of violence has been shaped by the degree of military pressure they were under in a specific locale. Based on the privately held data set referenced above, there appears to be a degree of geographic correlation between international forces' military activity and insurgent attacks deliberately targeting civilians. This data is drawn from 2016 through early 2019, and no earlier data is available for comparison. What this data suggests is that military pressure was likely not the only factor driving attacks, and there is a degree of complexity involved in interpreting these patterns. The accounts and evidence discussed above support the idea that this dynamic existed, at least to some degree, from the early days of the insurgency (see also Giustozzi, 2008; Suhrke, 2008; Sexton, 2016).

This line of reasoning helps explain why targeted killings of inform-ants (see Figure 3.3) varied so dramatically according to region over the years. Where and when the Taliban were under pressure, as peo-ple interviewed suggested, they more heavily cracked down on informants. Additionally, both civilian and Taliban accounts suggested the Taliban relaxed their selectivity, by choice or necessity, when and where they were under threat. We also know that their capacity to be selective with violence diminished where they suffered heavy losses and chains of command were disrupted (see also Hirose et al., 2017). More precise data regarding international military operations would, however, be required to fully test this theory.

UN data shows that targeted killings held steady long after the surge ended (2012–14), before increasing in 2015 and then declining again in 2016 and 2017. In 2018, targeted attacks on civilians, and attacks on informants specifically, sharply increased (see Figures 3.2 and 3.3). One possible explanation is that, with the dramatic rise in airstrikes that year, the Taliban relaxed prohibitions on violence and fell back on old tactics to eliminate spies and discourage civilian betrayal. In sup-port of this, interviews with Taliban and civilians consistently depicted a relationship between airstrikes and threats, intimidation and violence against suspected informants (see also Jackson and Giustozzi, 2012).

Targeted attacks, behavioural cues and civilian bargaining

The critical challenge for the Taliban was to use the power of violence to achieve their objectives, but without being so brutal that they turned the population against them. Outright rebellions against the Taliban were rare, but there were a handful of exceptions—in which Taliban behaviour was exceptionally, unrelentingly cruel. In Alishing district of Laghman, for example, civilians violently (if only temporarily) ejected the Taliban after the Taliban executed village elders and generally terrorised the population (Agence France-Presse, 2012). There is some evidence that the Taliban calibrated its use of violence to be just intense enough to generate compliance, but not so intense that it provoked confrontation and rebellion (Giustozzi and Ibrahimi, 2012). But another factor was that civilians had few alternatives to complying with the Taliban. Elders and local leaders who overtly opposed the Taliban were often harassed or killed; those that survived saw their ability to move outside their villages severely restricted. Because the costs of overt defiance were prohibitively high, civilians seem to have found more covert ways of undermining the insurgency. ISAF targeting intel—surely informed by civilian tip-offs to some degree—suggests some level of hidden resistance. But even the costs of covert resistance were high: the government and international forces offered little protection from retaliation if informants were uncovered. International forces promised to protect the population, but the Taliban repeatedly demonstrated to civilians that they could not.

If civilians instead complied with the Taliban, they could protect themselves from most targeted violence and, eventually, try to leverage their influence to make life under the Taliban more bearable. Yet it is nonetheless true that Taliban violence has never been so precisely targeted that civilians, if given enough information, could devise bargaining strategies that would keep them 100 per cent safe. There was little civilians could do, for example, to avoid suicide attacks, which often occurred on commonly travelled roads and busy public places. However, the Taliban tried to warn the population where and upon whom they were likely to attack. This practice started relatively early on in the insurgency, and was meant to shape civilian behaviour. A night letter that circulated in Zabul around 2006 issued the kind of broad warning that would become common:

> This is to inform government employees and drivers who work with Companies, which means they serve the government, to stop working with the government. If they do not, they bear full responsibility.

> In addition, this is to inform all those people who have their houses built near government offices to leave their houses. If they don't leave and get hurt due to explosions, they have no right to complain.

> Moreover, we hereby inform all the drivers driving in Zabul province to stop their vehicles. We have planted mines on roads. We are not responsible if you get hurt.[12]

Many of these warnings were unhelpfully broad, but some warnings were more specific. Several civilians recalled being told not to travel down certain roads at specific times, or being made aware of where IEDs were likely to be planted.[13] Nevertheless, the Taliban placed the onus on civilians to protect themselves. Without question, these 'warnings' functioned to pre-emptively justify civilian harm in Taliban narratives of the war.

At the same time, Taliban cues nonetheless informed civilian bargaining strategies. Taliban night letters outlined who was a target in a given village and which behaviours were unacceptable. Targeted assassinations of those siding with the government or working with security forces, for example, demonstrated the Taliban's ability to follow through on these threats. These cues helped civilians to gauge where there was room for negotiation and where there was not. A teacher from Herat explained:

> At first they will kill anyone, they were crazy people. But now, it is a little bit clear. Like me, my brother is working at NDS [the Afghan government National Directorate for Security] in Kabul and I have some other relatives in government. The Taliban have no problem with me. They have no problem with my relative working in the education department. My other relatives working in government, maybe they can come to our village but they are too scared. My NDS brother, he cannot come—unless he wants to volunteer as a suicide bomber for the Taliban.[14]

This nuanced understanding of how much government interaction was allowed—he as a teacher was safe, but his brother, working for the NDS, was not—only emerged over time. This reflects the Taliban's gradual sophistication in targeting, but also the extent of their civilian surveillance. When asked if the Taliban knew that his relatives worked for the government, the man interviewed said, 'Of course they do—everyone knows everything about the other people in the village.'[15] Through these kinds of anecdotes, one can begin to understand how civilians gained a sense of the rules through Taliban signalling. Where and when various forms of violence became more predictable, civilians understood it as a cue. Once they understood what the rules were and how they were enforced, civilians actively tried to influence them.

COERCION, CO-OPTION AND CO-OPERATION

Countering counterinsurgency and state-building

A key objective of insurgency is to separate the government from the people. In the Taliban's case, this extended to separating the people from international forces and the international community. There was a concerted Taliban effort, from the beginning of the insurgency, to undermine the ability of the state and the international community to provide benefits to Afghan civilians. Attacking symbols of the state: (a) undermines civilian confidence that the government can control security and protect civilians, (b) demoralises government supporters and (c) erodes the pro-government side's ability to provide benefits to the population (Shultz, 1978). Kilcullen describes the Taliban's exhaustion strategy as aimed at slowly draining the support and resources available to the Afghan government so that international forces would be forced to withdraw, leaving 'the government to collapse under the weight of its own lack of effectiveness and legitimacy' (Kilcullen, 2011: 52).

The shape and form of exhaustion tactics, again, evolved over time. In the early years of the insurgency, the Taliban attacked PRT projects, aid projects and basic services like health and education. Violence of this nature not only sent a message, but the cumulative nature of attacks ultimately weakened the incumbent government, impeded their ability to protect and provide for the population and undermined civilian perceptions of the government's legitimacy. To be clear, early Taliban attacks on government workers and schools were not bargaining per se. They did, however, impact the prospects for civilian compliance, albeit not in the way the Taliban had planned. The Taliban ultimately faced a sharp backlash and was forced to reconsider their stance. They thus began to see aid and services as a bargaining chip. As they gained territorial control and faced the challenge of governing, the Taliban instead co-opted and claimed credit for the benefits provided by their battlefield adversaries.

Attacking symbols of the occupation

After the fall of the Taliban, there was a massive influx of aid money and aid actors into Afghanistan. International donors spent close to $18 billion on aid programs in the country between 2001 and 2008

(Cordesman, 2012). NGO and UN agency presence rapidly expanded. Around 158 NGOs were reportedly operating in Afghanistan in 2001; that number quadrupled by 2010 (Mitchell, 2017). While the international community presented this aid as a means of helping Afghans recover from the conflict and lift themselves out of poverty, the Taliban depicted aid as a symbol of the occupation. As discussed in Chapter 2, PRTs, and the aid activities they undertook, quickly became Taliban targets. Aid workers were similarly targeted as symbols of foreign occupation. For Afghans, supporting reconstruction or aid efforts became a costly choice.

Taliban spokesmen repeatedly claimed responsibility for violence against international aid workers and often accused them of spying for international forces (Jackson and Giustozzi, 2012; Reuters, 2003). After the killing of an aid worker in 2003, the Taliban claimed that they had 'confirmed information that most of the foreigners working in our country are American agents and have no sympathy for Afghanistan ... They are not doing anything for common Afghans but are preaching Christianity in Afghanistan or spying against the Taliban' (Reuters, 2003). A Taliban document circulated in 2006 claimed that:

> NGOs that came into the country under the infidel's government are just like the government. They came here under the slogan of helping the people, but in fact, they are part of this regime. That's why their every activity will be banned, whether it is building a road, bridge, clinic, school or *madrassa*, or anything else.[16]

The education system had been decimated during the preceding decades of conflict. Education, particularly female education, became a government and international priority. In response, attacking state schools became official Taliban policy. Attacks on teachers were encouraged in the 2006 *layha*, with the express purpose of forcing them to stop work:

> Anyone who works as a teacher or mullah under the current state—which is a state in name only—must be given a warning. If he nevertheless refuses to give up his job, he must be beaten. Of course, if a teacher or mullah continues to instruct contrary to the principles of Islam, the district commander or group leader must kill him.[17]

Although there had been earlier attacks on schools, Afghan government data shows that they increased substantially around 2006–7 (AIHRC, 2008; Giustozzi and Franco, 2012). The Ministry of Education reported that 357 students and teachers were killed in 2007, and the AIHRC reported nearly half of the schools in the south were closed as a result of violence in 2008 (AIHRC, 2008). That said, not all of this can be attributed to the Taliban. For example, in the south, there was an array of other actors who attacked or threatened schools, particularly girls' schools, for different reasons (CARE, 2009; Human Rights Watch, 2006). Nonetheless, we can assume that, given their overt anti-education policies, the Taliban were responsible for a fair share of attacks.

Education, it appears, also genuinely invited suspicion. A senior Taliban official explained that the insurgency believed that occupation forces 'were building schools but also using them to spy on us' and that 'the country did not belong to Afghans, so we were afraid of the education system'.[18] More broadly, opposition to education was also partly ideological. Female education is generally more controversial than male education, suggesting that attacks on girls' schools might have been more tolerable to some Taliban, as well as some civilians, than attacks on boys' schools. This in part explains why girls' schools were attacked more often than boys' schools (CARE, 2009; Human Rights Watch, 2006; Jackson and Amiri, 2019). Finally, schools may have also been practical targets for local Taliban. Schools were often the only government presence in a village, making them convenient objects of Taliban violence aimed at diminishing state presence.

The line between violence of this nature and cracking down on suspected collaborators was, at times, blurry. The Taliban often had multiple, complex motives for a given attack. Threats and killings of government workers, for example, not only eliminated regime supporters but clearly deterred other civilians from working with the government. These tactics had such a chilling effect that by 2010 the government struggled to find replacements for high-level officials who had been assassinated in the south (UNAMA Human Rights, 2011). Attacks on schools and threats against teachers and students not only deterred teachers from continuing work and parents from sending their children to school, but also led to widespread school closures in the south

(Jackson and Amiri, 2019). Violence of this nature not only sent a clear message, but the cumulative nature of the attacks ultimately weakened government capacity to deliver education. Additionally, these attacks raised the costs of pro-government collaboration and signalled to civilians that pro-government forces could not provide adequate security for basic outreach, aid and governance.

Taliban violence effectively turned intended benefits into a risk, right up until the Taliban started to feel a growing tide of civilian backlash. In seeking to eliminate services and benefits provided by the state and aid agencies, the Taliban failed to appreciate that most people desperately wanted these things. In many areas of the country, they lost more by attacking schools than they could gain by allowing them to operate.

During the surge, the US strategy once again provided more targets for Taliban attack. Increases in troops were accompanied by expanded efforts to improve governance and services, with a significant increase in aid devoted to bolstering the Afghan state and 'winning hearts and minds'. US civilian presence, geared towards addressing government weaknesses to counteract Taliban influence, increased across the country from 320 to 1,142 personnel (US Government Accountability Office, 2012). Counterinsurgency and stabilisation aid dramatically increased; project funds for US PRTs alone increased from $200 million USD in 2007 to $1 billion USD in 2010 (SIGAR, 2012).

The logic guiding this strategy was that civilians were uncertain about supporting pro-government efforts, given the high costs of doing so. Civilians needed to be convinced that the risks of supporting the government were worth it. Aid projects and governance interventions aimed to convince them, winning civilian trust and building reciprocal relationships that boosted the legitimacy of ISAF and the Afghan government.[19] ISAF guidance clearly articulated how it sought to influence civilian calculations:

> An effective 'offensive' operation in counterinsurgency, therefore, is one that takes from the insurgent what he cannot afford to lose—control of the population. We must think of operations not simply as those that target militants, but ones that earn the trust and support of the people while denying influence and access to the insurgent ... It is a contest to influence the real and very practical calculations on the part

of the people about which side to support ... We must undermine the insurgent argument while offering a more compelling alternative. Our argument must communicate—through word and deed—that we and GIRoA have the capability and commitment to protect and support the people.[20]

Similarly, one US counterinsurgency manual directed forces to 'employ money as a weapons system to win the hearts and minds of the indigenous population to facilitate defeating the insurgents' (US Army, 2009: 1). Such funds were spent on an array of activities from upgrading security infrastructure to improving healthcare and education facilities.

Predictably, the Taliban then targeted counterinsurgency aid and the communities receiving it. Aid disbursement painted targets for the Taliban. One senior Taliban figure explained that 'when there were 100,000 international forces and PRTs, we saw reconstruction activities together with their covert activities'.[21] These claims are backed up with empirical evidence. Using data on the geographic spread of counterinsurgency funding in Afghanistan from 2008 through 2010, one study finds that the Taliban orchestrated more bombings and live-fire attacks against pro-government forces in areas that received counterinsurgency compared to relatively similarly localities that had not received counterinsurgency aid (Sexton, 2016). As ISAF made civilian support their objective, the Taliban doubled down on its efforts to prevent civilian collaboration with the pro-government side. Violence and coercion increased, but the Taliban also sought to negate any benefits offered by the pro-government side. The Taliban systematically sought to demonstrate to the broader civilian population that there would be dire consequences for siding against them.

Co-opting aid and state-building efforts

This strategy would dramatically change once the Taliban gained significant territory, and after the drawdown of international forces was completed in 2014. The Taliban went from attacking symbols of the government and foreign occupation to systematically co-opting aid and state-building efforts within a few short years, something which senior Taliban figures directly attributed to troop drawdown, PRT closures and the decline of counterinsurgency efforts. Aid and services were less suspect, they argued, once they were no longer being used as a weapon against them. But another important shift was occurring within the movement, towards planning for life after the war. One Taliban interlocutor explained that 'with the international troops leaving, we could be less war-like and we could focus on government'.[22] A senior Taliban figure expressed similar sentiments when we met in 2018. 'NATO is almost completely gone, just a few thousand soldiers sitting in their bases and not fighting,' he said, referencing the post-drawdown period. 'Taliban are thinking, "we have our country again now, and we need to keep and preserve what has been done so that it can be used to help Afghans."'[23] As the Taliban exerted greater control over international aid, they became a stakeholder in the process, albeit a deeply coercive one. They began to feel more ownership and less suspicion as international forces pulled back, ceding ground for the Taliban to gain stronger control. The same appeared to apply more broadly to aid projects and basic services provided by the government. As the Taliban gained territory, it had to govern that territory and provide something for civilians.

It is important to emphasise that subtle policy changes on these issues started much earlier, with the caveat that one shouldn't paint too linear a picture: having lived through some of these changes on the ground in Afghanistan, I know firsthand that they were difficult to fully appreciate at the time and only became somewhat clear in retrospect. That proviso aside, we know that provisions condoning attacks on NGOs and aid workers were removed from the 2009 version of the *layha*, and the Taliban began to more proactively engage with aid agencies to negotiate the terms of their work afterwards.

The most dramatic change, however, was with regard to education. The sections of the 2006 *layha* on attacking education facilities were removed in the 2009 edition. The 2010 *layha* goes even further, stating that 'all the activities regarding education, within the designated organisation structure of the Islamic Emirate shall be according to the principles and guidance of the Education Commission' and that provincial and district authorities shall act in accordance with Taliban policies (Clark, 2011: 11). According to Ministry of Education data, attacks on schools dramatically declined by 2011.[24] Part of the reason for these changes was likely that the attacks were deeply unpopular with civilians (Jackson and Amiri, 2019). Some civilians might have understood attacks on PRT projects, but attacks on schools were unjustifiable (CARE, 2009). Most people wanted education and aid projects, and they sought to convince the Taliban to permit both.[25]

Persuasion

Research on persuasion more generally suggests that it is absorbed by its intended target(s) in a dual-process manner, both logically and intuitively (Ledgerwood et al., 2006). In other words, persuasion can be direct, and it can also be subtle and atmospheric. It is as much about the substance of the arguments as it is about the delivery, manner and general environment in which they are made. While we have already alluded to some aspects of this in discussing violence, this section takes a more holistic look at persuasion, considering all of the persuasive means that the Taliban deployed. Deconstructing Taliban persuasion is thus a complex task. This section attempts to untangle Taliban persuasion by breaking it down into three components: what they sought to persuade civilians of (the substance), how they did it (the means) and who they sought to persuade (their targets).

The substance comprises their themes and arguments. The primary objective of Taliban persuasion has been to elicit compliance by convincing civilians of the incumbent government's illegitimacy. To do this, they emphasised the civilian casualties and abuses caused by the government and international forces. Further, they framed the government as a puppet state propped up by the West. They played on both Afghan anger at government ineffectiveness as well as pride and nationalism. They argued that the post-2001 international intervention was actually foreign occupation in disguise, and the occupiers sought to destroy Islam and Afghan culture. They pointed to examples of government corruption and warned that the nefarious influence of the West was eroding Afghan and Islamic values. To persuade civilians to comply, the Taliban also needed to convince them of their staying power, which they did primarily through publicising their battlefield victories. Finally, the Taliban sought legitimacy. They did this in two main ways. The first was by grounding their arguments in Islam and promising to restore 'true' Islamic values. In doing so, they sought to bestow upon themselves unchallenged moral authority. The second was by demonstrating that they were capable of governing, which became critical as the insurgency gained control of territory.

The means of persuasion are the Taliban's mechanisms, techniques and strategies. How a message is packaged and transmitted might hold as much weight as much as its intended meaning. A given message will be received differently by various individuals, based on their underlying preferences and experiences. Not all means of delivery will reach all audiences, so messages must be delivered in a targeted way. Familiar and accepted forms of communication are more likely to be impactful than unfamiliar methods. We have already discussed how the Taliban used night letters and preaching at the mosque; they deployed these and other means (i.e., public statements, poetry and social media) differently to maximise their resonance with specific audiences.

Finally, persuasion was targeted based on Taliban perceptions of underlying civilian positions. Drawing on Mason's work on insurgency and Johnson's work on Taliban propaganda, targeting is broken down here into three core groups: undecided civilians, overtly supportive civilians and overtly oppositional civilians (Mason, 1996; Johnson, 2018). An important caveat is that the Taliban's use of persuasion cannot be entirely divorced from coercion and violence. Night letters, as we have already discussed, were 'armed propaganda' both meant to convince and terrify; that the Taliban delivered on the threats it issued demonstrated their commitment. While this section attempts to delineate the distinct elements of persuasion that the Taliban employed, it unavoidably overlaps with the preceding discussion of violence and coercion.

Themes and arguments

Civilian casualties

When asked to describe how and when the Taliban came to their village, many described a similar set of events. The Taliban would meet people in the mosque at night. Few who had attended these meetings could remember exactly what had been said, but they most commonly recalled that the Taliban had argued that the foreign forces were occupiers fighting a covert war against Islam and not, as they claimed, there to help Afghans. Many people recounted how Taliban night letters circulated around the same time, decrying the illegitimacy of the international intervention and threatening those who supported it. Many of those interviewed said they were initially unconvinced in early encounters with Taliban and Taliban messaging. The Karzai government had brought a degree of security, their children were going to school, and life had generally improved. International forces might patrol the bazaar or the village, but their behaviour did not typically line up with Taliban claims.

This changed once the insurgency emerged as a violent force. International forces increasingly targeted villages where Taliban were believed to be present with night raids and airstrikes. Many people recalled civilians being killed, relatives and neighbours being detained on spurious grounds, and their growing fear of international forces. The Taliban used civilian casualties as a wedge between civilians and pro-government forces. Taliban messaging on this was highly responsive to local events: where people had been killed or arrested by pro-government forces, these events were often incorporated into preaching and night letters. As ISAF military pressure on the Taliban intensified, it gave the Taliban ever more material to work with in the form of civilian death, seemingly arbitrary detentions, damage to property and the general trauma inflicted on the population.

Things only worsened with time. With the 'kill or capture' strategy specifically, ISAF were, like the Taliban, casting a wide net in targeting.[26] Anger over night raids and airstrikes spurred greater sympathy with the insurgency (see Gaston, 2009; Kolenda et al., 2016; Open Society Foundations and The Liaison Office, 2011). While ISAF gradually took measures to limit civilian casualties and compensate for harm done, it did not undo the damage to civilian perceptions. Many Taliban interviewed talked about how valuable civilian anger was in their efforts to recruit fighters and elicit support. One senior Taliban member claimed that 'whatever you see now, it is because of revenge. The airstrikes in the provinces result in the ambulance bomb in Kabul. In [the Taliban's] mind, whatever is happening is because of something that was previously inflicted on them'.[27]

While dynamics were undoubtedly more complex and transcended revenge as the sole motivation, civilians interviewed repeatedly emphasised the egregiousness of abuses committed by international forces in a way that was far more pronounced than their anger at Taliban violence. In other words, civilians were seemingly more outraged by international forces' abuses than they were by the Taliban's. It could have been that they expected less of the Taliban than pro-government forces. A study of Afghan attitudes towards civilian casualties in insurgent-influenced areas in 2011 found similarly asymmetrical dynamics. ISAF-inflicted harm reduced support for ISAF and increased support for the Taliban, but Taliban-inflicted harm had only a marginally negative impact on support for the Taliban and did not translate into greater support for ISAF (Lyall et al., 2013). UN data indicates that the insurgency has been, for the vast majority of the conflict, responsible for more civilian casualties than international forces, yet the impact of inflicting civilian harm has been disproportionately detrimental to international forces. In their persuasion campaign, the Taliban exploited this asymmetry to maximum effect.

Collective honour and nationalism

The Taliban employed a broader retinue of cultural and historical motifs. Emphasising the brutal, unjustified nature of airstrikes, for instance, the Taliban compared them to the widespread bombings of the countryside during the Russian occupation (Johnson, 2018). This resonated with any Afghans old enough to vividly recall the horrors of Russian airstrikes, but also with younger Afghans who heard these stories from older relatives. In this way, the Taliban drew a parallel between two foreign 'occupations' and invoked the collective trauma of the past. More broadly, notions of nationalism and Islam were employed to appeal to Afghan identity. Afghans were portrayed as brave warriors with a history of resisting foreign occupation, from the invasion of Alexander the Great to the British and Russian wars.

The Taliban drew on notions of courage and honour, deeply important concepts in Pashtun culture as well as broader Afghan identity, in other ways. Night raids and searches were, quite obviously, terrifying and deeply humiliating. Civilians were dragged out of their homes, women and children separated from the men, family members often taken away and damage done to their property. But the humiliation was what the Taliban seized on. Within the Pashtunwali notion of honour (*Nang-e-Pakhto*), unavenged injury is a deep source of shame. The honour of a person or tribe can only be redeemed by performing a similar action against the wrongdoer (Benson and Siddiqui, 2014). With the idea of proportional retribution (*badal*), damage to honour or property is expected to result in reciprocal damage.[28] The Taliban played on these cultural elements to make the case that Afghans should fight back against the occupying forces.

Jihad and Islam

Jihad (or striving) has been a powerful ideological and rhetorical tool. Jihad in the strictly religious sense, and as most Afghans interviewed understood it, is about internal and external expressions of what it means to be a good Muslim. Military jihad is a subset of this ideal, which not only justifies but obligates one to protect the faith in instances where Islam is under attack.[29] The Taliban thus portrayed the foreign occupation as not just a threat to Afghanistan but to Islam itself. Yet it is important to underscore that the Taliban's jihad is not a global jihad, but a local one. In contrast to transnational Islamist groups like the Islamic State, Taliban notions of jihad were strongly tied to nationalism and Afghan identity, and not framed as part of an international armed struggle. While they might have portrayed the occupation of Afghanistan as a threat to all Islam, the struggle they were advocating was nationalistic at its core. In these narratives, the Taliban were drawing on a positive sense of collective identity as much as a negative portrayal of a common enemy. Mullah Omar's 2007 Eid message illustrates how these themes were interwoven:

> All Muslims must help their Mujahidin brothers fighting against the forces of evil, putting aside their personal interests and desires for power. Now you know your religion and Afghanistan are in danger, so pursue the path of bravery, righteousness, nobility, dignity and generosity by following the footsteps of pious religious leaders and leaving cowardliness, haughtiness, stinginess and the ways of dishonesty by joining Jihad.[30]

Jihad has been a consistent theme in Taliban appeals to civilians, preaching by Taliban-aligned mullahs, night letters, press releases, website articles, online videos and DVDs, and nearly all other persuasive means the Taliban employ. When asked what drove the insurgency, jihad was almost always the answer that civilians and Taliban interviewed gave. Typical of this, a fighter in Logar said, 'When infidels occupy an Islamic country, it is obligatory for all Muslims to fight against them, so I joined the Taliban based on the Quran.'[31] A Taliban-aligned mullah in Helmand said that the Taliban were 'motivated by Islamic studies, and they are taught that jihad is our Islamic duty'.[32] When the Taliban assumed control over schools after 2014, teachers and students interviewed reported that Taliban commanders or mullahs gave lectures on the importance of jihad, and often this covered jihad in both the sense of striving on the path of Allah, as well as the obligation to wage a holy war against the foreign occupation.

The meaning of jihad was often adaptable to circumstance, and its obligations—as the Taliban saw them—were not limited to males of fighting age. In a 2008 Taliban DVD, a Taliban commander made an impassioned plea to mothers, arguing that a 'mother can give birth to martyrs, youths, and people who have guns to sacrifice their lives … By killing them [foreigners], the door of paradise opens to us'.[33] Over time, jihad has also shifted from a purely religious and military fight to a cultural and intellectual one. A 2018 Taliban statement called for 'intellectual struggle against the propaganda and intellectual invasion of the occupiers [as] a religious obligation' (Islamic Emirate of Afghanistan, 2018a). The Taliban called on 'all educated strata of society' to 'inform the youth about the dangers of the immoral plots of the invaders, enlighten them about our pure religious traditions and culture and dangers of foreign cultural invasion', in order to ensure 'future generations can continue following their Islamic traditions that ensure success and prosperity both in this life and the hereafter' (Islamic Emirate of Afghanistan, 2018a). Further, jihad was not just about Islam. The Taliban's deployment of the concept evokes the fight against the Russians and more deeply rooted notions of honour and nationalism. It has evolved from a rallying cry for fighters into a more broad-based appeal to all Afghans. In this way, the Taliban has used jihad both to argue that all Afghan Muslims are obligated to support their cause, and to justify their actions (even when they seemingly violate other Islamic or common values).

Corruption

Taliban narratives pit a positive portrayal of Afghan identity (i.e., brave, nationalistic, pious) against a negative portrayal of the post-2001 Afghan government. The Taliban has consistently described the incumbent government as a corrupt, inept, un-Islamic, morally bankrupt puppet of the West. The Taliban also sought to undermine the legitimacy of the Afghan government in more subtle rhetorical ways, referring to it as the 'Kabul administration' and 'Karzai government' (and later the 'Ghani government'), and this terminology was parroted by some of the civilians interviewed. That the post-2001 government re-empowered various *mujahedeen* or so-called warlords routed by the Taliban in the 1990s, and that they resumed their abusive behaviour, added to the resonance of the Taliban's claims to the government's illegitimacy.[34] It is unsurprising then that these Taliban narratives resonated most strongly in rural conservative areas, particularly where local government and security forces were weak or abusive.

In the Taliban's narrative, government corruption was a moral danger. By talking about state corruption as moral corruption, the Taliban affirmed civilian grievances and framed state weakness as an affront to Islamic and Afghan values. In an appeal for pro-government supporters to switch sides, the Taliban argued that President Ghani was guilty of 'profanity towards monotheism by the head of this regime, support for international ban on Islamic veil by his wife and launch of a concentrated campaign against Islamic rituals and religious sanctums inside the country' (Islamic Emirate of Afghanistan, 2016). As this quote suggests, the Taliban also played on the fear of immorality via the desecration of women's honour. As in many other cultures, Afghan women are the keepers of male honour, and any infringement on female honour is a threat not only to the family's honour but to wider social norms and values. The reality is far more complex, but the key point is that in as much as the international community has trumpeted the progress made for Afghan women's rights and status in society since 2001, the Taliban used fears about women's changing roles to support their case for war.

Numerous men interviewed expressed this fear. A man from Baghlan said that the women in Kabul were now going out in public naked and that government officials routinely kidnapped children for sexual purposes. He had never been to Kabul but was convinced this was true because he had heard it from the local (Taliban-aligned) mullah.[35]

Projecting power

Finally, the Taliban sought to project their power and make their victory appear inevitable, rendering civilian resistance futile. They did this initially by publicising, and exaggerating, their military successes. Early night letters showed pictures of the aftermath of attacks (reversing a regime-era ban on images) and praised the heroism of Taliban fighters. People relayed how preaching in the mosque often trumpeted Taliban victories and created a sense of momentum. At a broader level, media coverage amplified the impact of the Taliban's violence. Even in its early years, the Taliban sought to seize the narrative in news coverage of the conflict. Announcements of attacks, casualty estimates and photos were sent via email or text to both Afghan and international journalists after attacks. Reports, videos and interviews about recent victories were posted to their website and, later on, circulated via social media. Taliban poetry and chants (*tirana*) glorified victories, mourned losses and celebrated the courage of fighters. That the Taliban were generally more proactive and responsive to media requests than either the government or international forces gave them an upper hand in the battle for press coverage. National and international media coverage mattered to the Taliban because it could embarrass their enemies and create foreboding among civilians, far beyond the areas they influenced or controlled.

What actually happened on the battlefield mattered far less to the Taliban than a good headline. Particularly early on, the Taliban distorted the impact of their military activities to suit the circumstances. A former Taliban spokesman interviewed admitted that, in the early years, they had claimed credit for attacks and incidents which were not of their making.[36] He added that they had later denied, or refused to comment on, attacks that they were responsible for but which might have had adverse effects on how they wished to be perceived. They also used the media and Taliban-produced propaganda to justify attacks. Claims of Taliban victory were contrasted with reports of pro-government 'atrocities'. The Taliban grossly exaggerated civilian casualties caused by pro-government forces in the early years of the insurgency.[37] After the Taliban established mechanisms to investigate civilian casualties from 2011 onwards, this exaggeration lessened somewhat; they broadly shifted towards minimising and justifying their own violence.

Mediums, mechanisms and strategies

Outreach

Throughout the insurgency, religious figures have played an essential support role to the Taliban. As discussed in Chapter 1, the mosque is the centre of village spiritual and political life, clerical networks have immense reach and influence in transmitting messages, and religious figures play a central role in organising and promoting collective action among the community. The Taliban wanted to harness the social power wielded by these figures. Many rural religious figures allied themselves with the Taliban—either willingly or under the threat of force—and used their authority and capacity for mobilisation to influence civilian behaviour. In villages under Taliban control, people typically described mullahs as mouthpieces for the Taliban. Their Friday prayers aligned with Taliban messaging, they aided recruitment, they participated in Taliban governance structures (as with the adjudication of disputes) and they played a role in meting out Taliban punishments.

But outreach was often more subtle than formal Friday prayers. The Taliban also urged its fighters to make their case to civilians and their adversaries more generally. Taliban fighters were part of the communities where they fought, which meant that they interacted with civilians in various ways. Each interaction was an opportunity for them to exert influence over the political opinions and views of their family and acquaintances. People talked about the way the Taliban sought to gain converts, often referencing individual or informal group conversations in mosques, homes, schools and elsewhere.[38] While things like night letters and Taliban propaganda are more obvious to detect, these inter-personal reactions seemed to have more of a chilling effect on civilians with no affinity for the Taliban. Some talked about how relatives or friends had completely altered their political views under the influence of others, conveying a sense of betrayal at how their relationships had irrevocably changed as a result. For young men especially, there was a sense of naïve, macho rebellion—as well as more deep-seated notions of honour and pride—that seemed to draw them to the Taliban. One man talked about how, after his adolescent nephew began parroting Taliban propaganda about 'infidels' and the 'occupation' at a family gathering, he had instinctively turned around and smacked the boy, but then recoiled. 'But then I realized, it was already too late—he could already be with the Taliban,' he said. 'I just wasn't hitting my stupid nephew. Maybe I had hit a Taliban fighter.'[39]

Night letters

Night letters are simple in form, but complicated by virtue of the fact that they serve many purposes: to persuade, to transmit information and to threaten. The target might be an individual, as discussed above, or they might be addressed to the whole community. They are a cost-effective, familiar medium, easily understood and accessed by Afghans. They are designed to be brief and direct. One night letter circulated in Kunar around 2007 reads, in part:

> As all dear Afghan citizens know, a military invasion happened and our national dignity has been disrespected and stepped on. Allah and his messenger Mohammad and the book of Allah (Quran), women, Ulemas and tribal elders have been disrespected. Therefore, is it not legal to conquer the invaders? The Mujahedin announce again: Don't cooperate with the government, don't be recruited to the military or police.[40]

Another from Wardak (undated, but believed to be circa 2006) fol-lowed a common format for night letters targeted at the community. It began by justifying the insurgency's actions, and levelled a series of 'requests' to civilians:

The Afghan Muslim Mujahedin state the following related guidelines to ensure obtaining our goals, and ask earnestly all Afghans to respect them seriously:

1. All those who work and are at the service of the crusader army, cooperate military [sic] o[r] logistically with them, and carry oil, food and similar things for them, are warned strongly to stop cooperating with them promptly; otherwise, they will face serious consequences.

2. All those who do business with the crusaders are asked to avoid doing business with them, so as not to suffer during the exalted strike of the mujahedin on the crusaders.

3. We seriously ask all persons not to expose the holy names of the mujahedin to the crusaders army and to their Afghan slaves during the exalted strike of mujahedin on them, and likewise, we ask those Afghans who spy for Americans and for their Afghan slaves to stop doing this evil act, otherwise, they will be punished at the hands of the holy mujahedin according to Sharia.

4. We ask all Muslims to cooperate whole-heartedly with their mujahedin brothers and to join their ranks and to support jihads, so as to perform their religious duty properly.

5. We ask all those who spread false allegation against mujahedin to stop their evil acts.

The mujaheds' power is not based on any foreign support, it is founded on Allah's blessing and the will of the Afghan Muslim people.

(God grant success to the mujahed everywhere and always).

The Mujahedin of the Islamic Emirate of Afghanistan

Religious scholars say: Cooperation with infidels, under any circumstance and any reason and excuse, in any form, is an open blasphemy that needs no deliberation.[41]

This night letter is quoted at length because it invokes so many of the themes and tactics discussed, using a combination of threats, argumentation and religion to make the Taliban's case. Posted in public places, its contents might have been orally translated by literate people for the illiterate, a husband might come home to tell his wife that he saw a night letter in the bazaar or it might become subject of village conversation and gossip. That the Taliban delivered on the threats it issued provided civilians with proof of their commitment and strength.

Poetry and *tirana*

Poetry is a beloved Afghan art form and pastime, often verbally transmitted. In Taliban hands, poetry communicates insurgent messages in ways that move beyond psy-ops and into the realm of emotion, ideals and fantasy.[42] Poetry might communicate familiar messages around occupation, honour, the bravery of Taliban warriors and Islam. It might even transmit tactical instructions. Yet it often uses imagery not likely to be found in other forms of Taliban persuasion. Romantic symbols, like roses and flowers, are juxtaposed with brutal descriptions of battle and suffering, with the primary purpose being to evoke emotion.[43] Afghans might text each other these poems, or post them on Facebook or Twitter, and a volume of this poetry has been compiled and translated into English (see Strick van Linschoten and Kuehn, 2012b).

Some, although not all, Taliban poetry is overtly political. The topics covered in Taliban poetry are vast, from calling upon women to show more modesty to expressing the desire for a truly Islamic, independent Afghanistan. One, entitled 'Goodbye', is written by a poet named Qatin and reads much like a battle cry. It is framed as an explanation of why the war must be waged, portraying the Taliban as defending Afghanistan and Islam:

> We have the proper *shari'a* and believe in it at all times,
>
> *Shari'a* is my light and I am light of heart in its light,
>
> I am an Afghan *mujahed*, I am an Afghan *mujahed*.
>
> We want a free life, we want stability in every place,
>
> Because I love truth and will never tolerate injustice:
>
> I am an Afghan *mujahed*, I am an Afghan *mujahed*.
>
> We hate war, but we are fighting in war.

If war is imposed on us, then I am a man of the field,

I am an Afghan *mujahed*, I am an Afghan *mujahed*.

Oh cruel colonizer! Take it from me, Qatin,

I avenge the people, I am committed to my promise:

I am an Afghan *mujahed*, I am an Afghan *mujahed*.[44]

Taliban *tirana*, melodic chants or unaccompanied songs, served a similar function. Music, like poetry, is an integral part of Afghan culture. The *tirana*, however, are unique for their absence of musical instruments, and they usually have just one singer. While the Taliban regime banned various musical instruments in the 1990s, they never expressed a problem with singing, and *tirana* took off in popularity during this period. *Tirana* are simple, melodic, and repetitive. A simple, direct way to describe them to the uninitiated would be that they sound like pop songs without the backing music. Taliban *tirana*, similar to *narcorrido* associated with drug gangs in Mexico or the rebel songs of the IRA, are designed to be infectious. They use production effects, like autotune, commonly heard in Western pop music. In rural Taliban areas, I would hear *tirana* from passing car windows, in shops and as cellphone ringtones. One man from a village in Kunduz, where the local mosque played *tirana* from its loudspeakers on Fridays, described them as a 'brainwashing drug' that stuck in his head, even though he despised the messages they conveyed.[45]

Media engagement

There is some irony in the fact that the post-2001 Taliban embraced many of the means of communication (i.e., videos, photographs, television, the internet) that they had banned or severely restricted in the 1990s. They did so seemingly out of necessity. Access to media and telecommunications flourished after the fall of the Taliban in 2001. In 2004, Afghanistan had 60,000 mobile phone subscribers; by 2017, there were nearly 24 million mobile phone users.[46] By the end of 2014, 90 per cent of residential areas had telecommunications coverage (SIGAR, 2018). Internet usage increased, albeit primarily in urban areas, from less than 1 per cent of the population in 2004 to 11 per cent in 2017.[47] In rural areas, access to the internet increased rapidly via the spread of cell phone usage and coverage.

The Taliban, like many modern insurgencies, produced their own media, ranging from magazines to DVDs. An official Taliban website has existed in some form since 2005, produced in at least five languages and frequently updated. While Taliban media and web communication once mostly focused on attacks, they now also highlight the Taliban's 'civilian' activities such as enabling (male) children to go to school and Quran recitation competitions. The Taliban website, for example, features a much broader range of materials than even a few years ago, including Q&As with shadow governors and other notable figures, media statements and civilian casualty reports.[48]

One consequence of Afghanistan's increased access to the internet, social media and cell phone usage was that the Taliban's traditional forms of communication could now gain greater reach. Night letters could be transmitted via email or messaging apps; poems and imagery could be replicated through Instagram, Facebook posts and tweets; and *tirana* could be turned into ringtones. Official Taliban social media accounts, and accounts run by supporters, provided rapid comment on events and spread Taliban messages. Messaging apps meant that Taliban spokesmen were immediately available for comment and had an unfettered line of communication to journalists.

A media commission based in Pakistan was established sometime around 2002 or 2003 to manage these efforts. The senior leadership of the Taliban gradually tried to impose a structure and rules that would enable consistent messaging. In the early years, some commanders would give interviews without permission and often to the dismay of the leadership. In 2005, Mullah Omar released a statement telling the media to ignore all statements not officially issued on the website (International Crisis Group, 2008). The 2009 edition of the *layha* stipulates that to 'avoid disunity and chaos', no one other than the official spokesmen 'has the right to talk to the media as a representative of a group, unit or as individuals' (Clark, 2011: 20).

The media commission, like other Taliban commissions, became increasingly coherent and effective over time. It is worth going into this in some detail, simply because so little is known about the internal dynamics of the media commission, and it illustrates just how important the Taliban felt this work was. According to a former Taliban spokesman, the media commission's work was as much about effective communication as security concerns.[49] Spokesmen were repeatedly arrested by Pakistan intelligence or international and Afghan forces, particularly during the surge. Being in constant communication with the media and with other Taliban meant that their locations and activities could more easily be detected. While an individual ran the commission, the spokesman role was divorced from this position to shield the head of the commission from detection around 2009.

To further improve security and capacity to respond to events, provincial and district media officers were appointed sometime around 2011. Each link in the chain only had contact with one or two other individuals, but the information was vetted and disseminated from the top via the website and the two official spokesmen, Qari Yusuf and Zabiullah Mujahed (*noms de guerre*, and the role of each has been assumed by a succession of individuals over the years). To deal with claims that the Taliban was exaggerating or falsely claiming attacks, which they came to see as hurting their credibility, a system of event verification was set up. The decision to claim or report individual events lay with four or five individuals at the top of the commission, who consulted with the senior leadership *shura* on statements of significance. A former Taliban spokesman estimated around 200 people worked for the media commission in 2019.[50]

The media commission not only disseminated messages but monitored media. It tracked coverage to see who was speaking about them (i.e., politicians, community leaders, religious figures). At times, members of the Taliban approached, threatened or targeted with harassment those who commented negatively on social media or reporters who painted them in an unfavourable light. This was true of every single one of the nearly two dozen Afghan journalists I worked with or interviewed as part of my research. The Taliban, particularly early on, directly threatened media and claimed credit for several journalist kidnappings. The late Mullah Dadullah, a Taliban commander who shaped the early years of the insurgency, claimed in 2006 that 'if in future they use wrong information from coalition forces or NATO we will target those journalists and media ... we have an Islamic right' to kill them (Norton-Taylor and Walsh, 2006).

Dadullah was one of the Taliban's most outspoken commanders, and frequently at odds with the leadership, so his statements should not necessarily be seen as official Taliban policy.[51] Nonetheless, this quote was widely picked up by the international and Afghan media at the time, shaping public perceptions of Taliban policy. Over time, the threats they once openly levied against journalists were largely replaced, at least publicly, with chiding commentary urging fairer coverage. In a way, the softer tone doesn't much matter. They still occasionally kill journalists and members of the media,[52] and the long, brutal legacy of Taliban violence against the press casts a coercive shadow.[53] One journalist I worked with in Helmand said Taliban media officials have indeed become more 'professional and try to make relationships with us, and I'm not afraid to write the truth about them, but I carry a gun because a crazy Taliban is still a crazy Taliban'.[54]

The Taliban used the media to get their side of events across, project power and indirectly influence civilians, and this wasn't based on threats alone. For journalists, information—particularly on attacks in Taliban areas—was often difficult to verify directly. Plus, the government and international forces were typically far slower to respond than the Taliban. The Taliban significantly invested in its media operations to shape the public narrative of the war to their advantage. As with night letters and poetry, they consistently articulated the same themes of foreign occupation, national pride, defence of Islam and government corruption. By telling their story in a variety of ways, directly and indirectly, they aimed to convince civilians that there was no choice but to comply with their rule.

Targeting

Local networks and intelligence gathering allowed the Taliban to gauge civilian attitudes, and persuasive efforts were tailored to targeting specific civilian preferences, attitudes and positions. This section divides Taliban profiling of civilians into three core groups: overtly opposed, undecided and overtly supportive. It captures how the Taliban viewed and dealt with different civilian preferences, and helps illuminate why bargaining dynamics played out differently in various cases.

Overtly supportive and sympathetic civilians

Messages to sympathetic or supportive Afghans aimed to shore up support, rather than bargain. In terms of understanding civilian–insurgent bargaining, the dynamics of preaching to the converted aren't terribly illuminating, so this section will keep it brief. Suffice to say, approaches to already sympathetic civilians emphasised many of the themes outlined above, particularly the misdeeds of pro-government forces, the weaknesses of the Afghan government and the idea of Islam under threat. These messages inspired and affirmed, rather than seeking to coerce. They exaggerated Taliban victories and more heavily praised the courage of their warriors. Messaging underscored the inevitability of Taliban victory, and that the sacrifices required to achieve it were for the greater good of Islam and the nation.

Sympathetic civilians received these messages in many of the same ways as neutral ones. However, sympathetic civilians were more likely to also be targeted with materials of the variety aimed at fighters, such as videos portraying Taliban victories or good deeds, statements extolling battlefield victories and so on. They were more likely to have closer links to the insurgency in direct and indirect ways. This meant that they likely knew local Taliban personally, might be on messaging groups with Taliban and sought out or more frequently received Taliban messages via social media and the internet. They also had access to materials with which they could demonstrate and project their support. They could, for example, download *tirana* and *tirana* ringtones which were sure to project their support for the Taliban to everyone within earshot. (This was, incidentally, also a tactic deployed by those with no love for the Taliban. A journalist I worked with reliably switched the car stereo from Afghan pop music to *tirana* whenever we drove through Taliban areas, as a 'security measure'.)

Undecided civilians

With regards to undecided or neutral civilians, the Taliban aimed to get them to turn against, or at least not support, the government and pro-government forces. The Taliban's arguments drew on Islam, culture, tradition, history and lived experience. They focused on the misdeeds

121

of foreign and Afghan forces, exploiting civilian casualties, abuses and insensitive behaviour. Alongside this, they needed something to offer in place of what they sought to destroy. As they gained territorial control, the Taliban aimed to convince civilians that they could provide better governance than they did in the 1990s, and that they would be less corrupt than the Afghan government. They emphasised the fact that Taliban victory was assured and their morale strong. Political talks between the United States and the Taliban from 2018 onwards added credibility to Taliban claims of strength. For many civilians in Taliban areas, the deal signed between the United States and the Taliban in February 2020 signalled that the Taliban would likely exert unchallenged control of their areas for the foreseeable future.

Many of those interviewed remarked, unprompted, on the effectiveness of these mechanisms and messages. They worked partly because they affirmed civilian biases, reflected their values and stoked their fears. Many individuals attributed the pro-Taliban behaviour of friends and relatives to the power of the Taliban's persuasion. One man from Kunduz recounted that they 'use the mosque as their voice in the world'. When I asked how much people actually bought into these messages, he offered a story:

> They started targeting the government through the mosque loudspeaker saying, 'the government is an infidel government, all the ANA [Afghan army] are not Muslims.' My uncle, he believed this but then he saw the ANA in real life, he saw that they were Muslim, saying 'Alluha Akbar' and then he was like, 'Wait, they *are* Muslim.' He wanted to start supporting them and he was talking to them when they were on patrols. I had to tell him: stop, they [the Taliban] will kill you!

He told the story to make a fundamental point he felt I needed to understand: 'This is how uneducated the people in the village are. The mosque is the authority, so a lot of people—without education, without reading news or things like this—believe what they hear.'[55]

Most civilians—this man's uncle being a possible exception—were keenly aware that the Taliban surveilled them for any hints that they might act against or disobey the insurgency. A man from Baghlan, for example, said that he was sure to attend prayer five times a day because the Taliban 'targets the people who are absent and punishes them'.[56]

Offhand comments in casual conversations might be relayed to the Taliban by informants. Several people recounted instances in which a person was summoned by the Taliban and asked to account for comments they had made during what they had thought was a private conversation. One man from Kunduz, who had made negative comments about the Taliban to a friend, was later approached by another acquaintance linked to the insurgency. This acquaintance, he recounted, was 'warning me, as his dear friend, to be more careful, to consider my opinions in light of Islam and try to see the good changes our brothers [the Taliban] have brought'. To be clear, such an exchange would have had menacing undertones. The man, understandably, felt betrayed by his friend: 'He was my close friend for 20 years, I went to school with him and he informed on me; it was the mosque, the *tirana* and things, it changed his mind.'[57]

In targeting undecided civilians, violence was deeply intertwined with persuasion. Anyone working for or helping the government or pro-government forces was warned to either stop or leave the area; attacks on those who defied Taliban threats magnified persuasive effects. In Helmand and Kunduz, recorded confessions from government workers and spies that had been executed were routinely broadcast from mosque loudspeakers.[58] Even civilians in cities ostensibly under government control were subject to such tactics, indicating that the Taliban could get to anyone anywhere. Night letters, text messages, poems and *tirana* traversed the boundaries of control.

Overtly oppositional civilians

Civilians opposed to the Taliban encompassed outspoken critics from all walks of life, as well as those explicitly associated with the government (i.e., government officials, Afghan soldiers and police, and politicians). This group was subject to various forms of armed persuasion like threats in the form of text messages, phone calls and night letters, as well as targeted violence. As time wore on, threats of violence might be accompanied by more benignly worded invitations to surrender to the government.[59] Oppositional civilians were also often subject to direct outreach from the Taliban or their proxies, attempting to convince them to switch sides, blackmailing them into helping the Taliban or otherwise inducing them to complying with Taliban demands.

The Taliban maligned government officials and supporters, portraying them as weak and corrupt (i.e., puppets, slaves to the West, tyrants, quislings). But as Taliban attitudes and tactics evolved, the Taliban started to frame their persuasive efforts in vaguely more respectful terms, as appeals to misguided fellow countrymen. The Taliban argued that oppositional civilians could see for themselves how corrupt the government was and that they deserved to work for a more honourable system. Through their rhetoric, the Taliban empathised with civilians' plight and offered an alternative. In a message on its website announcing the 2016 amnesty for government workers, the Taliban said it hoped 'to pull away the misled countrymen from allying with the infidels and invites them to the open arms of its nation and Islamic system' (Islamic Emirate of Afghanistan, 2016).

The Taliban further undermined government legitimacy through its attacks on military and government facilities, and on government supporters. The argument that lay beneath these attacks was that the government and military could not protect its people or its property, so why would anyone continue working for them? In their amnesty policy statement, the Taliban appealed directly to government workers and members of the security forces:

> Do you not understand that your corrupt officials not only play with your lives but loot the chastity of your honor after your death? So why would you throw away your lives and destroy the future of your children and families for such corrupt and immoral officials? For the sake of your own lives, for the protection of your children and for deliverance in the afterlife, leave the support of the Americans and accept the invitation by the Islamic Emirate of a life of peace and honor for you and your families.[60]

As the Taliban gained greater territorial control, they could move more openly and interact with civilians more frequently and directly. Their shadow governance reinforced persuasive efforts and gave them greater reach to communicate their messages. Because the Taliban system sought to co-opt many government institutions, such as schools and clinics, they more frequently interacted with government officials.

COERCION, CO-OPTION AND CO-OPERATION

This created new opportunities for coercion but also for more subtle persuasion with pro-government civilians.

In their behaviour and messaging, they consistently sought to convey an image of shared interests and values with these government officials. This varied, of course. Some described the Taliban as harsh and unreasonable, but most government workers I spoke with had more nuanced attitudes. They had to deal with the Taliban to deliver services, and in this capacity they often portrayed them as interested in the well-being of people, and not overly obstructionist. In other words, they had a common interest and needed one another's co-operation to fulfil it. An official working in Kunduz for the Ministry of Rural Rehabilitation and Development (which oversees several important internationally funded, government implemented development programmes, and thus had to negotiate with the Taliban on delivering these) described it like this:

> You can work with them because they want services and projects in their area. They don't allow the people to use government logos on our project and they take all the credit, but still this means they want the project. They want to show they are less corrupt and better than us, but that means they are willing to make deals with us and they will make sure the work is implemented.[61]

Whether this was an objective opinion or a relative one (in which initial expectations of Taliban behaviour were so low that the reality of Taliban being even remotely reasonable was graded on a curve) is debatable. And this is to say nothing of the objections government officials might have had to their ideology or other practices.

There is another factor, which became increasingly important as the Taliban gained ground: as with undecided civilians, oppositional civilians knew that the insurgency was watching them and gaining ground. This was true even where the Taliban had been pushed back by pro-government forces, but particularly pronounced where they had a consolidated presence. As we talked about the security situation more generally, the government official in Kunduz said the Taliban had checkpoints a five-minute drive from his home. 'You see why I have to have good relations with my Taliban brothers,' he laughed. 'Someday soon the government I work for will be in their hands.'[62]

Incentives

While ad hoc and highly individualised incentives are further explored in Chapter 4, this section explores the Taliban's organised and systematic efforts to provide incentives with the explicit goal of inducing civilian compliance. The Taliban first attempted to implement its shadow governance around 2007–9, but the US-led military surge all but decimated these efforts. After 2014 and the reduction in international military presence, governance efforts expanded considerably and became more sophisticated as the Taliban gained more territory. Parallel governments are exceedingly difficult to establish and maintain, particularly when one is constantly under attack. Taliban governance—and, by extension, reliable incentive provision—has been shaped by military pressure and the exigencies of waging an insurgency.

Once insurgents control territory, they must govern. Governance is the means for resolving a persistent insurgent dilemma: they rely on civilians, yet this reliance puts them in constant danger of betrayal. Enabling access to services and opportunities, such as education and healthcare, can placate the population. By creating systems of governance, an insurgency seeks to further dissuade and better prevent the population from collaborating with the other side. Governance is both coercion and a value proposition to civilians: we can provide benefits and protection as long as you obey our rules. Moreover, governance systems create greater capacity for systemic coercion. The structures and policies of shadow governance allow an insurgency to collect intelligence and punish non-compliance in a more organised, predictable and precise manner.

Insurgent governance can also be a means to further drive a wedge between the population and the incumbent government. For this to work, the insurgency has to present a credible alternative in the form of relatively 'good' governance (or, at very least, it has to be perceptibly less corrupt, abusive or ineffectual). What counts as good or less bad governance will likely be weighed against what has been provided in the past, or is currently provided in areas of government control.[63] As Nelson Kasfir has argued, because governing presents immense organisational challenges and resources, insurgencies tend to co-opt what already exists, even if it belongs to their adversary (Kasfir, 2015).

The Taliban co-opted resources provided by the state and international community. In short, shadow governance is complex, with many different objectives pursued through the same or overlapping means.

What the broader study of insurgent governance has largely overlooked until more recently is the importance of performativity. In other words, one way in which the Taliban shadow government becomes 'real' is through the Taliban acting like a state. The fact that, for example, the Taliban issues tax receipts and electricity bills that often look exactly like those issued by 'legitimate' state entities might defy credulity, but they do. They certainly don't need to mimic the state, but doing so gives them an added layer of legitimacy. In the case of electricity bills, the Taliban very obviously has nothing to do with providing the electricity—that's down to the state power company—but it's the performance that counts.

It is also worth pointing out that this kind of performativity predates any significant degree of Taliban territorial control, and its practice can be found even among groups who do not have significant territorial control. Kasper Hoffman and Judith Verweijen argue that the Mai Mai in the Democratic Republic of Congo (DRC), who neither control much territory nor have built much in the way of state-like structures, nonetheless employ a 'looping effect' to cultivate the appearance of state-likeness (Hoffman and Verweijen, 2018: 369). Even where they lack firm control, insurgencies can deploy techniques of power to shape civilian subjectivity and self-conduct. The performance of governance (as a means of influencing civilian behaviour) may precede, or exist in the absence of, territorial control. Indeed, the Taliban used this kind of performativity both as an incentive to induce compliance, even before they established firm control over the population, and as a technique to manage and enforce that compliance once control was established.

Justice

The first collective benefit the Taliban offered was justice. Justice was ideologically important to the Taliban, but it was also the most straightforward, strategic incentive they could provide. From the very beginning, justice was a hallmark of the Taliban regime. When they first emerged in the 1990s, they established local sharia courts to settle disputes and restore order as they took territory. Punishments were swift and brutal, but effective. They restored law and order and provided a sense of relief for many Afghans who had suffered relentless violence and uncertainty during the civil war. The courts also signalled the Taliban's commitment to deliver on its promises to rid the country of crime and create a pure Islamic society. An oft-repeated anecdote is that Afghanistan was so safe under the Taliban in the 1990s that a man could walk from Kabul to Kandahar (roughly 500 kilometres) carrying a hundred pounds of gold and face no problems.

The Taliban began appointing judges early in the insurgency, sometime between 2003 and 2007, according to those interviewed. This was a practical move; the Taliban unquestionably struggled with other aspects of governance during the 1990s, but they knew they could deliver justice. This tactic had the added benefit of being cost-effective, as judges could be cheaply trained and deployed quickly to cover large swathes of territory. Many of these judges were roving, covering several districts, while others were stationed in a fixed location.

Justice provision also allowed the Taliban to capitalise on the government's weaknesses. The Afghan state's post-2001 efforts to build a justice system had badly faltered. In 2006, just one-fifth of Afghans surveyed said they would approach a government court to resolve their disputes (Asia Foundation, 2006). This improved over time, but state justice is still widely regarded as ineffectual, corrupt and difficult to access (Asia Foundation, 2018). For a rural Afghan to reach the court, they would have to travel to district centres or the cities and engage in costly, wholly unfamiliar processes. Western-inspired legal codes and time-consuming, bureaucratic processes have left many such Afghans disillusioned.

Corruption was also a persistent issue, with social connections and bribes often deciding the outcome of a case. Government courts could take years to come to a ruling, usually costing the parties a series of ever-increasing bribes before they reach a decision. Additionally, lack of access to justice has been an acute security problem in many rural areas where land conflicts are pervasive. Land and resource disputes steadily intensified after 2001, erupting into violence and dragging on for years without resolution (Wily, 2013; UNAMA Human Rights, 2014). One former member of the leadership described the reintroduction of the Taliban judiciary after 2001 as influenced by a combination of opportunism and ideology. 'The government was very corrupt, so justice was the first need,' he recounted. 'Even people in government-controlled areas were referring [cases] to us. These were not people who wanted the Taliban, you see, but they wanted justice.'[64]

Many Afghans interviewed had few good things to say about the Taliban regime of the 1990s, but often caveated their remarks with appreciation for Taliban justice. This nostalgia, brought about by weak state capacity and corruption, worked in the Taliban's favour. Bribes are uncommon in Taliban courts. The social power of litigants and their extended family or tribe mattered less than in government systems. The Taliban's legal logic and norms were familiar to rural Afghans. They were well-known for ruling on the spot and quickly settling cases that had been trapped in limbo in the state courts for years or decades.[65] Unlike the government, the Taliban's coercive power meant that it could enforce judgements. Few dared to disobey a Taliban ruling. The Taliban judiciary was less sophisticated than state systems, but that was an advantage in the eyes of many rural Afghans. What counted most was that it was more accessible, faster and perceived as fairer than any alternative. Justice, as one of the earliest incentives provided by the Taliban, showed that they had something to offer the population beyond coercion and violence. Sharia bestowed the kind of legitimacy that only religious authority could. Further, the courts signalled Taliban intent to establish an alternative political order.

This strategy with the courts similarly foreshadowed how the Taliban would compete with the Afghan state on the battlefield as well as in governance. The Taliban would engage with the Afghan government in what Kilcullen refers to as the battle for 'competitive control' (Kilcullen, 2013). With its justice system, the Taliban established a pattern that characterised their governance in the years to come: they would offer services and build a parallel administration, alienate civilians from the government through a combination of persuasion and violence, and eradicate government influence at the local level through direct attacks on government officials and state courts. Much like its expansion of civilian governance later on, the provision of justice helped the Taliban exert control over civilians more effectively. Taliban-run legal systems and dispute resolution mechanisms provided incentives for compliance in the form of order and security, but they also functioned as 'civilianised' mechanisms of coercion. They enhanced the Taliban's ability to collect intelligence and punish non-compliance in a more organised, predictable and precise manner. Alongside this, the Taliban actively sought to identify, harass and punish those who opted instead for the state courts. For a mix of these various reasons, many people saw Taliban justice as the only viable option.

Governance strategies and structures

In talking with current and former Taliban, it was clear that the Taliban did not have a 'grand plan' for governance. What began with a gradual recognition that unbridled violence would ultimately hurt them grew into more sophisticated planning policy and structures geared towards providing incentives for compliance. Members of the leadership and provincial officials described the policy formation as iterative and 'step by step'.[66] Although the justice system was the most well organised, consistent and widespread service the Taliban delivered in the early years, there were other, more uneven, attempts to provide or regulate health and education, to impose control over private-sector entities and aid organisations activities, and often to profit from them. These were ad hoc at best, and more often appeared to be driven by local commanders' prerogatives than any intentional or more general strategy.[67] In principle, the leadership set up a parallel civilian structure including provincial and district governors. However, leadership at both levels were primarily military figures in practice, more concerned with waging war than with insurgent governance.[68] Taliban sources claim that similar to the military commission, civilian commissions covering health, education and other sectors existed—at least in theory—at the leadership level from sometime around 2006 or 2007.[69]

'When we got control of many areas, we started thinking that people will want services from us,' a former member of the Taliban senior leadership said. 'We got together as the *shura* and thought we have to find a way to start providing services.' The solution was to mimic a formal government, in both form and personnel. 'All the commissions are meant to be equivalent to ministries,' he explained. 'Like the former Minister of Health [under the 1990s Taliban government], Abbas, he became head of the health commission. Anyone who had experience in a relevant field, we brought them back to work on the area they had experience in from before.'[70] These civilian commissions, however, had nowhere near the same level of control or strategic organisation as the military commission. They might have existed in the Taliban shadow-state imaginary, and perhaps to some extent inside Afghanistan, but their real impact on the ground did not materialise until many years later (Jackson and Amiri, 2019). Whether a company would be charged taxes, whether a school would remain open or whether an aid agency was permitted to implement projects were, until much later, determined by commanders on the ground.

Taliban governance might have become more systemic and uniform sooner had it not been for the US-led military surge that began in 2009. Only with the 2014 international forces' drawdown did the Taliban begin to gain stable control of significant territory and systematically expand their programme of governance. 'With the international troops leaving, we could be less war-like, and we could focus on government,' a Taliban official involved in policy discussions explained. 'We were also more prepared than in the 1990s because we knew the government would disappear, and we would have to be ready with our own systems to help the people.'[71] This suggests the Taliban took time to think about their system of governance. While they were under enormous military pressure during the surge years (2009–12), they also knew it was only temporary.[72] The Taliban were confident that they would take more control once it was over, and knew they would need to be prepared to govern.

While there was local adaptation within the broad boundaries set by the leadership, there was nonetheless a roughly discernable pattern and progression at village level. By relying on coercion and justice to gain a foothold, the Taliban re-established themselves where they had once been routed and entered new villages. As their influence grew in a given area, the Taliban gradually imposed their rules on civilian life. To enforce them, they recruited a force of insurgent civil servants, ranging from electricity-bill collectors to clinic and school monitors. Yet the Taliban had to incorporate room for civilian bargaining into their governance structures. They knew from experience they could not enforce a uniform set of rules in a country as diverse as Afghanistan.

In the 1990s, they faced outrage over repressive initiatives or policies that were wildly out of step with local custom. Regardless of how harsh they were during that period, they were still instances in which political imperatives forced them to accommodate local norms (i.e., allowing girls' education in parts of Ghazni and Khost).[73] They also needed civilian manpower and expertise. Elders, teachers and religious figures could be co-opted into the system if they were given influence and their preferences taken into account.

The shift from fighting force to government-in-waiting required organisational restructuring. An important piece was separating out military functions from civilian governance. This created not only a division of labour but a system of checks and balances. In my work with Rahmatullah Amiri on the Taliban's bureaucratic evolution, we document how messy and incremental this process was. The Taliban leadership gradually introduced a civilian structure, in theory separate from—but in practice intertwined with—the military chain of command. While civilian commissions and civilian positions existed in theory from the early years of the insurgency, their actual existence was variable. Where they did exist, in the form of the odd education focal point or NGO negotiations point person, they generally had little influence, and most power lay with military commanders.

By creating civilian structures, the Taliban gradually took away civilian governing responsibilities from the local military commanders who had hitherto been responsible for things like negotiating with aid agencies. They were also subtly diffusing power within the movement. Some military commanders resisted this shift; others cared little about things like schools or aid projects, and so hardly objected. The final result, though, was that the Taliban moved in the direction of having a civilian wing. There was still a strong relationship between military and civilian actors, in which military actors ultimately had far more power, and military imperatives trumped all in a conflict between the two. Dedicated civilian structures nevertheless allowed the Taliban to more systematically function like a government and bring more strategic coherence to incentive provision.

In line with this, the Taliban shifted their attitudes towards private-sector entities, aid agencies and government service delivery ministries. The Taliban would win little compliance by obstructing economic activity and denying people services, as they had done in the early years of the insurgency. Acceptance of government service delivery ministries and aid agencies was instrumental to pacifying civilians; if they were satisfied, they would theoretically be less likely to betray or act against the Taliban (Jackson, 2018a). So instead of attacking government schools, the Taliban would allow them to operate under supervision. Rather than refusing aid agencies entry, they would require them to work according to Taliban rules.

There has, however, been a long-standing tension between fear of betrayal and potential gain (Jackson and Giustozzi, 2012; Jackson, 2018a). Where Taliban control was fragile or threatened, they typically forewent the potential gains to be had through greater engagement with the government and private sector in order to mitigate the risk of betrayal. In areas where control was consolidated, the Taliban had much more to gain by allowing these entities to operate under their rule: businesses could be taxed and services provided by others could be regulated and taken credit for. Although these policy and rhetorical shifts began to occur around 2009, they weren't necessarily always discernible or concrete on the ground until after 2014. Suffice to say, the Taliban established parasitic yet sophisticated systems to regulate essential service provision by 2017.

Education and health

By 2017, the government, aid agencies and customary authorities were coercively entwined with the Taliban shadow system. They developed a parallel system of civilian administration. In the education sector, a shadow provincial education representative was appointed by the education commission in consultation with the provincial governor. The shadow representative appointed district focal points, who were usually aided by 'helpers' and school monitors. People sometimes described these monitors as 'educated' men, mullahs or *maulavi*, who observed classes, gave religious lectures and worked with school management and finance personnel to monitor and accurately record teacher attendance. Others were less well regarded. Regardless, Taliban monitors typically ensured that any absent teachers—a chronic problem in government schools—were docked pay and that students attended class. They also played a regulatory and support role with regard to *madrassa*-based education, which in many places was complementary to the state education system.

Schools were also fertile ground for recruitment and intelligence gathering. The Taliban regularly enlisted male students to inform on their teachers, but also more broadly as lookouts and helpers. Taliban commanders or mullahs regularly gave lectures in schools about the importance of jihad and the Taliban's objectives. Most teachers interviewed knew they had current or future members of the Taliban in their classes. One teacher in Wardak said:

> They do not do well, but you cannot fail them because the Taliban will call you up and say 'he has some family problems, he is a good boy ...' This is not true, he is fighting at night and that is why he is failing, but there is nothing you can do.[74]

A similar system existed for health, although the national health system is a hybrid system overseen by the government and implemented by aid agencies (the Basic Package of Health Services, BPHS). A shadow provincial health representative was appointed by the health commission in consultation with the provincial Taliban governor and supported by local focal points and monitors. These monitors were tasked to ensure that clinics had adequate medicine and that staff showed up for work. Taliban education and health officials also vetted and approved new hires. This allowed the Taliban to appoint people they trusted, but also to use these positions as patronage for supporters. The Taliban reported absenteeism of education and health workers to the government and aid agencies, who were obligated to dock the pay of absentee staff, lest they risk incurring Taliban ire. The Taliban coercively influenced hiring choices in schools and clinics, but only the government (and NGOs to some extent with BPHS) could approve hiring decisions.

When asked about the seeming contradiction of co-operating with a state that they were simultaneously fighting, a Taliban spokesman said simply that 'this is about meeting people's needs. It's not a part of the war'.[75] Nothing could be further from the truth. With education, in particular, the Taliban capitalised on high levels of corruption and dysfunction suffered by state schools (i.e., teachers do not show up, textbooks are sold rather than distributed), and the fact that state-provided education has been mostly top-down, with little community input. The Afghan government's own 2017 education sector assessment noted widespread corruption and suggested that in order to be hired a prospective teacher had to pay bribes equivalent to their first year's salary to secure the job (Independent Joint Anti-Corruption Monitoring and Evaluation Committee, 2017).

It is difficult to overstate how deeply most Afghans value education. There are, of course, regional differences in norms (as in any country). Helmand, for example, has historically had less access to education. But even in this province things are starting to change as more children attend school. Again and again, people talked about lack of education driving the conflict. When I asked what they wanted most from the government or the Taliban (aside from them to stop fighting), many people—particularly women—talked about access to education for their children. Parents and grandparents might have missed out on some level of schooling due to poverty, conflict, lack of physical access, early marriage or a mix of all of the above. Regardless of whether they received a formal education themselves, many people drew a direct link between education and a more secure, stable future. Lack of access to education and the poor quality of schools are frustrating on a deep, emotional level; they do not want their children to suffer in the ways that they have. Further, there is an enormous gulf between urban versus rural areas, with the quality of education being comparatively much poorer in rural areas (Global Partnership for Education, 2016; Molina et al., 2018). The Taliban played on civilian desires by showing that it intended to improve the quality of rural education, even if their primary means of doing so was terrifying teachers into showing up.

The majority of civilians interviewed felt that the Taliban had improved the functioning of government schools. They said that teachers showed up, children attended, books and supplies did not go missing and students behaved better in the classroom. Some asserted that girls, for as long as they were allowed to go to school, had also benefitted from the improved quality of education. Typical of this sentiment, a teacher in Logar said, 'The government could do nothing in the past ten years. The Taliban solved our problems right away.'[76] The reality, however, was not quite so simple. When pressed, most civilians noted that there were also significant drawbacks in the form of coercion and violence. Most teachers interviewed were fairly resigned to the situation, believing they had little say in who ran their schools.[77]

Many people expressed similar feelings about the Taliban's regulation of NGO and government health clinics, although corruption has historically been far less pronounced in healthcare than in education.[78] Few government officials or NGO workers interviewed felt that the Taliban excessively interfered with healthcare or impeded access. What was more problematic, they typically said, was government interference, government corruption and occupation (and theft) of clinics by Afghan security forces and militias.[79] Some government and NGO workers even described Taliban attendance monitoring as helpful, noting that the Taliban had more power to force people to show up than the institutions did by themselves.[80]

In the battle for competitive control, the Taliban only has to be seen as less bad than the government, something which it for the most part achieved in its co-option of essential services. It was also an area in which civilians could, and did, bargain. As Chapter 4 details, civilians advocated for health and education to be allowed and protected, and they continually engaged with the Taliban to negotiate its implementation.

Taxation

As of this writing, the Taliban has established an extensive and remarkably state-like taxation system. In early 2020, I began to specifically research Taliban taxation with Rahmatullah Amiri and others. Taliban taxation was not just ad hoc extortion (although the Taliban at times engages in that too). In its areas of influence, the Taliban appeared to be collecting revenue more systematically than the government. They charged a 10 per cent tax on construction companies building infrastructure. They taxed major multinational corporations. They charged a 10 per cent registration fee on most NGOs delivering aid. They charged a tax on goods at all border crossings, produce on its way to market, poppy harvests, minerals being transported from mines and almost anything else one could think of.

A table on Taliban letterhead listed fees for the transport of everything from perfume and cigarettes to marble and motor oil (see Figure

3.4). They collected the money in cash, in kind and via *hawala* transfers to Pakistan. If someone refused to pay, they could expect their goods to be impounded, threats to be levied and potentially to receive a Taliban beating. The Taliban issued receipts to those who paid, which meant that tax payers could avoid requests for double payment. As with other sectors, there was a hierarchical structure (i.e., various commissions and rules) governing tax collection and revenue generation.[81] In most of the country, taxes were predictable, extensive and almost impossible to avoid paying.

At least some of these taxes were framed in Islamic terms. They seemed to be a combination of taxes traditionally levied on income and the productivity of land, and an Islamic taxation regime. Ordinary Afghans would regularly encounter two forms of tax: *zakat* and *oshr*. *Zakat* refers to the Quran's prescription that Muslims should donate 2.5 per cent of their disposable income to the poor. *Oshr* was described by the Taliban as a tax of one-tenth of produce or harvest brought to market, collected in kind or in cash. The tax on narcotics, often framed as *oshr* in interviews, has been a vital source of revenue for the Taliban in poppy-cultivating areas. Taxes on private businesses were also at times referred to as *oshr*. But as the Taliban's taxation system became more systematic, Islamic justifications seemed to matter less. The Taliban's ideological framing of taxation initially derived from legitimacy concerns, and that Taliban taxes are framed in Islamic terms also implies mechanisms of ideological control. *Zakat*, for example, is one of the five pillars of Islam mandatory for believers and forming the basis of Islamic life. The payment of *zakat* is therefore not only about obeying the Taliban but about being a good Muslim. Like healthcare and education, taxation reinforced control. Linked to this, taxes were also part of the battle for competitive control. Several people reported that Taliban tax burdens were far less than what they would otherwise encounter in ostensibly government-controlled areas.

A whole volume alone could be written on Taliban taxation. The description above is a necessarily incomplete overview of how the system worked, as the central point here is to illustrate how civilians engaged and bargained with it. What is often overlooked more generally in works on the collection of taxes by non-state actors is that the benefits they incur from taxation extend far beyond income

Figure 3.4. Taliban duties list

Islamic Emirate of Afghanistan
Economic and Financial Commission
Directorate of Admin and Finance

No	Type	Quantity	Total Amount in figures
1	Spare parts (Machine)	Per truck	45,000/AFN
2	Medicine	Per truck	45,000/AFN
3	Spare Parts (Car)	Per truck	35,000/AFN
4	Steel bar (Construction Grid)	Per truck	35,000/AFN
5	Waterproofing (construction)	Per truck	35,000/AFN
6	Gas	Per big tanker	35,000/AFN
7	Gasoline	Per big tanker	35,000/AFN
8	Dishes	Per truck	35,000/AFN
9	Motor Oil (Car)	Per truck	35,000/AFN
10	Battery	Per truck	35,000/AFN
11	Carpet	Per truck	35,000/AFN
12	Black pepper	Per truck	35,000/AFN
13	Perfume	Per truck	35,000/AFN
14	Bicycles	Per truck	35,000/AFN
15	Mobile, chargers	Per truck	35,000/AFN
16	Mobile Phones / Chargers	Per truck	35,000/AFN
17	Blanket	Per truck	35,000/AFN
18	Tires	Per truck	35,000/AFN
19	Electric organize tools	Per truck	35,000/AFN
20	Jewelry (without precious stones)	Per truck	35,000/AFN
21	Dried fruit	Per truck	35,000/AFN
22	Watches / Clocks	Per truck	35,000/AFN
23	Food stuff	Per truck	35,000/AFN
24	Refrigerator	Per truck	35,000/AFN
25	Clothes	Per truck	35,000/AFN
26	Tea	Per truck	35,000/AFN
27	Cigarettes	Per truck	35,000/AFN
28	Marble	Per truck	33,000/AFN
29	Washing Powder	Per truck	33,000/AFN
30	Car lights (arrow lights)	Per truck	33,000/AFN
31	Unbreakable dishes	Per truck	33,000/AFN
32	Ceramic Tiles	Per truck	30,000/AFN
33	Plastic Materials	Per truck	25,000/AFN
34	Raw materials	Per truck	25,000/AFN
35	Plastic	Per truck	25,000/AFN
36	Hydraulic (oil)	Per truck	25,000/AFN
37	Paper / Cartons	Per truck	25,000/AFN

Source: Obtained from Herat province in 2018 and translated from the original Pashto.

generation. While the Taliban was clearly interested in collecting revenue, Taliban taxation was also about performativity and legitimacy, and that is what is of most interest vis-à-vis civilian bargaining. Taxes are perhaps the most obvious way in which insurgents 'perform' governance and act like a state. Taxes imply a social contract in which payment is made to an authority in exchange for protection and security. Levying taxes is coercive, but paying them is deeply symbolic and theoretically enables the taxpayer to access incentives. It doesn't always work that way in practice, but it creates the grounds for a civilian argument that taxes imply a quid pro quo.

Taliban taxes have historically been negotiable, and that negotiation was about generating legitimacy through securing compliance. When the Taliban faced resistance to taxes from individuals, NGOs and private companies, they often argued that they provided security in return. Coercion was always in the background, but it was this state-like function that framed the Taliban's arguments on taxation. (Never mind that the Taliban started levying taxes long before there was much Taliban shadow governance to speak of, but this claim to provide security was how they legitimised taxation.) In numerous cases, the Taliban relented, at least temporarily, or reduced its demands where it encountered organised, steadfast resistance.

Social capital

The Taliban is a grassroots insurgency, grounded in a specific version of rural social relations and beliefs. As discussed briefly in Chapter 2 and in this chapter, social capital has enabled the Taliban to gather intelligence, craft propaganda and develop a set of incentives enticing enough to compel civilian compliance. Social capital has, however, been a double-edged sword for the Taliban, both a powerful asset and a source of vulnerability. Local links were essential to establishing influence and to governing, but the Taliban as a group required the obedience of its fighters to the movement above all. Local ties advanced the Taliban cause, but external loyalties also threatened to undermine group cohesion. Ultimately, the Taliban has walked a fine line of wanting to use social capital as leverage over civilians while limiting civilian ability to use social capital as leverage over them.

To overcome the vulnerability created by social ties, the Taliban attempted to reconfigure the nature of social capital among their ranks. They have also sought to de-emphasise certain features of Afghan identity, such as tribe or ethnicity, which might undermine or challenge leadership authority and movement cohesiveness. At the same time, they cultivated a unique collective identity among their fighters, keeping the elements that suited their objectives and minimising what threatened them. The Taliban deployed ideology to regulate the beliefs, behaviour and social orientation of their ranks, emphasising Islam as a unifier above all else. An ethos of comradery (*andiwali*), or the idea that all Taliban are obligated to serve and support one another, has also helped unite the movement (see also Ruttig, 2010). Cultivating common social capital was incredibly important as the insurgency evolved, and essential in unifying the disparate, personality-centric factions that comprised the early Taliban. Just as they could not achieve their political goals if fighters were more loyal to local commanders than the leadership, the Taliban could not afford for fighters to be more loyal to their family, tribe or community than to the movement as a whole.

Yet the Taliban has still had to retain local links and shared capital with civilians. Social capital can almost be thought of as a toolkit, which the Taliban reaches into when it needs to achieve specific objectives. In his study of the Taliban's tribal roots, Ruttig delineates three types of social capital that the Taliban accesses: religious, political and tribal (Ruttig, 2010). The remainder of this section expands on Ruttig's observation, exploring how the Taliban used these three different types of social capital in their relations with civilians.

Religious ideology and institutions

Religious institutions have been an invaluable asset to the Taliban. Preaching at the mosque and the transmission of Taliban messages by mullahs gave the Taliban a legitimacy they could not have achieved through military might alone. Through the co-option of Islamic practice and belief, the Taliban have sought to legitimise themselves to civilians. There is a consistent emphasis on Islam and the restoration of morality in the Taliban's attempts to explain their objectives to the

Afghan public. That the movement is headed by an Amir, presiding over an Emirate, implies that he is naturally a leader of all faithful Afghans. But, most importantly, Taliban efforts to capture and capitalise on the power of Islam enabled the insurgency to access specific sources of rural social capital.

One such source of power lay in rural religious networks. Particularly in the south and east, the religious networks the Taliban drew upon were partly grounded in new or pre-existing Deobandi *madrassas*. *Madrassa* networks in these areas are also often linked to similar ones on the Pakistani side of the border. In Pakistan, these networks supported recruitment and logistics, provided a safe haven in which fighters could rest or recover and created safe spaces where fighters met with senior commanders to receive instructions and resources.[82] The Taliban drew on these structures, and the linkages they created, to sustain their fight, make appeals, recruit fighters and gain civilian support. Taliban village activities—from strategy and planning to recruitment, indoctrination and outreach—routinely centred around mosques and *madrassas*. Even in areas outside Deobandi networks, mosques were an anchor for Taliban presence and organisation.

Most rural Afghans of a certain age would have attended a *madrassa* or *hujra*, which used a similar curriculum. That the Taliban went to the same schools and mosques and learned the same things as the civilians they were trying to persuade was an important asset. As Gopal and Strick van Linschoten have argued in their authoritative work on Taliban ideology, the Deobandi curriculum echoed, or was interpreted by the Taliban in ways that echoed, the pre-existing logic of cultural practice within rural Afghanistan (Gopal and Strick van Linschoten, 2017). The Taliban drew on this common background as cultural capital. Where the Taliban's appeals resonated, it was partly because they were rooted in the specific Islam of village life.

Religious education and knowledge, and the shared values and symbols they instilled across rural society, were important features of the Taliban's social capital. Islamic values mingled with local beliefs in these narratives: their fight was not an insurgency but a jihad, and the Taliban's objective was not to take power but to create a truly Islamic government that reflected rural values. Afghanistan's conflict fault lines have long revolved around modernising, state-building and largely urban intellectual forces on the one hand, and conservative, rural forces urging a return to tradition on the other. When the Taliban spoke of moral corruption in Kabul, they called to mind commonly held rural prejudices about the hedonism and debauchery rife in the cities.

Political networks and *mujahedeen* alliances

Chapter 2 argued that political and economic life in Afghanistan revolves around networks, and the same is true of the Taliban. After 2001, these alliances were knitted together to extend the Taliban's reach in what Giustozzi has called a 'network of networks' (Giustozzi, 2012: 20). The Taliban's networks vary in size, with some totalling thousands of fighters across multiple regions, and others only a few hundred in a single province. These include, and are not limited to: the old guard 'Kandahari' Taliban; the Mansur network; the Haqqani network in the southeast; Hezb-i-Islami Gulbuddin (HIG); small Salafi groups in the east, mainly Kunar and Nuristan; and a miscellaneous category of unrelated ex-mujahedeen who joined the Taliban after being alienated from government. Among these, several old mujahedeen networks became integral to the Taliban's early growth.

The Haqqani network, founded by Jalaluddin Haqqani in the late 1980s, is one of the most prominent and strategic of such alliances. After 2001, the Haqqani network effectively demobilised but remained unified under the leadership of Jalaluddin Haqqani, setting itself apart from the new government. In mid-2002, Haqqani began remobilising his front, and Haqqani fighting groups began operating in Paktia and Khost later that year. While the Haqqani faction operated somewhat autonomously in its strongholds in Loya Paktia (the broader southeastern region), its *madrassa*, training and logistics networks provided the Taliban with greater reach and enhanced appeal. In his definitive study of the Haqqanis, Vahid Brown and Don Rassler write that the Haqqani network 'acts as a regional bridge' through which the Taliban localises its representation and adapts 'its strategy to the political, social, and tribal landscapes of Loya Paktia' (Brown, 2013: 2371). Haqqani's local tribal connections and its history in the region make it more trusted and credible, and thus far more capable in navigating southeastern social dynamics and infiltrating villages than other sections of the Taliban.

Hezb-i-Islami Khalis (HIK) was another such network. Founded in 1979 by Maulavi Mohammad Younus Khalis, Mullah Omar had fought with HIK during the civil war. After the death of its leader and an internal power struggle, HIK fractured after 2001. Its power waned, but it remained a minor political force in the east. Numerous old eastern HIK commanders, under the leadership of Khalis's son, subsequently allied with the Taliban (although the alliance was fragile and rocky). These patterns were replicated by the Taliban with other *mujahedeen* groups, too numerous to count here. How this happened varied according to the positions, strength and coherence of these old networks. As with Haqqani and HIK, these networks generally acted as a 'bridge' that gave the Taliban local legitimacy, added capacity and ultimately more significant geographic influence.

Not all places had strong *mujahedeen* networks that could be readily co-opted. In fact, the Taliban more commonly encountered deeply fragmented power dynamics at the local level. Competition between local powerbrokers and networks often created problems, particularly in the early years of the insurgency. Ethnic and resource tensions, particularly in the north and west, also came into play. Different cliques within the insurgency might also vie for power in a given province or district. And in several instances they ended up going to war with each other. A study of Taliban micro-politics could, again, fill volumes, but the key takeaway is that these kinds of local internal conflicts illustrated the difficulty of reconciling the Taliban's seeming internal cleavages with its rapid expansion throughout the country.

The leadership's objective has been to balance power among these factions to create enough coherence to wage an effective insurgency. If the Taliban leadership allowed commanders too much leeway, they risked undermining the Taliban's central authority and the ability of the movement to unite against their adversaries. However, if the leadership tightened the reins too much, local factions might rebel and the movement could fracture. There is another element to this balance: accommodating local civilian preferences. In certain instances, following a strict directive from the leadership would have compelled local commanders to act in ways that would have undermined civilian compliance. They might have been forced to ignore civilian interests for the sake of a unified policy, even if meeting those interests would better serve the insurgency's overall objectives. Too much centralisation and uniformity endangers the adaptive ability of the movement overall. By carefully striking this balance and keeping internal disagreement largely inside the movement, the Taliban has often managed to appear more coherent than the government, which also helps to strengthen the movement externally.

If coherence is about maintaining balance in a volatile environment, it must be seen as a dynamic that is continually managed rather than a perfect end state to be achieved. The Taliban manages its internal diversity and cultivates greater coherence in two main ways. The first is representation. The various factions that comprise the Taliban on the ground are, at least to some degree, represented at the leadership as well as the provincial and district levels. The composition of the supreme leadership *shura* is consequently comprised of key figures from across the movement's ideological, ethnic, tribal and geographic spectrum, even if it remains dominated by major southern networks. Various factions come into conflict with one another from time to time, but acrimonious splits have been exceedingly rare.

The second is decentralised decision-making. Policies exist at the top, but there is broad scope for negotiation and local adaptation. Or as one man from Faryab explained, 'They leave the local level open for interpretation.'[83] There is a tension between local interests on the one hand and leadership interests on the other, and this room for manoeuvre relieves some of that. Most importantly, local decision-making has created leverage and space for civilians to negotiate. Accommodation means allowing local Taliban flexibility in negotiating with civilians.

Family, tribe and ethnicity

In 1956, anthropologist Louis Dupree wrote that Afghan 'loyalties and obligations decreased in roughly the following order: family, clan, tribe, confederacy' (Dupree, 1956: 26). While Afghanistan's tribal and ethnic landscape is incredibly complex, and these systems are living, evolving structures, Dupree's observation remains salient: links with those closest to you often matter above all else. What is most important for the Taliban in this context is the role that various social structures play in maintaining and reproducing social order. Family, tribe, ethnicity and so on have helped the Taliban make inroads, ever more so as local recruitment increased. All other things being equal, civilians were more reliably sympathetic to and less suspicious of fighters from their community. The Taliban could cultivate intelligence based on their pre-existing relationships. They knew who might be most sympathetic and who might be most likely to oppose them, and they knew who to ask for the most reliable information. And they understood how to exploit local histories and grievances. Local fighters also knew the terrain, giving them a military advantage over international forces. Social capital enabled the Taliban to differentiate among the civilian population and target pro-government collaborators and adversaries more selectively.

At a broader level, tribal and familial links enabled the Taliban to draw on reciprocal relations to infiltrate villages. The exclusionary practices and abuses perpetrated by the government also often tracked on ethnic or tribal lines, which further allowed the Taliban greater leverage with the persecuted and marginalised. This, however, was tricky territory to navigate. Tribal authority has threatened to undermine Taliban authority, and tribal and ethnic rivalries among Taliban have created internal conflicts.[84] This is the last thing an insurgency wants to deal with when it's trying to get everyone to work together for a common purpose. Emphasis on tribe or ethnicity also risked creating the appearance that the Taliban might exclude or unduly favour one tribe or ethnicity over another. This perception would undermine Taliban claims that it was fighting on behalf of all Afghans and open to all. The Taliban recognised this problem early: the 2009 *layha* stated that '*mujahedin* shall protect themselves completely from any tribal, linguistic, and regional prejudice' (Clark, 2011: 23).

Too much reliance on personal connections, in any form, could also create perceptions of corruption. The Taliban defined themselves as the antithesis of the morally, financially corrupt Afghan government and appealed to civilians on that basis. A Taliban commander providing special treatment to his family or tribe undermines that, and so there was perpetual tension between using these relationships strategically and the need to appear impartial. When interviewed, people talked about how favouritism nonetheless occurred, due to the unavoidably reciprocal nature of relationships in Afghanistan. But they also talked about how the Taliban sought to prevent such things from happening: by typically ensuring provincial or district governors did not serve in the province that they were from and rotating them frequently, by deploying judges to courts from outside their home areas to guard against partiality, by making examples of several high-level Taliban officials who were removed for 'corruption' and so on.

4.

NAVIGATING FOREVER WAR

CIVILIAN BARGAINING STRATEGIES

'All the fighting is useless. The area is 90 per cent Taliban controlled but the government won't leave. The Taliban can't force them to go because the government has the Americans behind them, but the government can also do nothing.' This is how a farmer named Haseeb explained the situation in his village in the east of Afghanistan. What little was left of government presence was, in his eyes, pointless. 'They are just sitting in their check posts or in the district centre. They can't protect the people, they can't control the area, they can't deliver services. The Taliban are the ones with the courts, coming into the schools, collecting taxes. They are doing everything and they are the only ones controlling things.'

He talked about how violence had escalated in recent months, with several airstrikes and ground operations in the area. 'Last night there was a raid and they are saying there are seven women and children who were killed or wounded,' he said. 'What is the purpose? They say there were Taliban in that house. But there are Taliban everywhere.'

The situation Haseeb described was hardly unique; he could have been talking about any number of villages across the country. The United States responded to growing Taliban control mainly by increasing airstrikes.[1] This might have kept the Taliban at bay in some places, but it failed to halt their momentum or enable the government to retake much territory. The human cost was staggering: airstrikes killed more civilians in 2019 than at any time since 2002. To ward off the bombings, the Taliban took to assembling children outside their meetings or gathering in schools or during events like children's Quran recitation competitions. Sometimes it worked, and sometimes it didn't.

The objectives of the US-led strategy were increasingly difficult to parse, let alone justify. Some Western diplomats and US military officials would say they were simply buying time until some turning point. But the goalposts were constantly moving. They might say that international forces were holding the ground for the Afghan parliamentary election in 2018, or the presidential election in 2019. Later, this shifted to be until the United States could secure a deal with the Taliban, or, after that deal had been signed, until intra-Afghan negotiations could begin. As time passed, the space they were 'holding' was increasingly illusory. The government kept getting weaker and the Taliban kept gaining influence.

Other Western officials talked about achieving a 'mutually hurting stalemate'. The idea is borrowed from negotiation theorist William Zartman, who argues that a moment can occur during wartime when belligerents, so fatigued by the fighting, come to believe that they cannot win militarily and therefore become willing to negotiate (Zartman and Berman, 1982; Zartman, 2000; Zartman, 2001). The application of Zartman's theory in Afghanistan was, however, a grotesque distortion of the premise.[2] The logic seemed to be that inflicting more violence would force the Taliban to the negotiating table. In reality, the Taliban had long been insisting—for many years at this point—that it wanted to negotiate. The issue was that the United States demanded that the Taliban talk directly to the Afghan government, while the Taliban would only agree to talk to the United States. The Taliban was willing to talk to the Afghan government, but only after it negotiated with the United States on the withdrawal of forces. This is, of course, how talks ultimately progressed, albeit several years and tens of thousands of dead civilians later.

The civilians I met during this period felt they had little choice but to somehow engage with the insurgency. Many, even in areas where the government still had a foothold, saw indefinite Taliban rule as the most likely outcome. But people viewed and approached this differently, and some were able to exert more influence over the Taliban than others. This chapter divides civilians into three broad groups to better understand these differences. These groups overlapped and at times cooperated with one another, but they are distinct enough to illuminate the nature of wartime leverage and the bargaining process.

The first group is customary authorities, discussed at length in Chapter 2. In negotiations with the Taliban, customary authorities' interests focused on group problems or on advocating on behalf of individual constituents, in line with their mandate to provide a buffer between the people and the ruling authorities. Their primary leverage lay in their ability to deliver the collective compliance of their constituents. As the social 'glue' of village life, keeping these authorities on side had considerable value to the Taliban. Particularly as the insurgency sought to govern, elders became an invaluable bridge between civilians and the Taliban.

The second group is civilian organisations, encompassing a wide range of different international and Afghan NGOs, UN agencies, farming co-operatives, governmental entities, local businesses, multinational corporations and so on. Their core interest was obtaining guarantees from the insurgency which would allow them to work safely, and their core leverage was the benefits they could provide to the Taliban. Comparing the way some different types of organisations negotiated reveals a great deal about why certain actors were able to secure more advantageous deals than others.

Lastly, this chapter looks at individuals. Many people found themselves, either by choice or necessity, negotiating with the Taliban. In comparison with customary authorities and organisations, their leverage was typically meagre. At times, they provided minor benefits to incentivise the Taliban to meet their demands (i.e., intelligence, small favours). Thus, access to social capital—such as relationships with customary authorities who would advocate on their behalf, or links to individual members of the Taliban—was essential.

Customary authorities

An elder is a traditional social position typically bestowed on widely respected, trusted older men who are mandated to mediate and solve problems. Elders are defined by their social influence, insight and ability to broker agreement, rather than their lineage or social status. They work to maintain community cohesion, settle disputes as they arise and enforce rules governing communal resources. A village *shura* comprises a group of elders usually, but *shuras* are not fixed groups; rather, they are fluid and, ideally, responsive to events. Amidst decades of civil war, *shuras* and elders have been the most reliable interlocutors for all sides. For their constituents, elders act as a bulwark against the ruling authority; for the ruling authority, they are a conduit to the people and a source of conferred legitimacy (Brick Murtazashvli, 2016).

These are all, of course, generalisations. The lived reality of these dynamics varies enormously in shape and form across the country, and elders vary in the degree to which they are accountable to their constituents. Some *shuras* may be more rooted in patron-politics while others are more impartial; elders may be more respected and play a more significant role in some communities and less so in others (see Pain and Kantor, 2010; Pain 2016). Understanding how this works in a given locale is less than straightforward. To speak to most elders, one might think their role was immutable. When I asked how the role of customary authorities had changed, one elder in Baghlan insisted that 'the village *shura* is the *shura*, whether it's Taliban or government or *mujahedeen* or some other group, it doesn't matter who controls the area—we remain the *shura*'.[3] In reality, the relationship between ruling authorities and elders has typically been more fraught.

The Taliban was—at least initially—overtly hostile. In some places they targeted elders (particularly those seen as aligned with the government) while in others they employed subtler strategies of divide and rule. Over time, however, the Taliban began to recognise that the elders could be useful. Elders could provide the first port of call for civilian problems, effectively running interference for the Taliban. If elders could not solve the problem, they could be induced to refer the issue to appropriate Taliban authorities (and, in so doing, reinforce Taliban authority). Elders effectively lightened the burden of governance for Taliban district governors, judges and commanders. This was particularly useful where they were overstretched. Crucially, elders and *shuras* communicated civilian desires and discontent to the insurgency, thus helping the Taliban to maintain and manage civilian compliance.

Interests

First and foremost, elders sought to protect their communities. They often did things like ask the Taliban not to fight in populated areas, to remove mines from frequently travelled road and to temporarily halt fighting so that farmers could safely collect their harvest. Unfortunately, their success rate in these endeavours was fairly low. Anything that impeded on the Taliban's ability to wage war was difficult to sell, particularly where and when the Taliban were under acute military pressure. Making matters worse for civilians, when this was the case the Taliban tended to loosen its restrictions on what tactics were permissible and justifiable. The southern province of Helmand embodied many of these dynamics. Abdul Qadir, a teacher in Helmand, said that 'the stupidest thing the elders do is to ask the Taliban to stop fighting, which they will never do'.[4] Qadir told of how elders had once tried to convince the Taliban to remove an unmarked mine placed at the steps of a local school. The Taliban had denied the request, recommending that the teachers and students instead be mindful about where they walked.

In another heavily contested area, an elder recounted that he had heard of Taliban plans to destroy a village water source because Afghan security forces also relied on the source. He tried to persuade the Taliban not to do this, arguing that everyone, including the Taliban and their families, would suffer. The Taliban contaminated the water source anyway.

Even where they knew their chances of lessening the damage were slim, elders often initiated negotiations anyway. So why did they persist? The need for protection was so critical that even a small chance of success meant that negotiations were still worth pursuing. Even when the elders did not get the full protection they sought, they might at least get a little more protection than they would have had otherwise. With regards to protection, even a second-best outcome was preferable to not negotiating at all.

Negotiating for individual protection was more likely to be successful, in part because it imposed lower costs on the Taliban. Elders could often secure the release of someone in Taliban detention by vouching that whoever had broken Taliban rules would not do so again. But if elders vouched for someone who broke Taliban rules and that person then reoffended, there was likely little they could do the next time around. As Taliban governance became more systematised, elders' influence became more clearly bound. If the Taliban arrested someone, that person would likely be tried in a Taliban court. Elders could testify on behalf of the accused at that trial, which might influence the outcome or punishment, but the verdict would ultimately rest with a Taliban judge.

Negotiating over access to services and benefits was typically easier, particularly after the Taliban had consolidated control in a given area. Abdul Qadir, the teacher from Helmand, rattled off a litany of examples where the Taliban had accepted elders' demands on things which brought important benefits to the village: a drain-cleaning project, a separate canal rehabilitation project, a government initiative to build a girls' primary school and so on. These kinds of things, in the Taliban's view, were less likely to conflict with their military objectives. At the same time, they would get credit for allowing these activities to take place. Elders thus had to make a persuasive case that the Taliban would not only benefit but also not incur undue risk.

These kind of negotiations could be relatively easy, fast and straightforward where both sides perceived the risks as low and the benefits as substantial. When I visited Faryab in the northwest of the country in 2019, I was surprised by how some of these negotiations had become practically bureaucratised. Almar district was a case in point. It had once been deeply contested but now was nearly completely controlled by the Taliban. When I spoke with various elders from the district, they had many examples of the kinds of deals they had been able to strike with the Taliban. The most elaborate concerned a hydropower dam. Nearly a decade prior, the government had allocated $51 million for work on the dam but had ultimately been able to do little due to the violence. Construction had begun years earlier, but it had stopped and the dam had subsequently been badly damaged by the fighting between Taliban and pro-government forces. Once the Taliban had effectively taken over Almar, it was a clear community priority to try to restart the project. And so, an elder spoke to the Afghan Ministry of Agriculture, Irrigation and Livestock about repairing the dam and resuming construction. They said they would be willing to restart work if the elders could guarantee their protection.

The problem was that the Taliban considered government workers as legitimate targets. The Taliban periodically attacked the only two government buildings left in the district centre: the police headquarters and district governor's office. Government employees could not safely leave the premises and were forced to send out others for food and supplies. Dam construction would have been impossible without a Taliban guarantee that government staff and contractors working on the dam would be safe. The elders decided to approach the Taliban to lobby for the dam reconstruction to resume. Almar district had been almost entirely under Taliban control for at least a year and a half at that point, and violence (aside from the occasional airstrike, raid or rocket) was fairly limited. The elders met the Taliban shadow governor, arguing that the community and the Taliban would both benefit from local electricity production. They reasoned that electricity would be cheaper, and the government could not cut the supply to undermine the Taliban. The shadow governor agreed. Five days later, the elders met a team of engineers deployed from Kabul at the local airport and brought them to Almar, with an escort of Taliban fighters, to conduct a survey.

It was, however, difficult to predict what might cause a perceived conflict with Taliban military imperatives. Had the Almar Taliban district governor been more suspicious or in a weaker military position, he might have denied protection to the engineers, arguing that they could be government spies. Requests for permission to undertake road construction or irrigation rehabilitation were at times denied for similar reasons, or because they would interfere with the Taliban's ability to plant IEDs. Taliban perceptions were fluid and subjective, and heavily influenced by local dynamics. Where the Taliban felt relatively secure, they might allow government officials or aid workers to undertake projects. Where they were under pressure, the Taliban often saw outside intervention as presenting new risks or worsening existing ones. Where the Taliban was weak, it was prone to seeing almost any intervention—from polio vaccinations to re-opening schools—as a potential threat to its survival.

Leverage

Elders' leverage derived from a combination of their customary legitimacy and their usefulness to the Taliban, in that they could deliver (or
withhold) collective compliance. In practice, they used this leverage to
mediate Taliban behaviour. To retain their legitimacy with the population (or at least keep discontent at bay), elders had to deliver something
that their constituents wanted. Yet these dynamics were more complex
than this implies. Their strength vis-à-vis the Taliban, and the respect
and legitimacy they commanded from ordinary people, varied according to local political histories and dynamics. Elders also had to balance
relationships with the government, international and Afghan forces, and
others. Elders are best thought of as walking a tightrope, under pressure
from all sides (i.e., civilians, the Taliban, pro-government forces, various other actors) and forced to contend with sharply different expectations and demands.

Regardless of how their influence might have varied, it was rare to
speak to someone who did not recognise the importance of elders in
dealing with the Taliban on their community's behalf. But people also
recognised the complexity of their role. Farhadi, a teacher from Logar,
described the elders' role as important, but emphasised that there were
strings attached. 'The Taliban consult with the elders on most things,'
he said. 'But it is two ways: like when they have a new rule, they introduce it to the elders who communicate it to the people. But also if
there is a problem, the elders bring it to them. They can negotiate with
them, and the Taliban will find a solution.' He however conceded that
there were still problems that the elders could not solve, explaining
that 'people are upset about some things where the Taliban will not
compromise, like the older girls not being able to go to school'.[5]

Farhadi insisted the elders were able to advocate for the community
because they spoke their mind, and he felt the Taliban 'respects the
elders'. Indeed, effective elders rarely cowed to the Taliban. They
expressed the needs of the community, framing them in ways the
Taliban was most likely to be receptive to. That said, Taliban and those
close to them in Logar viewed this dynamic differently than Farhadi
did. They underscored that elders were given authority in Taliban systems, but in a manner that was subordinate to and designed to service

Taliban systems. So long as elders co-operated and did not challenge Taliban authority, their efforts to negotiate were generally respected (even if their requests were not always granted).

Even in places like Helmand, where customary authorities appeared (in general) to have markedly less leverage with the Taliban than elsewhere, people felt they were still important. Jamal, a mechanic from Nawa district, felt that 'they do things no one else can: the Taliban arrested our youths for being with the national army, and the elders had them released, and women have access to health clinics again through elders' efforts with the Taliban'. Yet Jamal was clear that the situation was a quid pro quo. 'At the same time, the Taliban have some conditions that they put in practice through the elders,' he explained. 'The elders communicate these to the people.'[6]

There is, it would seem, a delicate balance between the autonomy that preserves elders' legitimacy on the one hand, and securing concessions from the Taliban by essentially serving their objectives on the other. People wanted the elders to push for positive change, but elders could only do so if the Taliban did not perceive them as challenging their authority. The tension at the core of this relationship rarely erupted into open conflict or rebellion. Fayeq, a mechanic from Faryab, described how elders in a nearby village had once evicted local Taliban because people were 'not satisfied' with the Taliban's behaviour. He said that 'they took all the weapons off the Taliban and told them to leave'.[7] In this instance, provincial Taliban commanders replaced the evicted fighters with better-behaved ones. When I said that it seemed as though the elders were more powerful than the Taliban, Fayeq was quick to correct me. The Taliban were still ultimately in charge. 'Every Friday at the prayer, they tell the elders what to do,' he said. 'So it looks as if the Taliban are more powerful than the elders but they do accept the decisions of the elders.'[8] Still, few people would dare disarm the Taliban or even demand that cruel commanders be replaced, for fear of retribution. When I asked Fayeq if elders in other villages had the kind of power they had in his village, he said that 'elders are not so strong in some other places, either they are corrupt or they are so weak that the Taliban do not listen.'[9]

The perceived effectiveness of elders seemed to depend on a combination factors. The first was their connections with the Taliban. One

elder insisted, for example, that he was respected by and able to negotiate well with the Taliban because people in the village viewed him as
an honest and good person. Only after I continued to prod him on this
point for several minutes did my translator interrupt the interview to
explain that the elder's son was a prominent Taliban commander. The
elder grinned and said, 'Afghan sons must show respect to their
fathers.'[10] While not all elders had sons in the Taliban, many had cultivated strategic relationships with members of the group.

The second factor was the elders' perceived responsiveness to the
needs and desires of the community. This is where their legitimacy lay,
and the Taliban appeared to weigh whether the elders genuinely represented a broader constituency in individual negotiations. Where elders
sought benefits for themselves, rather than the community, they were
seen as 'bad' or 'dishonest'. Elders who unduly favoured some members of the community over others also fit this description, as did those
who were seen as 'stealing' from aid projects, grabbing land or 'too
lazy' to do much for the community. If elders were illegitimate or
disliked, the Taliban had little incentive to listen to them.

People did not typically attribute 'bad' elder behaviour to the
destructive impact of decades of conflict, and it might be that the
elders in some of these areas had never been very effective at all. In
looking at the issue of customary authority and public goods, Adam
Pain finds that some Afghan villages are more 'developmental' in character than others and have a long history of being so (Pain, 2016: 7).
Others have a long history of being run largely for the exclusive benefit
of the elite. Pain argues that customary authorities are more likely to
promote social welfare and public goods provision in villages where
there is a low degree of inequality and competition among customary
authorities for legitimacy among the population. Where elites are few
in number and well off, and there is a higher degree of inequality,
customary authorities are less likely to promote social welfare and
public goods provision.

When it came to bargaining with the Taliban, communities with
more responsive, active authorities unsurprisingly fared far better than
those with elites removed from their perceived obligations to the
population. This matters because the Taliban's calculus revolved around
striking an advantageous balance between what they could deny the

elders and what they had to grant them. 'Bad' elders could be more easily ignored than 'good' ones. And that had ramifications for the protection and well-being of the entire community.

Thirdly, elders' leverage with the Taliban lay in their broader ability to mediate with 'outsiders'. Customary authorities have long occupied the role of intermediaries between Afghan rulers and the populace. One elder from Logar described his role as 'like connectors between the government and the people and the Taliban'.[11] Being seen as honest brokers conferred trust and made possible deals between entities that would otherwise not trust one another enough to reach an agreement on their own. This kind of mediation was expected of them, and so elders were typically willing to assume the risks of negotiating with the Taliban.

A story from the northern Helmand district of Musa Qala helps illustrate how this worked. Musa Qala is the de facto Taliban capital of southern Afghanistan, owing to its strategic importance to the Taliban and the group's unparalleled level of control. There is little to no government presence left. While the Taliban had invited a BBC journalist to Musa Qala in 2017 to show off their state within a state (something which they later started doing more frequently), they allowed few if any NGOs or government service providers into the area. One day, a group of elders from Musa Qala showed up at an NGO's hospital in the provincial capital and asked them to come work in the district.[12] The elders offered security guarantees, insisting it would be completely safe for them in the district. While they didn't explicitly mention the Taliban, a staff member at the NGO surmised that 'they could not do this without Taliban say so, so either they gained Taliban permission, or they were sent explicitly by the Taliban to get us up there to treat their women and children'.[13] The Taliban would never have approached the NGO directly; the security environment was too volatile, meaning that elders were the only ones who could obtain services on the Taliban's behalf. The NGO subsequently negotiated with the Taliban, entirely through elders, to support maternal and child medical services in Musa Qala.

Fourth, as the Musa Qala story illustrates, the degree to which the elders could provide a useful function for the Taliban was important. The role of elders within Taliban systems has gradually become more systematic and formalised, and by incorporating customary authority into their governance strategy, the Taliban has mobilised it for their own ends. This, however, creates new avenues of influence for the elders: through direct participation in the Taliban's agenda, they might be better able to shape the conduct or outcome of Taliban processes. One example is the Taliban justice system. In my research into the Taliban courts with Florian Weigand, we found that, in many areas, people relied on elders as conduits to the courts and advocates within them.[14] Elders were at times consulted in Taliban judgements, particularly in family disputes where they had knowledge of the backstories of those involved and were better able than strangers to devise an appropriate remedy. In divorce cases, for example, elders were typically consulted on whether the marriage should be dissolved (particularly if the case was not clear-cut, i.e., if both parties consented to the marriage, if one party objected to the divorce). If the elders advised that the divorce should not be granted, the Taliban judge might ask them to come up with another solution and put them in charge of monitoring the outcome.

The Taliban routinely called upon elders to provide guarantees that civilians would obey their rule in other ways. When the Taliban captured a civilian working for Afghan security forces or the government, the punishment in years past was technically execution. However, the Taliban frequently allowed that person one free pass, provided they promised to stop working with the government and an elder vouched for them. One elder emphasised the relatively formulaic and predictable nature of these interactions:

> I have to provide a guarantee the first time, this is my duty. Even if I think, you know, this person is not so smart and maybe they will not do what the Taliban is telling them to do. I have to do it anyway. I know that, the Taliban knows that, the people know that. I can do nothing the second time someone gets caught working for the ANSF [Afghan National Security Forces]. The Taliban can't blame me and the family of the person cannot blame me. If someone is given a second chance and the Taliban catches them doing something wrong, the Taliban could say to me, why did you protect this person? I will say, well, how could I know? I am not his father. Now you can do what you want with him. And I will not have any problems with Taliban.[15]

The Taliban later began to allow 'reintegration' in at least some cases where Afghan forces agreed to lay down their arms and apologise, and if they had a respected elder vouch for them. More generally, people who encountered trouble with the Taliban or had relatives in Taliban custody often saw local elders as the first port of call. In this way, elders mediated civilian compliance with Taliban rule while also appearing, to their constituents, to make efforts to protect them.

Tactics and strategies

The mechanics of elder–Taliban bargaining were fairly straightforward. Elders' negotiations with the Taliban generally began with a status quo conversation or meeting wherein the elders presented their request. They might claim that the initiative would benefit the Taliban in a specific way, or they might anchor their request in Islam or customary tenets. They often pledged to take responsibility for any risks or problems that arose. If the Taliban agreed, both sides moved onto implementing the agreement.

If the Taliban were asked to make a significant sacrifice, however, elders might offer extra incentives to persuade them to agree. This was often the case in instances where elders wanted physical protection for their communities. Elders might promise to shelter, feed and support the Taliban—and not provide intelligence to the government—in exchange for the Taliban keeping violence away from civilians.[16] Persuasion, however, had limits. When asked about the extent of his influence, Fathullah, an elder from Faryab, talked about how he had negotiated a quasi-ceasefire. He and several fellow elders had persuaded the Taliban to halt military activity in the bazaar for two days so that farmers could trade. The roads had been blocked due to intense fighting, and farmers were suffering. The reasons for a temporary ceasefire were evident to both sides: economic activity benefitted everyone, and the Taliban would gain goodwill from civilians.

Things went well the first day, and, sensing he could push the agreement further, Fathullah asked for an extension. 'I went back and said could you extend for one more day? And one of the Taliban, very angry, said, "okay you mean we have to stop our jihad, we have to stop our holy war so that you can have more of your bazaar?"' he recounted. 'So it means that when they say something like this, I cannot say anything back to them. It is not like all the time they listen to us.'[17] By invoking jihad, the Taliban commander effectively shut down the negotiation. While the Taliban commander was willing to accommodate civilian demands to hold the bazaar for two days, he reacted to the request as interfering with the Taliban's military objectives and, by extension, their religious obligations. If he had objected or pushed harder, Fathullah would have been implicitly challenging the premise of the Taliban's war.

While the Taliban commander was visibly angry in this instance, civilians rarely described the Taliban as overtly threatening or emotional in negotiations. They simply said 'no' or 'not now', or they used delaying tactics. Akbar, an elder from Logar, described a common dynamic in negotiating for aid projects. 'They would say "stop this work, Haji Sahib," they don't threaten,' Akbar explained. 'They just say "enough, don't involve yourself," there is no strong treatment.'[18] When I suggested that the Taliban, given their reputation for violence, probably don't need to articulate direct threats, Akbar responded, 'Exactly— they don't need to say anything hard, and we don't overrule them.'[19] The picture that emerged from such accounts suggested negotiating with the Taliban was akin to walking through a minefield. To be skilful negotiators, elders had to know exactly where the limits were (even if those limits were constantly shifting). The trick was to push just hard enough to maximise their leverage, but not so hard as to provoke the Taliban.

Levying threats was a tactic of last resort, and usually occurred only where the Taliban was not convinced by any other means. Elders attempting to re-open a school in Helmand after many months of delay from the Taliban side reportedly told local commanders, 'We will support you if you open the school, but we cannot support you if you don't.'[20] Euphemistic expressions like 'we cannot support you' or 'we cannot say what people will do' are common in such cases. Further, in Afghanistan, where communication is often opaque and indirect, these kinds of expressions carry heft and send a strong enough signal about the importance of the demand. Threatening the Taliban was, however, high risk. If, as in the case above, the Taliban had not agreed to re-open the school, elders would have faced a difficult choice: either follow through on their threat or relent. Following through would have meant withdrawing their compliance and exposing themselves and the community to Taliban retaliation. Not following through would have diminished their legitimacy and reduced their leverage in any future negotiation with the Taliban.

Another tactic was the mobilisation of allies, such as religious authorities or other connections with more significant influence over their Taliban interlocutors. In some cases, this entailed appealing to more senior figures within the Taliban structure. One rather unique example occurred in Ghazni after the Taliban closed a community-based girls' school. Community-based schools circumvent many of the typical objections to female education by doing it apart from formal schools, segregating the genders and holding classes in private homes. In the Ghazni case, the girls' school was in a private home, separate from boys and run by a female teacher. Theoretically, this should have been allowed under Taliban rules, but the local Taliban objected anyway. Some civilians claimed they were flexing their muscles ahead of the annual spring offensive, while Taliban sources said it was a precautionary measure to prevent children from being injured in the upcoming fighting.[21] When elders were unable to persuade the local Taliban to re-open the school, they used personal connections to establish contact with members of the Taliban leadership shura in Pakistan. Several elders from Ghazni travelled to Pakistan to meet those representatives and complain about the school closure. The school was subsequently re-opened.[22] This is an exceptional example. Accessing the Taliban senior leadership would be almost impossible for most elders, and there is a high risk of upsetting the local Taliban by doing so. While local Taliban might be forced to concede on this one issue, relations might also be irreparably damaged.

Finally, elders were persistent. When the Taliban articulated a firm 'no', many described that as the end of negotiations, but only for the time being. The elders might raise the topic at another time when they had more leverage or new arguments, or when the Taliban commander they had been dealing with was killed or replaced. 'No' generally meant 'no' under the prevailing circumstances. Dynamics were constantly shifting so that even if something was impossible now, there was no reason to give up entirely. Elders tended to bide their time and try again when new circumstances suggested a more favourable outcome was possible.

Civilian organisations

Aid organisations

Much has been written on Afghanistan's aid ecosystem, but, for the purposes of understanding civilian survival in war, the most important thing to emphasise here is the political power and economic importance of aid agencies after 2001. The post-2001 Afghan government was both financially and practically dependent on UN agencies and NGOs to function and deliver essential services. With state institutions in disarray, aid agencies became a cornerstone of the basic services Afghans needed, and this has not fundamentally changed in the subsequent decades. President Ashraf Ghani claimed in a 2018 interview with the US news programme *60 Minutes* that the government would collapse in six months if aid were cut and foreign troops withdrawn (Logan, 2018). In 2019, 75 per cent of the Afghan government's budget was funded by international aid (Haque et al., 2019).

As Chapter 3 detailed, this aid is deeply politicised.[23] Donors increasingly directed their aid to areas where they had troops on the ground as insecurity worsened, and placed significant pressure on aid agencies to align their work with the counterinsurgency strategy. While humanitarian needs undoubtedly also drew some aid agencies into areas of Taliban influence, so too did donor-funding requirements and political pressure to 'win hearts and minds'.[24] Yet many other aid agencies resisted this pressure, sticking to safer government-controlled areas and refusing to engage with the insurgency until it became all but unavoidable. This was partly because aid workers were targeted in the early years of the Taliban resurgence, but counterterror restrictions also effectively discouraged engagement.

Most agencies instead responded to growing insurgent presence by introducing increasingly heavy security measures and scaling back their programming. Some outsourced programmes (and the dangers of implementing them in Taliban areas) to Afghan NGOs. Others withdrew entirely from volatile areas and stuck to territory firmly under government control. Some NGOs, however, initiated dialogue with the Taliban through elders or other intermediaries. Two of the largest humanitarian agencies operating in Afghanistan, the International

Committee of the Red Cross (ICRC) and Médecins Sans Frontières (MSF), reported that negotiation and communication with the Taliban was occurring almost daily by 2010 (Trofimov, 2010; Crombe with Michiel, 2012). But ICRC and MSF were at the forefront of engagement; some aid actors working in Taliban areas only began to talk directly to the insurgency nearly a decade later.

Early negotiations with the Taliban were fragile, subject to disruption by new outbreaks of fighting. The Taliban did not have stable control of many areas at this point, which limited the degree to which they could hold up their end of any bargain. Often negotiations would falter when fighting broke out. If a Taliban interlocutor or decision-maker was killed, negotiations would have to start all over again with his replacement. This was particularly problematic during the surge, given the deleterious effect of 'kill or capture' on local Taliban command structures.

There was also dissonance within the Taliban. While much of the senior leadership exhibited greater openness and recognised the strategic benefit of these negotiations, fighters and commanders showed far greater fear and hesitancy.[25] The Taliban rank and file, not the leadership in Pakistan, would be assuming all the risk. Aid workers could, after all, be acting as spies for international or Afghan forces. As one fighter, who was initially supportive of service delivery efforts, said in 2011, 'After the killing of our brothers in an airstrike and arrests by the PRT, we became very angry … I am sure our hideouts were disclosed by these NGOs or their spies.'[26] These dynamics would not substantially shift until after 2014, when the Taliban began to gain more stable territorial control and had a higher level of internal coherence, but this suspicion would never entirely disappear.

Fear and fragmentation also shaped aid agency positions and strategies. Competition for funding and access to communities, fear of reputational damage and uncertainty were pervasive. These and other factors created formidable barriers to co-ordination and effectively blocked collective action. Even though negotiating with the insurgency was a necessity in many areas, few were ready to acknowledge that they were 'talking to the Taliban'. They feared that doing so might result in their funding being cut, or that it could be interpreted as breaking the law. Many aid agencies operated a 'don't ask, don't tell' policy, whereby field-level Afghan staff or subcontractors negotiated with the Taliban without explicit discussion or authorisation from their superiors.[27] They could not collectively bargain or effectively co-operate because that would have required them to admit, internally and externally, that they were negotiating in the first place. This ultimately undermined their leverage with the Taliban. As one NGO director told me in 2011, 'They get played off one another by the Taliban because they don't share information or coordinate.'[28] Again, this dynamic persisted nearly a decade later, even after the Taliban controlled more than half of the country.

Elders often acted as interlocutors, particularly early on when many civilian organisations were reluctant to deal directly with the Taliban (and, to some degree, vice versa). Key points of contention centred around how much control the Taliban could exert over the delivery of aid, and typical concessions made to the Taliban included paying tax, employing staff selected by the Taliban, employing only male staff, allowing the Taliban to choose project sites or other programme alterations. Many of these arrangements were ad hoc and informal. A service provider would ask community members to secure 'acceptance' or safety guarantees. Alternately, elders would offer to obtain such guarantees on their own initiative in order to persuade an aid organisation to initiate, or resume, work.

Syed, a Taliban fighter in Wardak, explained how this was handled in his district. 'When there is a budget for a project, the elders in our village get the information about the project,' he said. 'They go together to the Taliban, and they share the budget and discuss it. The Taliban agrees and accepts it in most cases.' When I asked if there were ever any problems, Syed conceded that 'some issues are more complicated, but if there is anything like a school or health clinic, there is no delay'.[29] In more 'complicated' cases, the Taliban usually asked to receive some benefit from the project, such as tax payment, although they occasionally had softer demands, such as for the agency to hire people recommended by the Taliban. Contrary to Syed's account, civilians insisted that it often did not seem to matter whether it was a school, clinic or road being constructed. And, according to them, what Syed left out was that the Taliban demanded taxes as well as influenced how the project was implemented.

Other negotiations were more formalised and structured, built into the design of aid interventions. The Ministry of Education and its partner aid agencies established school *shuras*, which largely reproduced existing customary institutions to monitor and facilitate education. NGOs delivered and ran the government health system, the Basic Package of Health Services (BPHS), at the local level, which similarly relied on health *shuras*. The National Solidarity Programme, a country-wide initiative to support local governance and rural development, established Community Development Councils. These bodies, similar in composition and function to traditional *shuras*, played the lead role in negotiating with the insurgency to ensure that these programmes could run in areas under Taliban influence. The *shuras* also offered a veneer of deniability for aid actors: aid actors were not necessarily 'negotiating' with the Taliban but relying on what they referred to as 'community acceptance' strategies.

As they gained more territory, the Taliban built various commissions to deal with NGOs and basic services in a bureaucratised manner. They also increasingly wanted to negotiate with aid providers directly. By 2017, service delivery ministry officials were directly involved in negotiating deals with the Taliban. Many provincial or district-level government health or education officials interviewed said they were in direct contact with their Taliban counterparts. In some areas, these deals were formalised in writing, either through simple Taliban permission-to-work letters or more substantial memoranda-like documents.

Notably, in February 2018, the Taliban and the Helmand provincial Ministry of Education formalised this working relationship in a ten-point memorandum of understanding, which set out clear penalties for absent teachers and stated that all sides would work together to re-open closed schools.[30] At the point this deal was negotiated, officials I spoke with at the Ministry estimated that something like 85 per cent of Helmand's schools were effectively under Taliban control. According to the provincial director of education for the government, thirty-three schools, or more than a fifth of those that had previously been closed, were re-opened after the agreement was signed. What was most striking was the seemingly mundane bureaucratic nature of such interactions at this point. Group pictures from the agreement signing surfaced on Twitter, showing black-turbaned Taliban sitting cross-legged alongside their civil-servant counterparts. The remarkable thing was just how unremarkable it looked; were it not for the give-away black turbans, one might mistake it for any routine government meeting.

The private sector

Like the aid economy, the private sector exponentially expanded after 2001. Afghanistan's Gross Domestic Product (GDP) grew by double-digits, and per capita income increased five-fold between 2001 and 2012 (SIGAR, 2018). Small businesses and industries rapidly expanded. In particular, telecommunications, transport and construction showed significant growth as reconstruction and foreign investment took off. The opium economy also expanded,[31] and by 2007 was equivalent to 53 per cent of the country's licit GDP, despite the international community's best efforts to counter it (UN Office on Drugs and Crime, 2007). Free-market principles, private-sector development and (licit) economic growth were positioned by Western policymakers as 'transformational, freeing the country from the "dead hands" of tradition, socialism, and the Taliban' (SIGAR, 2018: 6). As the conflict worsened, however, the Afghan private sector found itself increasingly having to deal with the Taliban. While deeply coercive, the Taliban used violence as leverage to extract profit and project power rather than to prevent economic activity, as they had done initially. There was room for negotiation because the Taliban's core interest was to profit and demonstrate state-like control. The dilemmas for businesses centred on the risks, both legal and in terms of setting a precedent by yielding to Taliban demands.

The Taliban has had a long, often mutually beneficial relationship with the trucking and logistics mafias that largely control cross-border and in-country trade (Johnson, 2007; Rashid, 2001; US House of Representatives, 2010). The Taliban as an insurgency established a racket relatively early on to tax the transport of goods, meaning that transportation and logistics firms were among the first private-sector actors to extensively engage with them. Many older firms had also established relationships with the Taliban in the 1990s. Unlike aid organisations or companies, they could not necessarily withdraw from areas of Taliban influence or outsource, because their businesses depended on being able to transit through those areas. They either had to cut deals on the Taliban's terms or they would lose business. Afghan government intelligence agencies estimated that, by 2009, security and logistics firms were paying as much as 60 per cent of their gross profits to insurgents in exchange for protection (cited in Sherman and DiDomenico, 2009). As early as 2007, some trucking firms were describing relatively standardised interactions whereby a Taliban commander would contact the firm to inform them that they would have to pay for safe passage and the two sides would come to an agreement fairly quickly.[32]

A similar type of opportunism existed with opium: the Taliban taxed and regulated its production and transport, much as they had done in the 1990s.[33] With opium, the Taliban were often taxing individual farmers rather than firms or organised entities. Payments to the Taliban on poppy crop yields, and broader agricultural production, have varied considerably over time and space, and in amount and form. Mansfield concludes that while this variance is 'a function of insurgent influence in the area and the state of the rural economy … there is, of course, also room for negotiation based on patronage and poverty' (Mansfield, 2017: 36). There are Taliban dealings with narcotraffickers and collusion with state-aligned entities engaged in opium production alongside this, akin to some of the trucking and logistic deals outlined above.

Interests

In exchange for guaranteeing their safety, the Taliban pressured a diverse array of organisations into making concessions that would benefit the insurgency. The Taliban was first and foremost concerned with minimising risks, and secondarily with maximising the benefits. The Taliban wanted these organisations to bring services, public goods, trade, jobs and so on to civilians, so that they could then claim credit for them, but they wanted this at no cost to themselves. Road construction might be rejected because it inhibited the Taliban's ability to plant IEDs. Elsewhere they might grant permission but impose conditions.

The Taliban sought to mitigate potential threats by regulating where and how an organisation worked: where pylons could be constructed, where aid projects could be implemented, when and how certain goods could be transported and so on. In Helmand in 2018, for example, the Taliban halted house-to-house polio inoculations over fears that inoculators were spies; they requested that polio drops be given in the village mosque.[34] Protection deals with telecommunications providers were subject to an agreement that the company shut off service from late afternoon through to the following morning (believed to be because the Taliban thought people were more likely to inform upon them at nighttime).

By controlling hiring, they could root out suspected spies and ensure that only trusted individuals were selected. Objections to appointments were often based on the candidate having ties to the government or international forces.[35] In most cases they simply vetted prospective hires, but, particularly with jobs that required little technical expertise, they also used it as patronage. Several people described polio inoculation jobs, for example, as perks allocated primarily to Taliban fighters and their families.[36]

The Taliban also levied taxes on aid and economic activity. They might justify taxation in Islamic terms, drawing on the concepts of *oshr* and *zakat*, or they might simply demand a certain percentage—usually around 10 per cent—of the project budget.[37] Taxes on construction or renovation—the transport of goods, harvests and small businesses— were standard by 2018 at the latest. Many of these taxes, such as those levied on aid agencies, went to the Taliban leadership and presumably were then redistributed from the top down, while others stayed local and may have helped fund things like the Taliban district governor's discretionary spending or local fighters' needs.[38]

Where they encountered sustained resistance, the Taliban at times either relented, at least temporarily, or reduced their demands.[39] Aid agencies faced a difficult choice: either cede to at least some of the Taliban's demands or stop work. But if they agreed too easily to Taliban demands, they often worried that they were setting a dangerous precedent for future negotiation. The Taliban would perceive them as soft, and only ask for more next time. Being seen as 'giving in' to the Taliban also posed serious reputational, legal and security risks. A perceived association with the Taliban put them at risk for retaliation from the pro-government side. Indeed, several interviewees from NGOs, UN agencies and private companies said that pro-government security forces had arrested staff members over alleged links to the Taliban.

Many people feared even worse consequences, pointing to the US bombing of an MSF clinic in Kunduz City in October 2015, which killed forty-two clinic staff, patients and other civilians, and injured dozens more. Prior to the bombing, MSF supported both a hospital under government control in the provincial capital and a small clinic a short drive away behind Taliban lines. It was widely known that MSF treated Taliban fighters. The more damaging accusation, which many people I spoke with repeated, was that the clinic in the Taliban area was 'under the control' of the insurgency. [40] There is little credible evidence of this. According to someone I interviewed with who actually worked at the clinic and another who sought treatment at the clinic during this period, as well as interviews with MSF staff, the clinic was staffed and run by MSF with the permission of the Taliban. [41] The complex reality of how the clinic was able to operate hardly seems to matter, though. As one aid worker explained, 'The US and Afghan forces, they did [the airstrikes] because they believed MSF was Taliban.' [42]

The risks of being seen to support the Taliban weighed heavily on those who had to negotiate with them. But, as the Taliban consolidated control, there also appeared to be gradual decline in the room for manoeuvre. By early 2020, for example, most aid workers I spoke with said they could no longer avoid paying Taliban tax. [43]

Leverage

Civilian organisations' leverage often depended on what they had to offer. An organisation without anything valuable to withhold from the Taliban had little power to influence them. An entity providing something the Taliban needed, which they would have difficulty replacing or obtaining by other means, could afford to drive a harder bargain. Without health clinics, for example, how would the Taliban treat wounded fighters and their families? Plus, civilians would be outraged if the Taliban did anything perceived as taking away their access to health-care. This perhaps helps explain why the Taliban has no ideological or political qualms with basic healthcare, and has been broadly accepting of health work since early on in the insurgency.[44] That health workers possessed specialised skills also endowed them with greater leverage.

In general, there was less Taliban interference in hiring for jobs that required significant technical skill, and that included medical personnel. In these cases, civilians frequently (and usually successfully) argued that, while they could defer to the Taliban on 'security' concerns, the person that they hired needed to be competent.[45] This was not the case with hiring teachers, where ideological concerns came into play. The Taliban believed they had teaching capacity among their ranks in the form of religious clerics, despite the fact that many had only a modest religious education and little or no formal education. When they pushed for Taliban-aligned mullahs to be hired in state schools, it was difficult to refuse.[46] Arguing that mullahs were ill-qualified might have been technically true, but it would have suggested that Islamic study was not important, something highly likely to offend the Taliban.

Negotiations were relatively more difficult in situations where the Taliban did not perceive substantial value in what was being provided, such as with higher education. When I met Abdullah, a university professor, Taliban demands for a construction tax had already delayed work to expand his university's campus by nearly a year. A 10 per cent tax on construction is commonly levied and paid in Taliban areas, yet the university had not factored this into their budget and so did not have the money to pay. They also felt that, as a public university, they should not have to pay, but the construction company would not start work without Taliban safety guarantees. As Abdullah described the negotiations, he laughed in disbelief about how naïve his university had been, saying, 'These crazy people actually expected the Taliban to respect higher education.' The university had little leverage because the Taliban saw no real benefit in the university construction, and the Taliban had no problem delaying construction for as long as it took to extract revenue from the deal.[47]

Sectors like telecommunications, utilities and construction presented both a threat and an opportunity to the Taliban. The Taliban generally wanted to profit from these sectors, but they also felt compelled to regulate them. The Taliban needed to regulate telecommunications to, as discussed, shut off mobile coverage when it presented a perceived threat to their security. They also sought to extract taxes, and the Taliban's desire for profit gave communications companies leverage to ensure that they would be able to continue to safely operate. Similarly, certain types of infrastructure, such as road construction, might be refused over security concerns. At the same time, however, the Taliban recognised the potential for hefty tax dividends on construction and the benefits of taking credit for infrastructural improvements, and that created some degree of leverage on the part of these sectors.

Tactics and strategies

Private organisations typically used incentives, or threatened to withdraw them, in negotiations. They might also try to convince the Taliban that it was in everyone's interest to allow them to work. At one private clinic in Kunduz City, the Taliban regularly requested a list of specific medicines as a form of in-kind tax payment. The clinic staff pushed back if they felt the Taliban were asking for too much, and the Taliban generally relented. 'They call our doctors and nurses in the middle of the night to treat their wounded fighters,' a doctor at the clinic explained. 'What if, one night, we don't pick up the phone? They know they can't be too harsh, that they have to give at least a little.'[48] The threat of entirely withdrawing services or refusing Taliban demands was never explicitly articulated in this case, but the possibility was always in the background.

The logistics and transport sectors offer a sharp contrast. Unlike most other types of organisations, these sectors use violence as a form of leverage. Employees were often armed, as some firms provided security in addition to other services, and many firms were run by or employed former *mujahedeen* or individuals with combat backgrounds. They had little problem countering Taliban coercion with credible threats of their own. A US congressional investigation into the Afghan logistics sector highlighted how firms used violence as a bargaining tactic, surmising that 'many firefights [between the firms and the Taliban] are really negotiations over the fee'.[49] These firms were frequently hired by international forces to transport supplies, and some used their easy access to weapons to buy off the Taliban.

Most other actors did not have the means for this kind of counterviolence. Instead, they often tried to mobilise allies. Some organisations relied on interlocutors with direct links to the Taliban leadership

171

or key commanders, while others relied on customary authorities. One Afghan aid worker went so far as to describe elders as 'the ones who do the real communication'.[50] Negotiation creates risks for the elders, but the promise of aid provided a significant incentive for them to bargain with the Taliban anyway. This aid worker claimed that his organisations didn't 'pressure them into it, but the incentive for them is this: we will quit if we are not safe … if you cannot negotiate for us we will go to the next village. So they say, "okay we will talk to local Taliban"'.[51]

Elders were not the only such interlocutors. Private companies, including telecommunications and media companies, and some aid agencies described hiring—and handsomely paying—individuals located in the Gulf to mediate with the Taliban leadership. Some also hired dedicated 'fixers' on the ground in Afghanistan, who had explicit links to the Taliban, to mediate at the local level.[52] Elders' primary objective was typically to deliver for their constituents, while 'fixers' were more driven by pecuniary interests. Both approaches relied on not only money or the delivery of services but trust; and that trust could only be established through reciprocal relationships.

Finally, collective bargaining enabled some private companies to negotiate their way out of, or at least reduce, Taliban demands. A group of the major telecommunications companies operating in Afghanistan met with the Taliban in Doha in 2016 to negotiate taxation demands, and have done so sporadically since.[53] The Taliban, reacting to a new government tax on telecommunications entities, requested a 10 per cent tax in exchange for not harming their facilities or employees. Representatives I interviewed from two of the organisations involved said they were able to sidestep Taliban demands through collective bargaining, but one admitted that local employees or fixers generally had to 'give something' to the Taliban on the ground to shield themselves from violence.[54] This varied, taking the form of cash payments in some places and gifts (i.e., fashionable sneakers and watches purchased in Dubai) elsewhere.[55] The leverage and savvy these companies exhibited—that they negotiated collectively and that they did so with the top level leadership on both sides—suggests that they were equipped to withstand Taliban pressure in a way few other actors could. But it wasn't only pressure from the Taliban that they had to withstand. MTN, a South Africa-based telecommunications company, withdrew from Afghanistan amidst a lawsuit accusing MTN of paying off the Taliban.[56] Negotiations over healthcare offer a sharp contrast to telecommunications. Public healthcare in Afghanistan is broadly provided under the BPHS, a donor-funded government programme in which health services are subcontracted to different NGOs in each of Afghanistan's thirty-four provinces. NGOs bid against one another for government-issued BPHS contracts every few years, meaning that their tenure is insecure. Similar to pressure to the telecommunications companies, these NGOs faced increasing pressure from the Taliban over time. The local Taliban monitored the attendance of doctors and teachers, checked clinic stocks and deducted from the salaries of clinic staff who were absent.[57] In the spring of 2017, this pressure became more concerted and strategic as the Taliban orchestrated a pressure campaign on providers in, by my count, at least twenty-one of Afghanistan's thirty-four provinces. The Taliban's rationale was that government areas had higher-quality healthcare than Taliban areas. Taliban demanded more staff, new equipment and the establishment of hospitals or health subcentres in their areas.

The Taliban's claims had merit. Most major health facilities are located in cities and district centres. This makes sense to the extent that urban areas are more densely populated than rural ones, but the government generally controls urban areas and the Taliban controls many rural areas. High quality care is consequently harder to access for Taliban fighters and civilians from Taliban areas who are afraid to cross into government territory. Afghan security forces have tried to arrest alleged Taliban seeking treatment in government areas, or after their release as they attempted to travel back to Taliban areas.

During the pressure campaign, most aid agencies were able to reduce Taliban bilateral demands through negotiation, but there was significant variation in tactics, strategies and outcomes. An Afghan NGO in Kunduz got away with making only minor upgrades, such as repainting the clinics, because they had argued that they were too poor to do much else. It's unlikely that a larger international NGO, however, would have gotten anywhere by pleading poverty. Elsewhere the Taliban ordered clinics closed until their demands were met, or NGOs pre-emptively closed them, fearing for their safety.

The fear of dealing directly with the Taliban, however, created obstacles for some. In one province, the Taliban made demands unacceptable to the NGO, so they shut the clinics for three weeks. Asadullah, who worked for the NGO's main office in Kabul, insisted that they couldn't contact the Taliban, as it just wasn't 'what we do'. He instead talked about how they relied on a community acceptance strategy, but the more he talked the less clear this approach seemed to be. He continually seemed to be blurring the lines between the 'community' and the 'Taliban' as he described events. 'We go through a local *shura*, but of course, we know some Taliban are in that group,' he said. 'When Laghman happened,' referring to the clinic closures, 'we convened people in Kabul for a meeting. They were threatening us in Laghman, so there was no way to meet there. Better to make them come to us, to meet where we feel comfortable.' When I asked if there were Taliban at the meeting, Asadullah was circumspect. 'I am sure that the Taliban were among them,' he said. 'But we do not ask, and they do not say.'[58] Dealing with the Taliban was hard enough, but the pervasive fear and inability to do it directly seemed to—at least in this case—make it all the more difficult.

Asadullah, and many other NGO workers interviewed, agreed with the Taliban argument that healthcare was worse in Taliban areas than in government areas, and they were willing to make some improvements (within what BPHS guidelines allowed). However, the Taliban typically also requested that NGOs improve their capacity to treat those wounded in the conflict: specifically, it would seem, Taliban fighters. 'They wanted surgical capacity, but we said: okay, we can only address small wounds,' Asadullah recounted. 'District level and everywhere, they wanted trauma treatment capacity, but of course we said no, and we gave them something small instead.'[59]

The director of another NGO in a different province, Uruzgan, faced almost identical demands:

> If they say, upgrade the health facility, or we need better staff, it is very clear to us what they mean. If I'm fighting, I know I will have injured people, and I need a surgeon. So verbally, they do not say. They say verbally there is inequality between Taliban and government areas ... but the issue is we say okay, we can send an extra midwife but we cannot give you what you actually need. They don't care about a midwife

if their fighter is injured. They want a surgeon. For the government, their indicator is the number of people vaccinated, how many contraceptives for x number of women. For the Taliban, it is how many injured fighters recover.[60]

This NGO attempted to make concessions to the Taliban. They mobilised allies within the UN to advocate on their behalf. They contacted others at various levels within the Taliban movement to try to resolve the issue. Nothing worked. As negotiations dragged on, the Taliban blamed the NGO. A Taliban spokesman claimed that the clinics were wrought with corruption and mismanagement, that staff were so poorly trained they often gave people the wrong medication. The Taliban said they were protecting Afghans from bad medicine, and would allow the clinics to re-open once these issues had been resolved.[61] Clinics in Uruzgan remained closed for more than three months. By contrast, the NGO in Laghman was able to resolve negotiations with the Taliban in twenty days. Negotiations were shorter still almost everywhere else, with most lasting between a few days and a week.

Health providers across the country received almost identical demands. Some made significant concessions, such as building new clinics in Taliban areas or doubling the number of staff in existing clinics, while others made hardly any. Each agency had different degrees of leverage, and varying capacity or willingness to bargain. Some NGOS that appeared to have the most substantial leverage made dramatic concessions, while some with little leverage at all were able to continue their work relatively unchanged. (This puzzle—of why seemingly similar bargaining processes had radically different and, at times, counterintuitive outcomes—will be revisited in the next chapter.)

The most striking aspect about this case is that these health NGOs—all working in different provinces—did not share information with one another about what was happening. Some thought they were the only ones facing these demands even more than a year later when I interviewed them. The health sector could have served as a prime opportunity for collective bargaining. The Taliban had no ideological objections, they wanted healthcare access and they recognised that health workers had unique technical expertise that the Taliban could not match or replace. Yet NGOs viewed sharing information and working together as a risk they were unwilling to take. The intense level of distrust and competition among NGOs rendered collective bargaining unfeasible, and painfully undermined their leverage. And, ultimately, people who needed health-care in these various provinces suffered the consequences.

Finally, it's worth noting that some organisations typically negotiated even when they knew they wouldn't get that many concessions out of the Taliban in the short term. While it doesn't neatly fit into a discussion of bargaining tactics, this is an important point to highlight because it demonstrates how these entities viewed negotiation: not as an isolated interaction, but one move in a longer game. Negotiating with a low chance of success was often part of a posturing strategy meant to build relationships and shape future bargaining dynamics. These organisations knew they would have to concede, but were not willing to do so without giving the Taliban a hard time. They wanted to be seen by the Taliban as formidable negotiators, hoping in part that concessions could be used as leverage in future negotiations (i.e., 'we gave you something in the past, and now we need something in return'). For aid workers in particular, many felt that this enabled them to demonstrate that they had at least tried to stick to their principles and preserve their autonomy, even where they had ultimately compromised both.

Individuals

The Taliban demanded different things of different people. If you worked for the government, the Taliban would demand that you stopped. If you were a teacher, they would demand that you obey the rules they set for education. If you were an elder, they demanded you use your position to deliver broader civilian compliance. If you were a mullah, they demanded—at minimum—that you feed and shelter them and propagandise on their behalf. If you were a young man, they would likely demand you keep your hair short, your beard long and wear traditional dress (i.e., no Western-style suits or trousers, and certainly no jeans). If you were a young woman, they would require that you wear the *burqa* or *chador* and travel with a male escort, and they would probably try to prevent you from attending secondary school or working.

But individual ability and willingness to bargain was, to some degree, shaped by intangibles. Some people displayed a high tolerance for risk, while others had a comparably far lower appetite for risk. Some negoti-ated to protect themselves, others to advance themselves and still oth-ers for a bit of both. Some had an affinity for the Taliban, while others expressed disdain or resignation. The thread that ran through these individual experiences, however, was the determinative impact of social capital. Tribe or ethnicity, individual relationships with custom-ary authorities or Taliban authorities, profession, education and one's broader life experiences all shaped individual negotiating endowments and inclinations.

Interests

The primary objective for most people in the early years of the insur-gency was just to keep themselves safe: they wanted to avoid Taliban violence, and the violence inflicted by pro-government forces in response. As the Taliban began to control territory, their presence became more invasive. Negotiations might centre around agreements to feed or shelter the Taliban, the detention or court case of a relative, the consequences of breaking a Taliban rule or damage done to one's property as a result of fighting. Nonetheless, there seemed to be more examples of civilians initiating engagement with the insurgency to their advantage as time went on. The Taliban were more present and more visible, thus easier to access and approach, and they had the capacity to provide more benefits.

Another change over time was that the parameters of negotiation became clearer as Taliban rules were more widely understood and uni-formly enforced. More civilians negotiated as time passed, which meant civilians had a larger evidence base upon which to make deci-sions and choose tactics. But civilians' objectives varied. Some informed on rivals or acted upon old grudges. Several sought Taliban favour, for example, so that Taliban judges would settle a dispute to their advantage. Other objectives were more prosaic. A man seeking a teaching position at a local school in Wardak made his case to both the headmaster and a local Taliban acquaintance, knowing he would need the approval of both to secure a teaching job.[62] Civilians also seemed to get bolder as time went on. Seddiqa, a mid-wife I met in Nad Ali in Helmand, was a case in point. The Taliban had used her clinic as a firing position, and she pulled out her cell phone to show me a video of her clinic in utter ruins as we talked. After the fighting died down, she summoned the pregnant wife of a Taliban fighter she knew to her clinic. Seddiqa told her the Taliban had to pay immediately for the damage they had done to be repaired, because she could not deliver babies until it was. Seddiqa gave the Taliban wife a handful of used shell casings from the wreckage to take back to her husband.[63] When I asked her if she would have pulled something like this two or three years earlier, her eyes went wide as she laughed and shook her head. The implication seemed to be that the Taliban were now the ruling authorities—or at least vying to rule Nad Ali at that point—and that came with certain expectations.

People continually calculated the value and costs of their compliance relative to their alternatives. Some were swayed by Taliban ideology, and either chose to join the fight or provided overt support. Others fled, often to nearby cities or towns. A typical pattern emerged where most of the family would flee, leaving behind a male family member to tend to the property and assets as well as monitor the situation, with an eye towards whether the rest of the family could or should return. Some calculated that it would be better to relocate en masse and abandon their villages entirely. This most often occurred among those who decided that life under the Taliban would be unbearable, and who had the resources to start over elsewhere.

Ali, a teacher in Chardara in Kunduz, explained how the Taliban in his village 'started their rules slowly, so people could prepare themselves and adjust little by little'. The Taliban's strategy of creeping control, and the back and forth nature of the conflict, gave civilians time to plan. People could gather information, test various tactics, and investigate their options. 'We all knew what was coming,' he said. 'And we all had to develop our own strategies.' Ali said that some of his colleagues immediately tried to cultivate friendships with the Taliban to protect themselves and their families. After the Taliban instituted a rule that all teachers should maintain long beards, he moved to a nearby city under government control. He joked that he could not 'grow his beard fast enough'. As he saw it, staying meant that you 'have to be their friend, you have to get their head in your hands because you need their support to survive'.[64] That was a sacrifice he was unwilling to make.

Many individuals at first attempted to avoid direct contact with the Taliban or did the bare minimum to comply. As time went on, however, avoidance became less viable. As discussed in Chapter 1, avoidance or neutrality is sub-optimal for an insurgency; insurgents require at the very least some level of compliance from civilians. This does not mean that civilians must overtly support the insurgency, but they cannot stay entirely separate from them. This might have been an option when the Taliban was weak, but not when it was strong, and their interference in people's lives intensified.

Ali talked about how the Taliban began to regulate the everyday behaviours and routines that comprise life in an Afghan village. Taking a dispute to a government court rather than a Taliban one became a punishable offence. The Taliban began setting caps on bride prices, midwives' fees for birthing babies and the markups on drugs sold at the local clinic or pharmacy. Attendance at the mosque became compulsory. Ali started attending the local mosque less and less, finding the recent shift towards pro-Taliban rhetoric distasteful. One day, however, he was forced by Taliban fighters to stand knee-deep in the local river, while the mullah chastised him for his absence from daily prayers and spectators from the village looked on.[65] As Ali recalled this humiliation, his eyes welled up with tears.

To be clear, everyone I met residing in areas of Taliban influence had a story about interacting with the Taliban. A farmer taking his crops to market had to negotiate safe passage and taxation at Taliban checkpoints.[66] A businessman cultivated relations with the Taliban to gain their favour.[67] Children going to school encountered Taliban monitors, who might recruit them as spies or seek to discipline them for misbehaving in class.[68] A woman seeking a divorce found herself pleading her case in front of a Taliban judge, after both the state and her village elders failed to help her escape an abusive situation.[69] A father whose son was abducted by the Taliban had to negotiate his release.[70] A teacher seeking employment at the village school had to earn the Taliban's trust to be appointed to his position.[71] To remain in these areas once Taliban control had been consolidated required obedience, and that was—in one way or another—almost always negotiated. How civilians navigated these situations was, however, highly individualised.

Leverage

Individuals drew on social connections, symbolic meanings, economic power and other features of this landscape to effectively negotiate with the insurgency. Social connections were often the most important feature of this embeddedness. For many civilians in Afghanistan, keeping a broad, diverse network or even doing an occasional favour for a Taliban fighter was the best way to navigate insurgent rule. Some of those running local Taliban operations were likely to be long-standing acquaintances or relatives, associations that in many cases pre-dated the insurgency. It would be unusual for people in a Taliban village not to have some connection to the insurgency, however tangential. These kinds of connections were the single most important source of leverage in individual negotiation strategies. While social capital was important for customary authorities and organisations, they had considerable leverage in other forms: they had concrete incentives to offer, and social capital seemed to strengthen their hand. For individuals, it was the other way around: their social capital was often the primary and most effective leverage they could access, and other forms of leverage enhanced that.

Tactics and strategies

When I met Hashimi, a university professor working in Wardak, his bravado, foul language and incessant chain-smoking charmed me immediately. He wasn't afraid of the Taliban, but he was a pragmatist and accepted that he had to deal with them. 'The Taliban examined schoolteachers in my area which, okay, fine,' he told me, describing the common Taliban practice of forcing government teachers to take competency exams.

> Under the current government, we have had terrible ministers, so the level and quality of education has been shit. They have done nothing for education, and there has been too much corruption. When security got worse, the good teachers left for Kabul, so the ones left are not as good or qualified. So at least the Taliban is trying to make sure we have qualified teachers.

His attitude changed when the Taliban tried to do the same with university professors. The Taliban head of education in the province called the university chancellor and ordered him to send all of the teachers to a specific location in Tangi, a local Taliban stronghold. 'Can you imagine being examined by a Taliban?' he asked. 'What does he know but fighting? It was ridiculous and humiliating. If we let them do this, where will they stop?'

'I called Zabiullah,' he said, referencing the Taliban spokesman Zabiullah Mujahed. 'And said to him: no, you cannot do this. If you do this, the Taliban examiners need qualifications. We professors all have a BA or MA, so the person who examines the professors with BAs must have at least an MA. The person who examines the MAs must have a PhD. He called back an hour later and said: it is okay, there will be no exam.'[72]

As a professor with a Master's degree, the prospect of being examined by, in his words, 'guys who were probably barely literate' was a non-starter. His anger was obvious and immediately understandable, but I pointed out that few people would have had the guts to challenge the Taliban like that. He laughed this off. 'You think the Taliban is going to kill a professor for being a pain in the ass? They have bigger things to worry about.'

The Taliban has, of course, killed people for less. But in calculating that he would not likely face any serious sanction for complaining, he saw little risk in voicing his discontent. His status as an educated man and a professor, he wagered, would allow him to make this logic-based argument persuasively. As ridiculous as his argument may have sounded—that the Taliban should, or even could, find someone with a PhD to administer exams—it worked.

A doctor in northern Helmand described how most clinic and NGO personnel had to negotiate with the Taliban focal point for health, Haji Laluck. He, however, did not deal with Haji Laluck. 'I am originally from Musa Qala, so I know other commanders and big Taliban and can find a faster way to solve problems,' he explained. 'Our family is big, so the Taliban can do nothing to us and we won't have any problems.'[73] Some felt, correctly or not, that their status protected them from the risks posed by dealing with the Taliban.

Arguments also mattered. People at times drew on religion, but more often employed logic or sought to evoke sympathy. Farmers interviewed often pleaded poverty or extenuating circumstances where Taliban taxes were unduly burdensome, and they sometimes received a break.[74] Habiba, a headteacher in Logar who was trying to keep her girls' schools open, argued, however, that the school complied perfectly with Taliban rules and Islamic norms. Habiba recounted trying to argue that her practices conformed to all of the Taliban's rules. 'I told them all the requirements that the Taliban want, we have,' she said. 'The school has a building and an outside wall, female teachers, just we have two men as guards, and the Quran says women should be educated, and the elders support me—so what is the problem?'[75] But in this case, even the elders couldn't help overcome the local Taliban commanders' ideological resistance to the only girls' high school in the district.

People might draw in elders at the outset, as Habiba did, or only after their attempts at direct negotiations faltered. In some places, such as Charkh, this appeared to have a procedural quality. 'If a person has a problem with the Taliban, the Taliban district governor is known to everyone,' an elder there said. 'They appeal to him directly and solve their problem. If they have a big problem, they approach the Taliban with a few elders and solve their problem. If their problem is bigger than that and the Taliban do not accept their arguments or their excuses, they have to leave the area, they have to flee.'[76] More broadly, elders acted in both ad hoc and more systematic ways as advocates. They could help make connections with the Taliban, where civilians could not do so directly, and advise on how to best deal with them (as with things like the Taliban courts).

Direct relationships with the Taliban came in handy, but one had to be selective. The key for individuals was not just knowing any Taliban fighter, but the right Taliban fighter. This meant a decision-maker, and ideally one sympathetic to their cause. A journalist from Kunduz mentioned that their childhood classmate was now one of the biggest Taliban in his district. 'It's funny to think about,' he said. 'But we used to play volleyball together, and he wasn't very good.'[77] Offhand recollections about casual associations like this were common, as though people almost couldn't quite believe how it could be possible for things to have changed so much in so little time. Notably, the journalist did not approach his former friend when he had a problem; he was sure this man would 'cut his throat'. Instead, he approached another Taliban connection, who he knew less well but who was both friendlier and more powerful.

Casual relationships with Taliban (or piggybacking on the relationships of those who knew them) could be incredibly and unexpectedly useful. Several individuals interviewed, who had little affinity for the Taliban, discussed having Taliban 'friends' who they continued to cultivate relationships with 'just in case'. One man from Uruzgan, where the Taliban has long controlled much of the province, described it like this:

> You give whatever you have to these people [the Taliban] to protect yourself. Maybe if you give one son to the Taliban, they spare you a little. You have an advocate if he becomes a big Taliban. You will have protection, information, everything. Otherwise, you are in a big mess. They will say give me your guns, give me bread, feed us and all of these things. If you know a Taliban leader, if you have a Taliban relative, you are safe.[78]

Individuals who didn't have these kinds of links often sought to build them, in whatever way they could. A woman recounted how a relative returning from his job in Pakistan by road had been detained by the Taliban while travelling back to his home village. She sent texts and Facebook messages to everyone she could think of who was from, or might know someone from, the area he was abducted from. Through these connections, she found someone able to contact the Taliban holding her relative. He was released a day later.[79]

These strategies worked because the Taliban needed civilian allies too. Networking, because it usually had some component of reciprocal exchange, meant that favours done now could be called in later. A Taliban commander I met from Baghlan explained his rationale in cultivating a casual relationship with a local police chief. 'We Afghans have been fighting wars for a very long time, and we need to be pragmatic to survive,' he said. 'Everyone needs two phone numbers, one for the government and one for the Taliban. Even me, I have many friends on the government side, and this is how we manage our lives.'[80] It was a wise strategy, given that in matters of life and death—such as the detention of a relative or blockage of aid access—these links often count the most. The Taliban 'rules' may still take precedence, but it is critical to have advocates to fight your corner.

5.

THE ART OF THE DEAL

EVOLUTION, VARIATION, ENABLING FACTORS
AND CONSTRAINTS

Throughout the research for this book, the theories I tried to develop
about how people might behave in a situation or how negotiations
should play out were routinely challenged. Each new place was, in
some ways, its own puzzle. Why did Taliban in this village or district
adopt certain policies that others didn't? Why did civilians seem to have
more power in one place than another? On the one hand, there was a
fundamentally similar civilian–Taliban dynamic across all of these
places. Yet on the other, local and even individualised dynamics seemed
to shape so many aspects of bargaining. When I asked people about why
things were the way they were, they would say things like 'that's just
Warduj, it's always been like that', or 'Sangin Taliban have always been
cruel'. While that might have been how people rationalised it, it wasn't
the full story.

   This chapter gets at some of the factors driving variation across time
and space. It starts with the evolution of these dynamics. Much of this
is down to the organisational development and maturity of the Taliban.
While some of the Taliban leadership recognised fairly early that violence alone would not enable them to achieve their objectives, it took
time for the insurgency to develop the internal consensus, coherence

and strategy that allowed them to shift course. As the preceding chapters have illustrated, only much later did civilian bargaining become integral to Taliban strategy. Civilians perceptions—of what they could demand from the Taliban, of what the Taliban wanted from them, of the risks of engaging and so on—and their capacities to bargain evolved alongside this.

The question of why bargaining dynamics varied across the country during the same timeframe is more complicated. Much of this is attributable to military dynamics, with the Taliban far less easy to negotiate with when and where it was under military pressure. Nevertheless, various forms of social capital were important in shaping these dynamics. An individual's status and relationships were vital, but social cohesion was particularly powerful. It created the ability to bargain collectively, which exponentially magnified civilian leverage. Plus, in tighter-knit environments, individuals were more likely to have useful links to Taliban or people who could influence them. Social capital was also essential for the Taliban, who leveraged local relationships, normative resonance and their own embeddedness in communities to further their military and political objectives. More broadly, social capital influenced the political alliances the Taliban cultivated, the rules they sought to impose and how they argued their case to civilians and external audiences.

Norms, ideology and argumentation were another dimension of this. Just as the Taliban sought to frame its ideology in ways that garnered sympathy and justified their actions, so too did civilians. The Taliban leadership allowed leeway at the local level, so long as these accommodations did not directly contradict core Taliban precepts. Where the Taliban perceived that negotiations threatened or undermined their core practices or beliefs, they were generally unyielding. The trick for civilians was to frame their requests in ways that did not explicitly reject Taliban ideology, but affirmed and appealed to it instead.

This does not, of course, explain everything. Civilians and insurgents alike are subject to near-constant danger, and live amidst pervasive uncertainty, rumour and suspicion. This made some individuals more risk averse and others, feeling they had little left to lose, more willing to take risks. It made some more empathetic or willing to compromise and others less so. Emotional impacts were unwieldy and unpredictable, but profoundly shaped people's perceptions, choices and interactions. This chapter looks at these various factors in an integrated way, bringing together the Taliban and civilian sides of the story discussed in Chapter 3 and 4, to understand what kinds of conditions and tactics best enabled civilians to negotiate for their survival and well-being.

The Taliban's evolution and civilian responses

In the early years of insurgency, the Taliban's heavy reliance on violence betrayed their profound distrust of civilians and left little room for, or interest in, negotiation. In general, civilians ultimately faced a difficult choice when the Taliban established a foothold in their villages: comply with the Taliban's rules or leave. Overt resistance and rebellion were rare, but the Taliban brutally suppressed hints of either. Those who stayed often found themselves in an impossible position. Complying with the Taliban might have meant providing them with food or shelter, but being seen to collaborate with the Taliban invited pro-government retaliation. There was also a distinct lack of accurate information. This made it hard to understand what the Taliban wanted or what 'the rules' were. At least through the end of the military surge, civilians typically saw the Taliban as unpredictable, unreliable and disorganised. But civilians paid attention to the balance of the conflict over time, and they slowly gained more insight into Taliban interests and behaviour. The better civilians understood what the Taliban wanted, the more willing and able they were to bargain.

Likewise, as the Taliban began to move more openly and present themselves as a government in waiting, civilians could more easily access them. Growing predictability of Taliban systems, particularly after 2014, allowed civilians to figure out how to influence the rules. More civilians negotiated, which made it seem less risky and created a kind of institutional knowledge on how to deal with the Taliban. At the same time, the Taliban began to feel they could present a less aggressive face to civilians. This relationship was nonetheless still premised on coercion: obey our rules, and we will provide governance and protection.[1]

Another important shift came about with the Taliban's quest for international recognition. At the Taliban's leadership level, engagement was gradual. During the surge era, tentative political talks and high-level engagement occurred between the Taliban and international community. The UN began holding regular, albeit confidential, meetings on human rights and humanitarian issues with the Taliban in the Gulf sometime around 2013. The ICRC and MSF had begun privately meeting the Taliban somewhat earlier, and several other NGOs followed suit. Repeated interactions created a virtuous circle, in that trust and greater openness was gradually built on both sides, and fear of engagement lessened.

Members of the Taliban leadership conceded that the decision to engage aid organisations and the international community was driven by their desire for political recognition. The desire for legitimacy was, however, more important to the Taliban leadership than to the rank and file. (And, to be clear, even the leadership did not want legitimacy for its own sake; they were pursuing recognition as a means to achieving their objectives.) The political commission in Qatar might have wanted to give aid agencies what they asked for because they saw the diplomatic and material benefits of doing so. Fighters and commanders, by contrast, saw recognition by the international community as an abstraction at best. Field commanders were willing to take what they could from the 'enemy' but openly expressed far more cynicism and distrust. When asked why he permitted aid projects despite distrusting aid organisations, a Taliban official in Faryab interviewed in earlier research in 2011 replied that 'a clever Muslim can use the sword of the *kafir* [a non-Muslim] against him'.[2] This attitude has, to varying degrees, endured.

Military pressure

While the Taliban had developed a sophisticated shadow government by 2017, they were still fighting for territory against a formidable opponent. They were also under increasing pressure from airstrikes and night raids. Consequently, options for bargaining were still heavily influenced by the degree of military pressure exerted on the Taliban in a specific time and place. Patterns of behaviour could be hyperlocalised and at times hard to delineate. Within individual provinces, and even within districts, there were complex patterns of influence and contestation.

In Kunduz, the Taliban's territorial control was a mélange of different levels of control and military dynamics, varying from village to village in some areas. Most district centres remained under government control, but that quickly faded beyond the immediate perimeter of government buildings. In some areas, white Taliban flags could be seen from district through-roads, indicating that government control ended twenty feet away on either side of the road. In the provincial capital of Kunduz City, ostensibly under government control, the Taliban moved freely, collected taxes from businesses and adjudicated disputes, while in Chardara district—a twenty-minute drive away—their control was almost complete. The nearly invisible and deeply permeable border between the two districts was marked by a lone and fairly barren-looking tree on the side of the road. Beyond that, Kunduz City ended and Chardara's Taliban checkpoints began.

Helmand was a different story. Northern Helmand belonged to the insurgency, but central and southern Helmand were subject to more complex dynamics. Nad Ali, much like Chardara, bordered the provincial capital, but the fight for control was more violent and visible there than in Kunduz. When I first visited, the government had recently and significantly pushed the Taliban back, deeper into the district. There were clear marks of the conflict: roadside craters from IEDs, bullet-pocked clinics and shops, and police checkpoints scarred by recent attacks. The Taliban could not move as openly, but they still regulated the schools, held courts in the district and taxed harvests. Parts of the district were under more complete Taliban control, but one needed to go village by village to understand how stable that was, how long it had been that way and what it meant for civilians.

Finally, Logar in Charkh district was under fairly consolidated Taliban control. The rest of Logar's districts each had their own unique patterns of control, prone to unexpectedly shift in the weeks between contact or visits. Baraki Barak, for example, neighboured Charkh but was more obviously contested. Logar wasn't deemed as strategic as Kunduz or central Helmand for pro-government forces (or by the Taliban, for that matter), so didn't face the same level of violence.

This surely paints a confusing picture, but it also helps explain why bargaining was so varied and dynamic. How could it be otherwise, amidst such volatility? In general, however, it is useful to think about two categories: areas of fragmented sovereignty (where the Taliban, the government and/or other armed groups engaged in an armed contest)[3] and areas of consolidated Taliban control. Fragmented sovereignty comprised areas where the Taliban were seeking to expand, reclaiming lost territory, or facing a severe threat of losing control. Historically, the Taliban have tended to be harsher and less open to negotiating with civilians where their control was threatened or tenuous. Once they have relatively consolidated control, the Taliban are typically more approachable and more amenable to bargaining. Perhaps unsurprisingly, people in Baraki described Taliban behaviour as more restrictive and less sympathetic than those in Charkh, where control was more complete.

Fragmented sovereignty versus consolidated control

Early on, when the Taliban tried to establish control over an area, they were more aggressive and violent, but as they consolidated control they became less brutal towards civilians. This broad pattern remains true, with some adaptations. Today, fighters might be drawn from outside the area or from the Red Units—specialised combat units deployed to lead offensive operations—to gain territory. The role of these forces' role is not to win the support of civilians but to establish coercive dominance, allowing local Taliban to then take over. The targeted killings, detentions and threats that characterised the Taliban's offensive operations were nonetheless accompanied by persuasion. These tactics—coercive as they might be—provided information to civilians, which informed their perceptions and course of action. Historically, there has generally been limited room for non-violent bargaining in these initial stages of Taliban infiltration. The Taliban does not possess the same kind of capacity—or the degree of trust and willingness necessary—to engage with civilians in this way. This initial phase nonetheless lays the groundwork for future negotiation.

This dynamic evolved over time, but the basic pattern persisted. After roughly 2014, the Taliban had greater capacity, institutionally, to create incentives in concert with coercion and violence. They effectively turned governance into a military tactic, via creeping control that softened the ground for infiltration. They often initiated the provision of incentives long before they could be said to control territory.

Security and related concerns were still a challenge but far less so than they had been during the surge (when there were far fewer civilian officials). One implication is that the rules were more explicit and more predictable as time went on. Another is that the Taliban arguably gained greater leverage over civilians by establishing a stable structure dedicated to regulating civilian life. Governance systems afforded them more coercive power. Justice, for instance, was not only a service but a means of enforcing civilian compliance with Taliban rules. Taliban school monitors recruited children as spies and ensured that nothing contradictory to Taliban ideology was being taught. At this point, military pressure no longer eradicated Taliban capacity to provide incentives, at least not in quite the same way as it had done during the surge (when dedicated civilian governance structures, separated out from the military hierarchy, hardly existed anyway). While counter-attacks still eroded the Taliban's capacity and willingness on this front, it was markedly more durable and resilient.

Much also depended on the Taliban's local history and the degree of military pressure being exerted. When they were exerting a new territorial claim, the Taliban was less likely to negotiate and more suspicious of civilians. Once they had established some degree of control over the area, the Taliban typically relaxed. Where local Taliban felt relatively secure, they were much more likely to bestow trust and provide rewards. Where they were seeking to recapture lost territory, both the Taliban and civilians already knew who and what they were dealing with. Even where the Taliban were routed, many on both sides tended to regard their return as inevitable. Some places had changed hands multiple times in recent memory. This familiarity enabled the Taliban to use its relationships to keep an eye on civilians. Civilian behaviour was shaped by prior experience: civilians knew what they were in for if and when the Taliban returned, how much room for manoeuvre there would be and what tactics might work best. On one visit to Nad Ali, I was initially surprised that little of the damage caused by operations to rout the Taliban six months earlier had been repaired. Taliban graffiti remained on the walls of the district government compound, and shell casings littered the courtyard. The district governor said that there would be little use in making repairs because the Taliban were sure to return. He even joked that maybe they would let him live if they saw that he had kept the compound to their liking.[4]

It is important remember that fragmented sovereignty and consolidated control are not necessarily distinct categories in practice, even though that is how I've presented them for the sake of rhetorical clarity. This dynamic is best envisioned as a sliding scale with consolidated government control on one end (as in much of Kabul) and consolidated Taliban control at the other end (as in the Taliban capital of Musa Qala, or a place like Chardara), with numerous permutations of contestation in between. Complicating this is the fact that even in many areas of consolidated Taliban influence or control, the threat of airstrikes and raids was always present. Where they felt intensely targeted, the Taliban devoted more energy to eliminating spies or increasing certain restrictions (i.e., cutting off mobile phone reception), but the rules governing civilian behaviour remained largely intact. Part of the reason was that airstrikes and night raids in these areas were rarely linked with attempts at establishing or expanding government control. The airstrikes and raids caused damage to the Taliban, but they rarely threatened their level of influence.

Pro-government operations to retake and hold terrain were, by 2017, usually reserved for areas adjacent to strategic major cities or towns. Remember that the strategy had shifted towards holding the ground in order to drive the Taliban to the realisation they could not win militarily and would have to capitulate to pro-government demands. Instead, the pro-government strategy focused increasingly on protecting cities (i.e., Kandahar, Kunduz, Mazar-i-Sharif, Jalalabad) and generally not on re-asserting government presence in rural areas under significant Taliban influence or control.[5]

The determinative impact of civilian cohesion

Social capital—defined as a public good, created by certain aspects of social structures, which facilitates co-ordination and co-operation—encompasses many of the most critical remaining factors that shaped contemporaneous variation. Communities with tighter horizontal linkages and functional institutions, for example, were better able to negotiate with the Taliban than those with deeper divides, marked inequality and weaker institutions. More united communities had better capacity to bargain than more divided communities, just as organisations that were able to co-operate with or mobilise allies were similarly better off than those who, for reasons of distrust or competition, could not. If elders could present a united front, for example, they limited the Taliban's opportunities to divide and rule (i.e., co-opting some elders while marginalising those who presented resistance). If they represented the community in its totality, they also could offer the Taliban a compelling incentive in the form of collective civilian compliance, and if the Taliban refused their demands, they risked turning the entire community against them. Where communities had fewer horizontal linkages or were internally divided, they were unlikely to be able to muster as much leverage (all things being equal).

In my and Rahmatullah Amiri's research into regional patterns of Taliban governance, we found that differentials in the strength of customary institutions drove sharp differences in Taliban policy in the south versus southeast of the country (Jackson and Amiri, 2019). Regional generalisations are perpetually subject to exceptions, but—in general—tribal structures play a much stronger role in society in the southeast than they do in the south. This had a clear effect on the Taliban's ability to impose its will on civilians. We looked at this dynamic from multiple angles, but schools provided one useful indicator of community strength. In the south, Taliban more frequently closed schools in the areas under their control, and pressured communities into closing schools in contested and government-controlled areas. The Taliban sent night letters, made threatening calls to teachers and spread propaganda forcing schools to shut and teachers to leave their jobs. The Taliban targeted or killed teachers who refused, both to punish them and to send a broader message to civilians. After these killings, elders interviewed felt sure that any attempt to engage the Taliban on the matter would result in threats, beatings or worse, so they were understandably reluctant to pursue the issue.

In the southeast, by contrast, local Taliban acknowledged the strength of tribal structures and knew that they would have to accommodate their preferences. The Taliban's early anti-education policy was curtailed, at least for boys' education. The Taliban closed girls' schools in 2008, although they later allowed them to operate until the sixth grade where communities demanded it. In 2012, elders said that the Taliban started to interfere with schools, in line with the broader Taliban policy shift towards co-opting education. In one example from Paktia, teachers' pay was docked for absences and teachers were required to pay a percentage of their salaries to a new military commander, who had come from the south. The community was outraged and pushed back. One elder from Paktia province said, 'We knew they hated schools,' but they 'continued to engage the Taliban with arguments that schools pose no threat against them, nor is the education system against sharia law.'[6] In the south, closing and attacking schools had not created real problems for the Taliban in the same way it would have in the southeast (even if some people were bitterly frustrated with these decisions).

Looking at whole regions provides a useful meta-comparison but obscures just how much the situation could differ between communities. There were instances in which one constituency within the community sided with the Taliban to gain an advantage. The Taliban used pre-existing grievances to gain a foothold among groups who felt disadvantaged or under attack. From the outset, these communities were in a weaker bargaining position than united communities. Whereas more cohesive communities did not need anything from the Taliban, various factions within these more vulnerable constituencies sought favour and help from the Taliban. These divides often fell along ethnic or tribal lines. In the southern province of Kandahar, for example, the Taliban heavily relied on tribal grievances to divide and rule. In the northern province of Kunduz and the western province of Faryab, these tensions fell along ethnic lines among marginalised Pashtun communities on the one hand, and predominantly Tajik and Uzbek constituencies on the other. Many of these Tajik and Uzbek constituencies received support from the government and international military forces to form quasi-state militias to 'fight the Taliban'. In practice, there was a blurry line between 'fighting the Taliban' and using violence for personal gain, or waging long-held grievances over access to resources and political power.

Another gradient was class and economic status. This was often, but not always, linked with tribal and ethnic identity. Many wealthy farm owners had their property seized, ostensibly because they had some affiliation with the government. The Taliban represents a predominantly

THE ART OF THE DEAL

poor, rural constituency. One landowner in Kunduz returned to his farm to negotiate with the Taliban only to find that the Taliban commanders he had expected to negotiate with were young 'angry, ignorant' men from the most impoverished families in his village. 'They were not even the dust off my shoes before, but now they are big Taliban,' he said.[7] He knew these men were unlikely to give his land back, regardless of what the Taliban rules said.

Among divided civilians, it was ultimately the Taliban who won out. But there are formidable obstacles to civilian unity and co-operation. If it were easy, more civilians would have done it. Violence spurred out-migration, disrupting networks of trust and customary governance structures. It also magnified cleavages and distrust within some communities and groups more than others.[8] All of this speaks to a larger debate about how communities or groups use social capital in situations of volatility and violence. More generally, research in other contexts has concluded that social capital generally increases as a threat approaches but withers as the threat materialises and violence increases (De Luca and Verpoorten, 2015; Jennings and Sanchez-Pages, 2017; Kalyvas, 2006). Civilian experiences in Afghanistan point to much more variable social capital dynamics, suggesting that social capital is more closely linked to pre-violence conditions and the nature of the violence inflicted upon the community.

Movement cohesion versus local imperatives

The insurgency evolved through the knitting together of a number of networks, of varying character and reach, under the banner of the Taliban. In at least the first decade of the insurgency, this created a debate over the coherence, and thus the staying power, of the Taliban. Some analysts saw the Taliban's internal divisions as a sign of chronic fragmentation. Proponents of this line of thinking argued that the Taliban could be divided and conquered by pro-government forces through military pressure and 'reintegration' incentives, and they later insisted that it would likely fracture were any peace talks to occur (see Christia and Semple, 2009; Farrell and Semple, 2017). There have, undoubtedly, been minor splits and disagreements, but none so fundamental that they threatened the future of the movement. The Taliban has instead become more coherent and capable of acting with greater unity of command. They were able to meet the challenges of taking and holding significant territory, while at the same time engaging in political talks with the United States and the Afghan government. The Taliban has exhibited, as insurgencies go, a remarkable level of operational coherence.

The Taliban, however, it is not a monolith. It encompasses a diverse set of factions and individuals with an array of interests. The Taliban leadership has sought to tighten the reins of control over its ranks while retaining the benefits of decentralisation and localisation. As argued in Chapter 3, they have achieved this by accommodating a degree of diversity on the ground, rather than attempting to eradicate it. All Taliban are united by common goals—ridding Afghanistan of foreign occupying forces and establishing a 'truly' Islamic government—and they act in a co-ordinated way in pursuit of those goals. Yet the networks that comprise the Taliban still largely reflect local interests, concerns and preferences.

When Rahmatullah Amiri and I set about trying to figure out how the Taliban made the 'rules', it quickly became clear that they were not crafted from the top-down. Across the country, local accommodations, influenced by civilian preferences, created the foundation for what became Taliban policy. The local Taliban initially worked without much practical guidance from above on how to deal with civilians. Violence would only get them so far, and many were simply making up the rest as they went along. The *layha*, from the revision issued in 2009 onwards, recommended a broadly conciliatory approach to civilians, but it was thin on the specifics of how to win people over.

The first time I heard about Taliban governance, beyond their sharia courts, was in a humanitarian co-ordination meeting in 2009. I was then working for a British NGO, and I remember a UN official reporting that the Taliban had started punishing absentee teachers and students in Chardara district, and forcing them to show up at government schools. The story stuck with me because it was so anomalous at the time. No detailed Taliban education policy existed then, and there were certainly no directives to discipline children for skipping school. When I tried to trace this story nearly a decade later during research for this book, I was lucky enough to find a school head who had worked in Chardara at the time. He recounted that the local Taliban had started intervening in schools because a group of concerned parents had approached a local commander and specifically asked that they hold the teachers accountable. At the time, corruption in schools had been a growing source of frustration among Afghans, with reports of 'ghost' schools and teachers—who only ever existed on payrolls and not in real life—proliferating. An NGO colleague sitting next to me at the meeting joked that the government would really be in trouble if the rest of the Taliban implemented 'Chardara rules', because people might actually begin supporting them.

To be clear, the Taliban did not simply accommodate community preferences. The commanders in Chardara threatening and beating absent teachers and students seemed benevolent when compared with some Taliban attitudes towards education elsewhere at the time. Fighters often had their own ideas about the rules civilians should adhere to. The divide between these and what the community writ large wanted was often shaped by where the Taliban were from, and the degree of shared social capital shared by civilians and Taliban. With outsider Taliban, it was more likely that these two sets of beliefs would diverge, narrowing the prospects for a mutually acceptable outcome. Where views between locally bred Taliban and civilians diverged, shared social capital typically increased the likelihood of a mutually acceptable compromise.

Where institutions are weak, charisma and the strength of personalities play an outsized role in shaping policy. Charisma is, however, a difficult quality to pin down. As James C. Scott writes, 'the relational character of charisma means that one "has charisma" only to the extent that others confer it upon one' (Scott, 1990: 221). Within the Taliban, charisma is conferred upon those with a mixture of battlefield accomplishments, political guile, leadership and the ability to acquire resources. The history of the Taliban movement is populated with such figures, often revered as folk heroes. Mullah Abdul Salam Akhund (the shadow governor of Kunduz from 2013 until his death in a drone strike in 2017) was able to go his own way partly because he had a strong personal power base and controlled the regional illicit economy. He was also widely respected for his military prowess. He was credited for orchestrating the fall of Kunduz in 2015, the first major Afghan city to fall to the Taliban after 2001. Yet, curiously, many of the people I met in Kunduz depicted him as a moderating influence: they described how he bent standard Taliban policies to enable local development projects, and how he showed leniency towards families with sons in the Afghan security forces.

Another such a larger-than-life figure was Mullah Abdul Manan, the shadow governor for Helmand until he was killed in a drone strike in 2018. BBC journalist Auliya Atrafi described Manan as 'mysterious, pragmatic and loved by his Taliban foot soldiers', but 'for the top leadership, however, he was said to be an argumentative, defiant figure'.[9] Manan controlled much of Helmand's substantial opium trade. During Manan's era, estimated poppy cultivation in Helmand alone surpassed production levels in all of Myanmar, which was at that time ranked the world's second-largest producer (Felbab-Brown, 2017). He also sought to aggressively expand Taliban control, sometimes in contravention of overarching Taliban policy and military diktats. While considered hardline for his opposition to peace talks, he had allowed schools and hospitals and negotiated for other public welfare programmes, at times in defiance of the leadership (Stanikzai, 2018).

Both Salam and Manan were revered by their fighters for prioritising local imperatives, needs and preferences, regardless of the leadership's desires. Salam and Manan ruled over arguably the two most important provinces to the Taliban at the time, and the leadership allowed Salam and Manan a degree of autonomy, so long as they stayed loyal when it truly counted. Many other figures, even less influential ones, have been known to violate a Taliban directive intentionally or show exceptional cruelty towards civilians to demonstrate their autonomy and authority. As with any organisation, the Taliban has its share of mini-dictators or charismatic individuals who get away with bucking the system.

There is, however, an important caveat to this: even where local commanders had different ideas about policy, or where they appeared to defy orders, they did not typically frame it in these terms. Taliban ideology discourages dissent, with an emphasis placed on obedience to the Amir above all else. A core Taliban text on this topic explains that 'any weakening of the spirit of observance of Obedience to the Amir weakens the implementation of God's system ... God has linked Obedience to the Amir to obedience to God and his prophet' (Ludhianvi, 2015: 503–11). Several Taliban interviewed who had gripes about movement policy, nonetheless talked about how open disagreement was not only disloyal but un-Islamic. A familiar refrain in interviews with Taliban—even where they had just complained about Taliban policy—was that any differences were inconsequential because everything the Taliban did was in line with Islam. Variations and debates were discursively reconciled as being consistent with group ideology, and this was what counted.

The Taliban leadership, for its part, appears to have been realistic about the limits of its authority. They knew that what works in conservative, rural and poppy-rich Helmand may not be feasible in more educated, ethnically mixed Kunduz. Local Taliban consistently indicated that governance orders came down from their superiors, but that they were also afforded discretion. In establishing rules, the leadership has, in fact, primarily been reactive. They have sought to create the appearance of unity and coherence atop a wide range of practices, and have had to negotiate norms and practices within the movement. Rahmatullah Amiri and I describe this as *ex post facto* policy recognition, in which the bounds are set wide enough to encompass diverse practices and local accommodations (Jackson and Amiri, 2019). Because mechanisms for civilian bargaining have been built into Taliban structures, variation can be more easily justified and given an orderly appearance.

When talking to a Taliban leader about why more girls go to school in the southeast than in the south, he explained—as though it were self-evident—that 'these communities are different, and we cannot force people to go against what they believe'.[10] This strained credulity. The Taliban has routinely demonstrated that it can, and will, force people to behave however it suits them. Where necessary and beneficial, however, accommodating civilians has become an integral part of the Taliban's ethos.

There is an enduring tension between the leadership's drive for control and the desire of the Taliban rank and file for autonomy. That tension created room for manoeuvre on the ground, which civilians were able to use to their advantage in negotiation. But by delineating broad rules and gradually narrowing them, the leadership is trying to compel those on the ground—civilians and fighters alike—to follow a relatively uniform set of practices. This attempt to bound, refine and influence behaviour is not a revolutionary process, but change by degrees.

Ties that bind: Family, clan, tribe, confederacy, qawm, etc.

Social ties, or lack thereof, tell us a great deal about why certain Taliban military tactics or strategies precluded, or conversely enabled, bargaining. In the early years, and when they were seeking to capture territory, the Taliban's reliance more on 'outsider' fighters limited their bargaining options. This partly explains why civilians described the Taliban as less open to negotiation when they initially arrived in an area. A fighter from elsewhere may have only seen civilians as a threat, or may have had comparably less empathy than local Taliban. As a result, they were seen as relying more heavily on the use of violence and intimidation.

That the Taliban often handed areas over to local fighters once they had established a presence helps explain why civilians saw them as easier to deal with as time went on. Local Taliban typically had a better understanding of how to elicit compliance through non-violent means, and more of an inclination towards doing so. For example, in 2012, the Taliban's new governor for Kunar tried to close the province's schools.[11] The governor was from the south, where schools had largely been closed, and was surprised to see them operating at all in Kunar. He believed that allowing education was against Taliban rules and that state education undermined Islamic values. Local commanders were alarmed at the prospect of closing schools and advised him against it. Communities wanted schools, and local Taliban felt that permitting education generated civilian goodwill and co-operation. Closing schools, on the other hand, would spur a backlash. The commanders, and the wishes of the community, ultimately prevailed.

The pull of local ties is powerful. Fighters from the community certainly recognised the potential threat posed by civilians, but among those civilians were family, neighbours, old classmates and friends. The bonds that a fighter possessed created a greater shared interest with civilians. All other things being equal, we can assume a local fighter would have a greater stake in ensuring his community's welfare than an outsider. He would want his family protected, his children to attend school and clinics open to treat his relatives. Based on his relationships, a fighter might believe that certain people could be trusted or that others could be peaceably convinced to comply. (And civilians used this to their benefit: from the elder in Faryab whose son was a Taliban commander to the schoolteacher in Logar whose brother was a Taliban fighter, these connections provided tangible protection and advantages.)

Social embeddedness accentuated tension between the leadership and local fighters.[12] Local Taliban at times described frustration, tension and subtle acts of disobedience when ordered by superiors to do things they saw as harmful, or going against the wishes of their communities. Distinguishing between 'good' and 'bad' Taliban is one way civilians made sense of the differences among Taliban. 'Good' Taliban came from the community, kept people safe from violent pro-government militias and crime, and did not overly interfere. Insider Taliban were generally seen as members of the community—known entities and 'one of us'—and thus easier to deal with. Anyone who repeatedly went against the will of the community and acted with excessive violence was 'bad'. 'Bad' Taliban were often seen as excessively influenced by the Pakistani intelligence services. The distinction may not always be borne out, and there were also locally born and bred tyrants. 'Good Taliban/bad Taliban' nonetheless offered people a way of explaining, analysing and rationalising a dangerous and unpredictable situation.

In Charkh and its neighbouring districts, for example, people often referred to the 'bad' Taliban as falling into one of two categories. The first category was 'Pakistani' Taliban or 'foreign' fighters. Insurgent fighters in Charkh are primarily drawn from the local population, which is itself fairly homogenous. Remarks about 'foreign' fighters usually referred to Taliban, most likely Afghans, who were transiting from Pakistan through Logar, rather than actual citizens of Pakistan or anywhere else. These transiting Taliban were uniformly reviled. They apparently had a different understanding of Taliban 'rules' and reportedly criticised local commanders for being too lax. A teacher described these dynamics in a way that suggested the community and local Taliban often sided together against 'bad' Taliban from outside. 'There was one foreign fighter—from somewhere else, maybe Paktika—who was trying to stop the polio vaccinations,' he said, referencing a nearby province to the southeast. 'The people complained. The Taliban beat him very badly and made him leave. They said, "if you do not leave in 24 hours we will kill you."'[13]

The second category of these 'bad' Taliban was of governors or high-ranking commanders, many of whom were deployed by the Taliban from outside. The Taliban ostensibly does this to guard against corruption as well as to prevent consolidation of local power by one individual or faction. An unintended by-product is that these appointed governors lack a basis for trust with local civilians. New district governors were often known to do things like blow up bazaars, lay IEDs indiscriminately on highways or arbitrarily limit aid access. In Logar, the appointment of a new provincial governor resulted in a brief uptick in seemingly haphazard attacks on the main highway running through the province, which most people felt was an ill-conceived, relatively pointless and unnecessarily dangerous show of force. Similar dynamics were observed in parts of Helmand, Kandahar, Nangarhar and Baghlan provinces.

In areas of ethnic or tribal heterogeneity, this played out slightly differently. This 'othering' of bad Taliban leaned on geographic stereotypes and longstanding resentments to create distance from undesirable elements of the insurgency. Bad Taliban were often described as 'Kandahari' or 'Pakistani', but what that meant was often dependent on the positionality of the speaker. In Kunduz and Faryab, for example, non-Pashtun Taliban or civilians might refer to 'Kandahari' or 'Pakistani' Taliban. In reality, they were referring to local Taliban belonging to Pashtun families that had migrated from the south generations ago. Local Pashtun Taliban or civilians might refer to 'Kandahari' or 'Pakistani' Taliban to indicate that they were commanders or senior officials deployed from outside.

As much as war remakes society and breaks down old forms of social capital, it also creates new ones. Civilian–Taliban relationships gave people access to information and a unique insight into the Taliban, which in turn informed their bargaining strategies. Mobilising allies who possessed relations with the Taliban was critical. Civilians went to great lengths to cultivate Taliban connections because they were often the only means of protection in an uncertain and volatile environment. This helps explains why, for example, some people spoke of giving sons up to the Taliban, because as a result the entire family would get better treatment and protection.

It also makes it clear why so many people with such little affinity for the insurgency proactively sought Taliban 'friends'. A large share of an individual's bargaining power rested on the ability to cultivate and mobilise relationships across the widest spectrum possible. When faced with a problem, civilians networked. They called around to see who might know someone (or know someone who knew someone) with influence. Each interaction helped them to collect information and build relationships, creating a basis for future negotiation and favour-swapping. Personal relationships had such power partly because they were also incredibly important to the Taliban. In the absence of gener-alised trust and in an environment of widespread suspicion, the Taliban relied on relationships for everything, from gathering intelligence to conducting background checks on prospective teachers, to securing aid deliveries (which they then sought credit for). It wasn't just emotion or obligation, but the guarantee of reciprocity, that made personal ties so powerful. Where a Taliban commander granted someone's request, they might well call upon that person to later help them.

Shared beliefs and norms

Ideology and prevailing norms shaped the discursive and cultural ter-rain of bargaining. Civilians acted according to, and were broadly con-strained by, a set of norms and social practices. The Taliban too had norms, encapsulated within the movement's ideology, which framed and justified decision-making processes. Civilian and Taliban norms and ideologies overlapped in some areas and diverged in others. Overlaps created common frames of references, beliefs and values, as well as a sense of familiarity. But what is important to bear in mind is that norms and ideologies, on both sides, were mutable. Taliban norms in particu-lar have historically had to be elastic enough to adapt to the practicali-ties faced by fighters on the ground.[14]

The Taliban drew on shared beliefs and symbols to persuade civilians that their cause was legitimate and worthy of support. As discussed in Chapter 2, they drew on ideals of masculinity, what it means to be a Muslim and an Afghan, and the collective Afghan trauma wrought by decades of war. They used common modes of communication and inter-action that communities would be readily familiar with, such as poetry and night letters. But they also adapted to the changing times, commu-nicating through cell phone, text, social media and messaging apps. The

Taliban's civilian commissions mirrored the incumbent state's ministries and they developed civilian councils to advise governors, much like the incumbent government's provincial or district councils might. Like many other insurgencies, the Taliban used shared frames of reference to enforce a system of civilian governance that served their objectives.[15]

Civilians did the same. They deployed Islamic or cultural justifications that they believed would resonate with the Taliban. They crafted arguments that drew on Taliban notions of collective honour, obedience to Islam and nationalism. They used customary authorities and interlocutors to intercede on their behalf. Aid agencies, too, geared their negotiation strategies towards what they thought would appeal to the Taliban. One agency hired mullahs to advise them on the best arguments around aid access, while a great many others appealed to the shared goal of providing services and alleviating poverty.

The difference is that the Taliban were more actively seeking to reconfigure social norms and practices. Their ideology ultimately privileged and accentuated the most conservative and traditional elements of a specific rural values system. Taliban ideology was thus both extreme and familiar at the same time, affirming common values and symbols while also seeking to impose new norms and practices. Some norms might be coercively enforced, but other times a process of bargaining ensued.

Sociologists Jack Knight and Jean Ensminger have argued that normative change, particularly when it has distributive consequences, comes about as a result of bargaining (Knight and Ensminger, 1998). They argue that compliance with new norms is most often achieved through a mix of incentives and sanctions. As the Taliban tried to create new rules and norms aligned with their ideology for civilians to follow, they typically sanctioned non-compliance and incentivised compliance. They also, at times, took a gradual approach, temporarily yielding to civilian preferences to elicit compliance. The latter seemed particularly linked to areas where there was little civilian resistance and tighter linkages between the Taliban and civilians.

There are numerous instances of Taliban ideology being mediated by concerns over civilian compliance. For example, communities were willing to fight for schools in the southeast (and, as argued above, had the requisite social cohesion to effectively negotiate for them). This contributed to a shift in the overall Taliban position on schools from banning to permitting them. In the southeast, where children had historically gone to school, the Taliban were also taking away a resource, thus challenging the status quo. Numerous studies of negotiation outcomes and behavioural economics find that there is often a status quo bias in negotiations: it is easier to preserve something than to take it away or introduce something new (Bazerman et al. 2001; Johnson and Goldstein, 2003; Ritov and Baron, 1990; Samuelson and Zeckhauser, 1988). Indeed, in Afghanistan, it was much easier to bargain to keep something than it was to bargain for something new.

Where communities argued for infrastructural improvements, by contrast, they were asking that the Taliban broaden its norms and policies to allow something new. These negotiations often took longer, but where they succeeded it was often because negotiators appealed to Taliban self-interest (i.e., money they would likely get from taxing the endeavour, jobs they could use as patronage) and self-image (i.e., obligations to civilians, aspirations to political legitimacy).

Where requests were perceived to directly confront or contradict Taliban ideology, they had little chance of success. This dynamic was not always clear-cut. Because the Taliban were waging a war in defence of Islam, any request that was perceived to interfere with military objectives was often seen as not only dangerous to the insurgency but as undermining Islam. Requests not to attack a school or a clinic were seen by civilians as being about protecting innocent people. However, the Taliban might argue the same requests as interfering with their defence of Islam. How genuine such Taliban reactions were is unclear; it was difficult to tell if the Taliban at times deployed Islam as a convenient tactic to shut down negotiations. Either way, perceived violations of ideological precepts were typically a recipe for failure.

Emotion

While most theories of war take a rational actor approach, requiring people to behave logically and dispassionately,[16] this book breaks with that idea. Taliban and civilians were not negotiating in a free and secure environment with laws and institutions that offer protection and security. They negotiated under enormous pressure, within a dangerously uncertain environment, rife with rumour and speculation. Fear, anger, pride, sadness, disgust and the instinct for survival all influenced people's behaviour.

While various theoretical and empirical works have illustrated how emotion affects decision making, its precise impact is notoriously difficult to analyse and theorise about, particularly in any predictive sense (Halperin and Schwartz, 2010; Lindner, 2006; Petersen, 2002). This is perhaps most evident with regard to risk tolerance. As discussed in Chapter 1, various studies suggests that risk tolerance varies according to an array of factors too diverse to account for in a conflict setting. The conflict—which is itself nebulous and far-reaching in its behavioural impact—is but one among many factors shaping someone's mindset, perceptions and decisions. Some civilians seemed to acclimatise to the high-risk environment and consequently took more substantial risks. Others became more afraid and less likely to take chances. Among the people I met, there was likely a selection bias skewed towards those with higher risk tolerance. After all, speaking to a foreign researcher about the Taliban posed at least some degree of risk. Yet, even within this, people's appetite for risk was difficult to foretell.

While emotion is not a predictive variable, it can help make sense of observed patterns of behaviour. A helpful starting point is Wood's idea of emotional mechanisms—such as moral purpose, pride in exercising one's own agency, pleasure in defiance—driving civilian behaviour (Wood, 2003). The need to stand up for something they perceived as moral and just drove some people to take extraordinary risks. Elders often displayed pride in being recognised as people who could cut deals with the insurgency. They felt they had a unique ability or privileged position, and felt compelled to use it. Pleasure in agency or defiance can help explain why people took enormous risks for what might seem (within the limits of a rational actor framework) like little gain. Habiba, the headteacher in Logar mentioned in Chapter 4, faced death threats for running her girls' school. Her husband was kidnapped, beaten and doused in petrol by the Taliban; they released him on the condition that his wife close the school.[17] She kept the school operating anyway. She was willing to face grave harm to herself, her loved ones and students, because she believed that what she was doing was right.

One might argue that if she had been acting according to a dispassionate or 'rational' assessment of her situation, she would likely have closed the school and fled long ago. That argument, however, implies that passionate conviction is inherently irrational. I met Habiba on the three separate occasions, and can't imagine anyone referring to her as overly emotional or irrational. She did not break down in tears talking about how the Taliban abducted and nearly killed her husband, or any of the other horrific things she had endured. She was deeply pragmatic, with a dark sense of humour. When the Taliban banned the girls from school, she found ways to get textbooks to their homes so they could keep studying for annual state exams and progress onto the next grade. When we discussed her various options, given the growing Taliban threats against her and her family, it was clear that she had thought them through many times before. She could move to a safer province and live with relatives, but she said that would be futile. The Taliban was practically everywhere, she argued, and she would only find herself having to deal with them again at some point. She could close the school but remain in the village, but she felt that would be akin to letting the Taliban win. Her teenaged son urged her to smuggle herself to Europe, but she joked that she didn't know where to buy a life jacket and didn't like boat rides anyway. Her self-sacrifice was not irrational, regardless of the danger she faced. Her conviction was carefully considered and calculated.

Her defiance seemed driven by strongly held beliefs and moral purpose. These were shaped by emotions, spurred at least partly by the conflict. When attempting to find a way to explain behaviour like Habiba's, most existing theory (Wood aside) failed me. I turned instead to civilian memoirs from other wars: from Rwanda, from Vietnam, from the First and Second World Wars. One of the most helpful was a woman's diary of the last days of the Second World War and life under Soviet occupation in Berlin, entitled *A Woman in Berlin*. In the space of the few weeks covered in the diary, the diarist is repeatedly raped, loses nearly everything and everyone she holds dear, her city and government collapse and she struggles to find enough to eat. Nonetheless, there is a sense that her very survival, with her values and wits mostly intact, is a kind of subversive victory. She writes: 'my own flame is stronger; I'm burning more fiercely than before the air raids. Each new day of life is a day of triumph. You've survived once again. You are defiant' (Anonymous, 2018: 37). At the heart of this defiance was a series of calculated risks and cunning tactics which allowed her to reassert her dignity and humanity despite degrading conditions and widespread brutality. Afghanistan is, of course, a very different kind of war, but there are echoes of this sentiment. Survival of the spirit and preservation of one's values can feel like a victory, even when all else feels lost.

Emotions, of course, worked in other ways. Some people aggressively confronted the Taliban, almost always to their detriment. One man punched a Taliban judge when he disagreed with the judge's handling of a property dispute.[18] He knew it wasn't a smart move, but he felt that 'at least he had stood up for himself'. Some people performed more creative acts of self-sabotage. A young man I interviewed in Helmand joked that his father was the only one in all of Afghanistan who didn't fear the Taliban. When I asked why, he explained that his father played jazz, loudly, in his rural Nad Ali village. This repeatedly provoked Taliban visits to the house (to whom annoyed neighbours, the son was convinced, had complained). His father refused to stop playing, and instead tried to convert the visiting Taliban. He told them that jazz would be good for their soul, and that the heart needed music to beat properly.[19] The jazz-playing father got lucky and, last I heard, avoided punishment. The son thinks the Taliban wrote his father off as a 'crazy old communist' and gave up, neither able to justify seriously punishing him nor able to stop him.

Surely these individuals knew at the time how badly it might go for them. After all, who in their right mind would try to turn the Taliban on to jazz? But this behaviour was about a different kind of survival. Under certain circumstances, what looks at first like self-sabotage can actually be integral to preserving one's sense of humanity and dignity. Enacting defiance or agency of any sort can be life affirming, particularly in an environment of terror and oppression. We might call it psychological preservation or spiritual survival, in which actions are pursued for the sake of holding onto one's sense of self, consequences be damned. The behavioural impact of fear, psychological trauma and stress in driving this behaviour should not be underestimated or oversimplified. James C.

Scott writes that 'conformity in the face of domination is thus occasion-ally—and unforgettably—a question of suppressing violent rage in the interest of oneself and loved ones' (Scott, 1990: 37). It should come as little surprise that suppression is not always possible for individuals con-tending with life under Taliban rule. There are always those who will not comply, or simply can't despite their intention to. After all, without an impulse for defiance, rebellion and insurgency would probably not exist in the first place.

CONCLUSION

The research for this book began in 2017, during a period when it felt as though the outside world had forgotten about the war in Afghanistan. Even inside the country, it felt like those responsible for the international effort had lost touch with what was actually happening beyond the heavily guarded walls of their compounds. I had trouble convincing donors and diplomats confined to their embassies in Kabul of what I was seeing in Taliban villages, about the extent and reach of the insurgency's influence. The fact that the Taliban effectively governed villages, just an hour or two by car from Kabul, was met with scepticism. The idea that the Taliban could return to power was, even then, still unthinkable to many.

During that time, I kept thinking about a security briefing I received during my first weeks in Afghanistan, in early 2009. The analyst leading the briefing pulled up a PowerPoint presentation showing the pattern of violence, tracing the spread of Taliban presence year on year. The violence was concentrated in the south and east, but the analyst insisted things would get worse. He clicked through a series of slides predicting how the Taliban would expand, moving further west and enlarging their existing pockets of influence in the north. He talked about how the *mujahedeen* had employed similar strategies to what he saw the Taliban now doing on the ground. It would not happen overnight, he said—it wouldn't be like the scramble to evacuate Saigon—but the Taliban would come back eventually, because we had failed to appreciate the fundamental nature of the insurgency. I did not take him seri-

211

ously at the time, and I doubt anyone else in the room did either. Few understood—still understand—how things could go so badly wrong.

A large part of the answer lies in the Taliban's relationship with civilians. This book has sought to do two main things. The first is to explore how civilians have interacted and negotiated with the insurgency in Afghanistan. In doing so, it puts forth a theory of civilian–insurgent bargaining, wherein civilians and the Taliban are locked in an interdependent relationship. Both sides use whatever leverage they can to secure the best deal possible under the circumstances, and the nature of this gave-and-take shapes the conflict. This idea places Taliban strategies and civilian responses in a slightly different light, and allows us to see how, even amidst widespread terror and intimidation, civilians exerted agency and influence.

A second, more subtle aim, has been to call into question some prevailing beliefs about civilian agency within the way we analyse and understand civil wars more broadly. The neglect of civilian agency and behaviour has fundamentally impaired our understanding of how wars are fought and won or lost. Afghanistan is a case in point, but the same is likely true of other past, present and future conflicts. This chapter first outlines some of the assumptions about Afghanistan that this book has sought to challenge. It then explores how some of the key conclusions about the relationship between Afghan civilians and the Taliban might be relevant to other conflicts, and to our understanding of civil war more broadly.

What we've got wrong about civilian–insurgent relations in Afghanistan

In writing about the Viet Cong, counterinsurgency scholar Bernard Fall argued that 'the "kill" aspect, the military aspect, definitely always remained the minor aspect. The political, administrative, ideological aspect is the primary aspect' (Fall, 2000: 2430–1). 'Once we understand this,' Fall wrote, 'we will understand more of what is actually going on in Viet-Nam or in some of the other places affected by RW [revolutionary warfare]' (Ibid.). More than a half a century later, policymakers and scholars are still grappling with this task of understanding 'more of what is actually going on' in Afghanistan. When violence—the 'kill aspect'—becomes the centre of inquiry with groups like the Taliban, their overarching objectives and political culture tend to get obscured. The Taliban has been consistently underestimated by their opponents, in part because their opponents focused almost exclusively on the Taliban's acts of violence and terror.

Given the dearth of evidence on civilian experiences, this book has sought to place Taliban violence and coercion within the group's broader social, ideological and political strategy. For observers and analysts, the Taliban's use of violence—particularly its more brutal tactics, such as executing civilians and suicide bombings—has had a blinding effect. It can be so grotesque or unrelenting that it obscures other aspects of their strategy. For the Taliban, however, violence is a means to an end and just one among many forms of power that they exercise. The analysis of the kill aspect is only useful if it is situated in a broader understanding of the political, administrative and ideological aspects of how they exercise power.

One way to understand the Taliban's power is to examine it from the vantage point of those over whom that power is exercised. Looking at the Taliban through the eyes of the civilians they live among is the fastest way to shake loose faulty but persistent assumptions. Few of the generalisations that proliferate about the Taliban hold up when examined through the lens of civilian experiences. This is in part because people's experiences and interactions with the insurgency were so diverse. Things were markedly different in, for example, Helmand than they were on the outskirts of Kabul. The Taliban's broader objectives, policies and ideology are important, but they were, and continue to be, mediated by exigencies on the ground, not least of all by civilian bargaining. It almost goes without saying that the Taliban has been brutal and uncompromising. That is true of many insurgencies (and combatants in general). Yet it is also true that what civilians demanded—and fought for—mattered.

Much of what we think we know about the Taliban relies on reportage or indirect research which has often turned out to be either incorrect, misleading or incomplete.[1] Part of the problem, as Alex Strick van Linschoten argues, is that many reporters and researchers 'come with preconceptions relating to the Islamic nature of the movement, and find it difficult to offer a balanced perspective' (Strick van Linschoten, 2016: 2). Correcting misperceptions about Taliban ideology and political culture has incredibly important implications for the future of Afghanistan. The idea, for instance, that the Taliban are unyielding zealots and hardline ideologues has been used repeatedly to argue that no political settlement to end the conflict is possible. Perhaps unsurprisingly, many of those who argue this have also been involved in prosecuting the failed war against the Taliban (see Petraeus and Serchuk, 2019).

Regardless, this line of reasoning continues to obstruct and diminish the prospects for ending the war. And, more importantly, there is scant evidence to suggest that it's accurate. The Taliban has, in fact, a well-established culture of negotiation. The preceding chapters have detailed how pragmatic deal-making has allowed the Taliban to strike bargains with civilians, forge alliances and even co-opt and capture essential services delivered by the Afghan government. The ability to bargain has been absolutely essential to their ability to expand and maintain territorial control. The Taliban can be fierce and ruthless negotiators, but they also have a strong capacity to compromise (when, of course, they feel it is in their best interests to do so). This is not exactly encouraging for those hoping for a political settlement to end the war such that it will preserve democratic ideals and human rights.

The point is not to downplay the role of ideology, but to demonstrate that its use and purpose within the Taliban is often misunderstood. Ideology is functional: it sets the parameters for action and provides a rationale. Perhaps most importantly for the Taliban, it has bounded and controlled the behaviour and conduct of fighters. It is the cohesive glue of the movement, but that does mean that it is immutable. This book has sought to show, from multiple angles, how ideology has evolved in step with the movement's objectives. The trouble with portraying the Taliban as unyielding zealots is that it tends to mask the complexity of how ideology works, which is to say: it exists to serve the movement's goals. When Taliban ideology conflicts with the group's ability to achieve their objectives, it is the ideology—not the objectives—that ends up shifting.

Finally, if there is one point this book hopes to make, it is that the way we talk about Afghan civilians needs to change. When we talk about civilians, we often talk about 'support' or 'resistance', or deploy other terms that imply a degree of taking sides. In Afghanistan, phrases like 'winning hearts and minds' and 'securing the population' drifted in and out of the lexicon, depending on the international strategy at the time. This book talks about compliance, bargaining and deal-making instead. For the Taliban, 'winning hearts and minds' was never the central military and political objective. Likewise, few civilians interviewed would say they 'supported' (or even liked) the Taliban. Support implies some affinity (and proactive behaviour to demonstrate that affinity). It also implies a freedom of choice that most civilians, faced with only bad and worse options, felt was not available to them. Compliance requires agency, but it also suggests an informed pragmatism. Further, compliance is not 'won' in a decisive victory. Rather, it is cultivated, mediated and maintained through continual negotiation. Misapprehensions about the nature of civilian behaviour have underpinned several fundamental yet deeply flawed assumptions about the nature of the war itself.

The civilian–insurgent relationship as a negotiation

The heart of this book is empirical evidence drawn from Afghanistan, and there is no one-size-fits-all theory of civilian survival. In closing, however, I hope to make at least a circumstantial case that similar dynamics might exist in other violent conflicts. We know that civilians strategise and take action in wartime: by assessing their available options, measuring risk against reward and weighing what tactics will yield the greatest chance of success. All of this is wedded to the specific context at hand. Because it is a social process, understanding of negotiation in any context must be grounded in social analysis. Any interaction between a civilian and an insurgent will inevitably be tied to how social order in a community or locale is maintained, how power has been historically mediated between ruling elites and citizens, the specific culture and norms of mediation and negotiation, and so on.

A particularly salient feature in Afghanistan is that, because the country has experienced conflict and upheaval since the late 1970s, most Afghans have been forced to cope with armed groups on and off throughout their lives. Capacity to bargain with belligerents is ingrained in the social fabric. One could envision parallels, in this regard, with other chronic conflicts, from Somalia to eastern DRC.

Various combatants targeted the very social institutions and safety nets that people relied on to provide social order and protection. Some of these civilians have nonetheless regenerated and adapted, and the process of conflict itself gave rise to new forms of social capital and alliance formation.

Linked to this, the internal coherence of communities had concrete effects on their ability to negotiate with the Taliban. There was a discernible difference in negotiating dynamics and outcomes between communities with strong customary organisations and a high degree of internal unity, on the one hand, and divided communities with weak institutions, on the other. The former had a much better chance of extracting concessions from the Taliban while the Taliban tended, among the latter, to exploit their differences and discount civilian desires in the process. Social capital gave rise to greater collaboration which in turn increased civilian leverage vis-à-vis the insurgency. Again, Afghanistan is not unique. We know social cohesion is a valuable commodity for civilians in wartime because it gives rise to collective survival capacities across a range of contexts, and that civilians in northern Uganda, eastern DRC, the Swat Valley in Pakistan and central Colombia, for example, relied on sharing tactics and collective analysis in engaging with insurgents (Baines and Paddon, 2012; Suarez, 2017; Sanaullah, 2020; Kaplan, 2017).

Information sharing and collaboration allow civilians to better craft persuasive strategies and appeal to insurgent ideology. Ugandan civilians invoked the Acholi belief that misfortune befalls a person who denies the requests of someone in need to get the LRA to release captives (Baines and Paddon, 2012). Mozambican civilians similarly seized on Renamo guerrillas' belief in spirits' control over their lives, afterlives, and battlefield outcomes (Schafer, 2001). As the guerrillas believed that they must make material sacrifices to the spirits, the civilians used this idea to covertly get a share of the food and goods that the guerrillas otherwise monopolised. In this case, civilians held the greatest leverage when guerrillas felt they might be losing, because it was then that they feared spiritual retribution most. And we know customary authorities can play an essential role in all of this. Religious authorities in the Aceh conflict, for example, leveraged their influence with the GAM to elevate their own status and influence: not wholly dissimilar to tactics deployed by elders in Afghanistan (Barter, 2015).

I have picked a handful of empirical studies here, and there are certainly others, to demonstrate a point. Many of these, and other, important insights exist on the margins and have yet to be fundamentally integrated into our understanding of civil war. There is a prevailing preference in the study of war to refrain from the kind of fieldwork that would better enable these insights, and a preference for more easily controllable (and undoubtedly safer) research designs. The result is a fundamental gap in our understanding of how wars are actually lived and experienced, and the complex realities of the civilian–insurgent relationship. This impacts how we think about war, but it also shapes the ways conflicts are fought, the design of peacekeeping missions and how humanitarians try to protect civilians in war.

Insurgent evolution

Where an insurgency is at in its evolution, organisationally and militarily, heavily influences how it relates to civilians. Chapter 2 talks about how many civilians described the Taliban as cruel and disorganised in the beginning. Like many insurgencies, the Taliban initially relied heavily on violence and coercion. They had little else to offer. Their persuasive arguments were rudimentary, centred on a sense of injustice and a call to defend Islam. They couldn't offer protection for civilians from the retaliation pro-government forces would inflict on them, and they could muster few incentives beyond exempting civilians from the violence they would otherwise inflict on them. Their limited command and control meant they could not reliably deliver on any promises, and they had not yet articulated an overarching strategy or vision. Only later on were they seen as less cruel and, in many ways, more competent at providing security and public goods than the incumbent government. (This is despite the fact that they were largely co-opting and regulating services provided by the government and NGOs, rather than actually providing them.)

Some insurgencies rely on brute force and have little interest in bargaining, but that strategy doesn't usually last for long. Those insurgencies that control territory or seek political legitimacy cannot rely on violence alone to compel civilian support. A young insurgency may not yet be seeking legitimacy or have the means to bargain with civilians, but that does not mean that it will never develop that desire or capacity. In 2005, it would have been nearly unthinkable to suggest the Taliban might try to bargain with civilians. Thus, an appropriate case for this bargaining framework would most likely be a 'mature', legitimacy-seeking insurgency rather than a young one. That is to say, an armed group that has established some degree of command and control, created or maintained roughly delineated areas of control and articulated a political vision or agenda. Conversely, not all civilians negotiate. However, where an insurgency is seeking to establish itself as the ruling authority, few civilians can altogether avoid it indefinitely. It is only a matter of time before both sides are compelled to engage.

The first major challenge for the Taliban leadership was creating the means to direct their growing ability to inflict violence towards the attainment of their political goals. Civilian compliance grew in importance, particularly as the movement sought to portray itself as having civilian support. As the Taliban gained greater internal control and its ideology came to bear on its practices, violence was deployed more strategically to compel civilian compliance. It became more targeted and was somewhat tempered by the Taliban's desire to be seen as 'legitimate'. Persuasion became more sophisticated and compelling, geared at re-shaping civilian perceptions instead of just inspiring fear. To cultivate and maintain compliance, they had to relax some of their harsher rules. Attacks on schools are but one example; they had to offer something in return for civilians' compliance. In this battle for competitive control, the Taliban strove to present themselves as less corrupt, more just and more reliable than the incumbent government. As they began to hold territory and develop the capacity to govern, particularly after 2014, the Taliban could also offer more predictable incentives, such as security, justice and access to services (again, largely co-opted from other sources such as the state and NGOs). The Taliban value proposition to civilians became more apparent, and opportunities for bargaining increased.

This evolution from disorganisation to discipline, from shadowy fighting force to shadow state is a common one among insurgencies. So too is the shift from indiscriminate to strategic violence, and this is usually accompanied by efforts to mimic state-like functions or behaviour. Insurgent groups with tighter structure typically use violence against civilians more discriminately and strategically (Hoover Green, 2016; Weinstein, 2006; Lidow, 2011; Staniland, 2014). Tighter structure generally evolves, as in the Taliban case, with organisational maturity and territorial advances. As groups take territory, they must begin to govern civilian life and develop some system for doing so. This will likely require some means and process of bargaining with the civilian population.

This does not imply, however, that insurgent evolution is strictly linear. This pattern reverses itself, or otherwise changes, when insurgencies come under attack, begin to lose territory or begin to fragment. When this happens, bargaining again becomes less possible and more constrained. The Taliban is one example of this trajectory, alongside Al Shabaab, the National Resistance Army and the LTTE, among others (see also Hansen, 2013; Kasfir, 2005; Terpstra and Frerks, 2017; Wood, 2010).

Insurgent strength

The opportunities for civilian–insurgent bargaining are often shaped by overarching military dynamics. On the whole, in a given locale, the Taliban was less likely to bargain when under significant military pressure. The same applied to new areas where the Taliban were seeking to exert influence or control. As and when the Taliban felt more secure, they typically relaxed their attitudes towards civilians, and bargaining became more feasible. Territory in many areas changed hands multiple times between the Taliban and pro-government forces. This enabled a glimpse into how civilian–insurgent bargaining worked in areas stuck in a tug of war.

What civilians feared most was the period of transition, not just the actual fighting but, as one elder described it, 'waiting until they can believe they are in control again, because until they feel like kings, they will be cruel'.[2] Civilians had to contend with an ebb and flow. Deals once brokered might only hold for a time and have to be later renegotiated with new commanders who might be more or less sympathetic. Civilians had to be resilient, even as they were increasingly exhausted and depleted by the relentless violence. They were inventive and creative by necessity, crafting new approaches as dynamics changed or new information emerged. Negotiation became routine, but the dynamics underpinning it were punishingly fluid.

In some places, Taliban control was remarkably consolidated. Life under the Taliban had assumed a routine quality. Things could hardly be described as peaceful; periodic airstrikes or internal Taliban problems still created headaches for many civilians. Yet there was a routine quality of interaction and exchange between the Taliban and civilians. The rules were clear, and civilians had tried and tested strategies of negotiating, bending them or subverting them. Particularly after the unilateral cease-fire the Taliban declared across the country in June 2018 and the progression of US–Taliban talks, there was a sense among civilians and insurgents that Taliban control in their areas was all but permanent. Most felt that they had no choice but to work with whoever was in control.

In other districts, fighting was more frequent, Taliban control tenuous and sovereignty fragmented. Nonetheless some standard Taliban rules and practices could be discerned: Taliban taxes, sharia courts, Taliban monitors in the schools and so on. Yet any bargains with civilians were hostage to military dynamics. Taliban suspicion towards outsiders in particular, and civilians more generally, was more pronounced. The sense of foreboding created heightened anxiety and fear, as well as pronounced fatalism. One man from Nad Ali described living under a 'fear government that existed between the Kabul government and the Taliban. The district governor is a trapped like a chicken in his cage and the Taliban are suspicious of everyone. No one has the power and everyone is scared'.[3]

The June 2018 ceasefire, and similar pauses that occurred after that, provide another angle on variance. The June 2018 ceasefire was a three-day freeze-in-place over Eid, accompanied by unilateral cease-fires on the pro-government side. It was not linked to any agreement or distinct political progress in ending the war per se. The Taliban in areas of more consolidated Taliban influence greeted the ceasefire with aplomb, seeing it as proof that victory was within reach. They visited nearby cities under government control to celebrate, embraced members of the Afghan security forces and took selfies with civilians. Taliban fighters in Nad Ali were less enthusiastic. One fighter in Nad Ali thought the ceasefire was merely a missed opportunity: 'Why should we stop fighting these cruel puppets and infidels even for one minute? We are not going on picnics. I went to Musa Qala with my leader to do some business and meet the other commanders [during the ceasefire]. No one should rest until the Americans leave.'[4]

Some scholars argue that civilians have the best chance of influencing insurgents where insurgent control is contested (Kalyvas, 2006). This assumes that each side is competing for civilian support and that each lacks the capacity to selectively punish civilians, which gives civilians both leverage and cover. Others argue that insurgents can only afford to cater to civilian demands where they have firm control (Kasfir, 2005). Still others take a more nuanced stand, arguing that civilian resistance to insurgency is more likely where insurgents are weak and civilian engagement with an insurgency is more likely where insurgents are secure (Barter, 2012).

This book argues something closer to the second position: firmer control is more conducive to civilian–insurgent bargaining. In situations of fragmented sovereignty, the Taliban were less amenable to negotiation and less likely to be able to deliver on their promises. Civilians had more to lose; not knowing who would win the battle for control increased the risk of engaging with either side. There was consequently little shared trust and a weaker sense of interdependence. This came out most clearly in places where the back-and-forth between the Taliban and pro-government forces had been prolonged. Because the dynamics had flip-flopped so many times in recent memory, people were quick to draw comparisons about dealing with the Taliban when they were weak versus when they were strong.

By contrast, people in areas of more consolidated influence or control described similar dynamics as having existed in the past, before the Taliban exerted more complete control. Some civilians described similar feelings of heightened anxiety related to this uncertainty and mutual suspicion before the Taliban can be said to have consolidated control. They often described a creeping Taliban presence. This manifested in some ways (new rules imposed by Taliban monitors in the school or the bazaar, the themes raised in the Friday prayers) which were subtler than others (executions, abductions, interrogations, night letters and other forms of intimidation). In the midst of this pervasive anxiety and the slowly tightening Taliban control over their lives, some of the peo-

ple decided to leave. Those who remained remarked on a clear difference between how the Taliban used to behave towards civilians in the
past versus how they began to behave once they assumed the posture
of the de facto authority. While it is a mischaracterisation to describe
things as having become easier once the Taliban took over, sentiments
like 'in the beginning it was bad but now it is easier to deal with them'
were common.

One might argue that once insurgents have complete control, they
may have no incentive to bargain at all.[5] But the logic here is off: for
insurgencies to have complete and secure control, they usually have to
have won the war. And insurgencies rarely win wars outright.[6] Many
contemporary insurgencies, from Al Shabaab to Boko Haram, feel very
much like forever wars in which no one decisively wins anything (or,
at least, that's the case as of this writing). There was nowhere in
Afghanistan where the Taliban had decisively 'won'—US forces could
always return to drive them away. Even in their most secure strongholds, like Chardara or Musa Qala, they still had to contend with airstrikes. This fluidity made bargaining essential. The Taliban strategy of
creeping control and its style of governance worked precisely because
they built bargaining mechanisms and decentralised decision-making
into their practices and structures. The willingness to negotiate was
integral to civilian perceptions of insurgent legitimacy.

Social capital as essential to both civilian and insurgent survival

If civilian–insurgent negotiations are social processes rooted in a specific cultural and political terrain, then social capital is what allows
both parties to work this terrain to their advantage. Civilian bargaining
power vis-à-vis the Taliban hinged on social capital. It enabled them to
cultivate alliances, identify champions and persuade influential interlocutors to intercede on their behalf. Whether there are strong customary institutions, whether collectives and private entities could
work together to achieve common objectives with the insurgency,
whether lone individuals could muster enough social clout to secure a
commitment from the Taliban, it all came down to social capital.

In more divided communities, some people were at an obvious dis-
advantage. In talking with a father and his daughters, all of whom were

CONCLUSION

teachers, from Nad Ali, it quickly became clear that they were on the disadvantaged end of the spectrum. Both ethnicity and politics had created an adversarial relationship with local Taliban. They were Hazara, and the father had joined a self-defence militia that had been supported by US forces to fight the Taliban. Unlike others from Nad Ali, who could draw on Taliban family members or extended linkages, this family had limited recourse as Taliban influence grew. The local Taliban had seized his land and property, and the father felt that there was little he would be able to do to get it back. He feared the Taliban would kill him for sure if he returned. The Taliban closed the school where his daughters worked. They had fled some months ago, and had no desire to return so long as the Taliban remained in control.

If one were to draw lessons on how to negotiate with insurgencies based on the Taliban case, the first might be to do extensive research. Civilians used persuasion and argumentation, appealing to Taliban self-interest or ideological imperatives. They sought to offer incentives, most often in the form of their compliance or assistance. Some even levied threats, although these threats typically centred on the withdrawal of civilian compliance and the risk of betrayal. What might work in one instance might not work in another. Tactics needed to be tailored to the situation at hand. One way to make that assessment was through trial and error, but—where they had the means to do so—civilians tried to gauge their prospects of success through gathering intelligence.

Thus, the second lesson would be to relentlessly network. Networks provide information, and civilian negotiators want to maximise the volume of information they have access to, cultivating as many sources and as much diversity among those sources as possible. When it comes to the actual negotiation, networks generate interlocutors, advocates and guarantors. Civilians leveraged their collective compliance through customary institutions, but also by building ad hoc coalitions. Individuals cultivated and drew on allies and interlocutors who might have more sway with the Taliban. It was easier to build these kinds of networks where social capital was high and communities were already more cohesive. Where divisions were deeply engrained along ethnic, tribal, political or other lines, such as in Nad Ali and some areas of Kunduz and Faryab, there was a clearer set of winners and losers. A third lesson is then to think creatively about how these networks might be used to further one's interests. In choosing among options, individuals typically (again) relied on social capital in the form of access to others' experiences and lessons learned.

There are a range of views on how war affects civilian social capital: some scholars suggest that violence erodes social capital, while others find that communities band together when faced with a threat. Both were arguably true in Afghanistan: some communities acted as one, others became further divided. Pre-violence social cohesion, and the nature of violence and divisions that communities experienced, were influencing factors. In Afghanistan, there has been a disproportionate emphasis on how social capital has been destroyed and the negative impact on everything from security to economic development. Michel Foucault argued that 'civil war is a process through which and by which a number of new, previously unknown collective elements are formed' (Foucault, 2015: 28). If we take this as our definition of civil war, then it becomes impossible to ignore the productive effects of conflict, particularly with regard to social capital. And it is through looking at civil war's productive effects that we can most clearly see civilian agency.

Shared social capital creates powerful leverage for both civilians and insurgents. This, however, is a double-edged sword: it creates leverage through personal ties, shared beliefs, and ideological sympathies, but it leaves one vulnerable to the pull of emotion, social obligation and manipulation. Social embeddedness creates tension within an insurgency. Local fighters are caught between their families, communities and extended networks on the one side, and their insurgent comrades and leadership on the other. Each side makes demands of the insurgent, and these demands are often competing.

These dynamics are not new, nor are they unique to Afghanistan. But they seem to work differently in different places and at different times. Insurgents during the Huk rebellion were torn between personal and sexual ties, on the one hand, and the demands of the rebellion on the other (Goodwin, 1997). The LTTE strictly discouraged fraternisation with the civilian population, lest it weakened the group's command and control (Terpstra and Frerks, 2017). Unlike the LTTE, the Taliban leadership wanted it both ways: they sought to benefit from the social networks their fighters were embedded in, while simultaneously attempting to guard against the vulnerabilities this created.

CONCLUSION

Towards a theory of civilian–insurgency bargaining

The arguments and insights most adaptable and applicable to other contexts pertain to the nature of civilian–insurgent dynamics and how they might evolve over time. The first is that, all other things being equal, as legitimacy-seeking insurgencies mature and gain territorial control, they are more likely to try to gain civilian compliance through bargaining. The nature of the bargaining will be shaped by cultural and social context, as well as the political objectives, ideology and norms of the armed group in question. A second, and related, conclusion centres on military pressure and battlefield dynamics. When insurgencies come under increased military pressure, civilian–insurgent bargaining becomes more constrained, or may not be possible at all. As military pressure fades and insurgents feel more secure, civilian–insurgent bargaining will likely resume.

While civilian–insurgent bargaining is, this book argues, a widespread phenomenon, it exists in the shadows of the literature on civil wars and insurgencies. In contrast to the civilian protection literature, which broadly implies that civilians are motivated by survival and altruistic motives, others in the more mainstream study of civil wars typically argue that civilian agency is exercised in pursuit of survival and self-interest (Jose and Medie, 2015; Krause, 2016; Kalyvas, 2006). Both theories are too simplistic. Acknowledging that motives in wartime are frequently overlapping, at times contradictory and often inscrutable, this book instead relies on the concept of interests to explore what drives civilian (and insurgent) action. Interests have been deliberately presented here in a neutral way, intentionally avoiding any normative judgement.

If there is one major argument this book hopes to make about civil war, it is that the way we think about civilians and insurgents needs to be thoroughly interrogated and reimagined. We cannot meaningfully understand insurgencies without understanding their relationship with civilians. That relationship determines insurgencies' survival and shapes their conduct. The experiences and strategies of those living among, married to, related to, resisting, repressed by or otherwise finding ways to co-exist with an insurgency are a vital, if poorly understood, part of the story.

INTRODUCTION

1. Interview with a Taliban education official from Rodat district, Nangarhar, March 2018.

1. NEGOTIATED REBELLION

1. There are, of course, notable exceptions. While there has been a wealth of writing about civilians in the humanitarian and human rights realms, they are still typically inert (i.e., victims in need of humanitarian assistance or whose rights have been violated). Part of the problem lies in the fact that international law, which governs both humanitarian action and human rights, offers a negative definition of civilians: they are defined by the fact that they are not combatants. Their non-combatant status (and the protections it secures) rests on the idea that civilians are neutral and somehow set apart from the conflict (Slim, 2008). There is often the sense that imbuing them too much agency might, however subtly, threaten the pillars of this normative framework. The emerging work on civilian resistance, by contrast, foregrounds their agency (see Kaplan, 2017; Krause, 2016). But by focusing on how civilians advocate for peace or protect their communities from violence, it tends to obscure how civilians might deploy that agency for ends other than non-violence.
2. Ideology, for instance, may play little role at all in some cases (see Reno, 2015).

2. DANCING WITH WHOEVER IS THERE

1. No complete census has been conducted; only estimates are available. World Bank 2017 estimate cited, retrieved 10 June 2018, https://data.worldbank.org/country/afghanistan
2. Ethnic figures from a US State Department population estimate no longer publicly available but cited in Lamer and Foster (2011).
3. For the sake of brevity, the text deploys 'rural–urban divide' as shorthand to frame Taliban strategy and orientation. That said, it is admit-

tedly a broad-brush generalisation of more complex social dynamics, as commentators including Ahmad Shuja and Thomas Ruttig, among others, have rightly critiqued (Shuja, 2011; Ruttig, 2011).

4. Interview with a woman from Saydabad district of Wardak, December 2018.
5. Interview with an elder from Almar district of Faryab, February 2019.
6. See USAID (2004).
7. See Ghani (1978) and Borchgrevink (2007).
8. Interview with a man from Khas Uruzgan district, Uruzgan, November 2017.
9. Tolo-ye Afghan article reproduced in Strick van Linschoten and Kuehn (2018: 1052–53, 1059–60).
10. See Agha (2014), Strick van Linschoten and Kuehn (2018), and Zaeef (2010).
11. A former Taliban finance official estimated the Taliban government had an average annual budget of just $60–70 million USD. Another regime era official felt this was a generous estimate. He claims that while he was in the education department the government had a planned annual budget of $60 million USD, but only $30 or 40 million were ultimately available, resulting in delays to civil servant salary payments by anywhere from six to nine months.
12. Statistics from UNHCR, 10 September 2001, https://reliefweb.int/report/afghanistan/unhcr-afghan-refugee-statistics-10-sep-2001. Retrieved 1 February 2019.
13. Interview with a Taliban fighter from Logar, July 2017.
14. Ibid.
15. Interview with a journalist from Logar, November 2017.
16. See also Giustozzi (2008) and Giustozzi (2017).
17. Antonio Giustozzi posits that training improved and the rate of failed IED attacks remarkably decreased around 2006 (Giustozzi, 2008); see also Strick van Linschoten and Kuehn (2014) for a slightly different narrative on IEDs.
18. Despite the fact that the United States officially declared an end to combat operations in May 2003, US forces increased from 9,800 in May 2003 to 13,100 in December 2003; by April 2004, the number of US forces had risen to 20,300 (Associated Press, 2016).
19. Twelve of the twenty-six PRTs in Afghanistan were run by the United States, while other ISAF countries who had contributed troops ran the remainder of PRTs. Figures for the primary US PRT project-funding source, the Commander's Emergency Response Program (CERP), are publicly available through the US Special Inspector General for

Afghanistan Reconstruction (SIGAR). No precise or systematic figures are available for non-US PRT project funding.

20. Up until that point, ISAF was primarily confined to Kabul, although the United States and other forces were present elsewhere in the country under a divided command.

21. The Taliban, however, cannot be given all of the credit. Part of the problem was that ISAF's expanded mandate was not backed up by sufficient resources (Suhrke, 2008). Another fundamental issue was that ISAF was deeply unco-ordinated, comprised of over forty different troop-contributing countries (often with different ideas of how to fight the war) and a substantial US presence that, until 2007, mainly operated outside the ISAF chain of command (see International Crisis Group, 2006).

22. Interview with former Taliban spokesman, Dubai, January 2019. See also International Crisis Group (2008).

23. Interview with a member of the senior Taliban leadership, January 2019. See also Giustozzi and Franco (2016).

24. Various author interviews with the Taliban leadership. See also Giustozzi (2008) and Gebauer (2007).

25. Interview with a former member of the leadership *shura*, March 2018.

26. President Obama announced in 2012 that US combat operations would conclude in 2014; however, Obama repeatedly delayed the full withdrawal of US troops, and his successor, President Donald Trump, partially reversed the withdrawal.

27. Interview with a former member of the Taliban leadership, Kabul, March 2018; interview with a member of the Taliban's political commission, Doha, November 2018.

28. UNAMA Human Rights documented 1,015 civilian casualties from airstrikes in 2018 and 590 in 2016. See UNAMA Human Rights (2019) and UNAMA Human Rights (2017).

29. NGO data set, provided in May 2019. The NGO requested not to be named, given the sensitive nature of its work.

30. Interview with a farmer from Nawa district, Helmand, January 2019.

3. COERCION, CO-OPTION AND CO-OPERATION

1. Interview with former Taliban spokesman, Dubai, January 2019.

2. Interview with an elder from Almar district, Faryab, February 2019.

3. Interview with an elder from Musa Qala district, Helmand, December 2017.

4. Interview with a former member of the Taliban leadership, Kabul, March 2018.

5. AIHRC (2008: 16).

6. Figures provided by Forces from Allied Forces Central Europe (NATO) cited in Wellman (2018).

7. Neither ISAF nor the Afghan government issued public Taliban casualty estimates, but ISAF commander General David Petraeus stated that pro-government forces had killed 2,448 insurgents between July 2010 and March 2011—a 55 per cent increase from the same period the previous year—and that they had detained an additional 2,870 individuals (Jaffe, 2011). Analysis of ISAF press releases reveals that, between 1 December 2009 and 30 September 2011, ISAF reported a total of 3,157 incidents (including 2,365 kill-or-capture raids) in which 3,873 individuals were killed and 7,146 detained (Strick van Linschoten and Kuehn, 2011).

8. Former Taliban spokesman interviewed in Dubai, January 2019.

9. A former Taliban spokesman interviewed stated that, among the Afghan population, only Afghan security forces, high-level civil servants not directly serving in a service-delivery capacity (such as governors and district governors) and state judges and prosecutors were considered legitimate targets of Taliban violence. He acknowledged that this had been different in the past. It is unclear when this shift happened, but the scope of targeting in practice appears to have narrowed gradually over time.

10. Interview with a member of the Taliban political commission, Doha, November 2018.

11. Interview with a UNAMA Human Rights staff member, Kabul, November 2017.

12. Reproduced and translated by Human Rights Watch here: https://www.hrw.org/legacy/campaigns/afghanistan/2006/education/letter7.htm. Retrieved 02/01, 2019.

13. Interview with a member of the Taliban political commission, Doha, January 2019; interview with a teacher from Nad Ali district, Helmand, December 2017.

14. Interview with a man from Khwajasabzposh district, Faryab, February 2019.

15. Ibid.

16. Quoted in Human Rights Watch (2007: 95).

17. Clark (2011: 26).

18. Interview with a former member of the leadership shura, March 2018.

19. See US Department of the Army (2006).

20. ISAF (undated: 3–4).

21. Interview with a former member of the leadership shura, March 2018.

22. Interview with Taliban interlocutor, March 2018.

23. Interview with a former member of the leadership shura, March 2018.
24. Cited in Giustozzi and Franco (2012). Interviews suggested that the picture was more complicated. Attacks may have decreased, but it also appears that the Taliban started to conceal their involvement in such attacks by simply not claiming responsibility. While the Taliban did not openly claim responsibility, many communities understood them to be behind the attacks. A senior Taliban official admitted in an interview that this was a common practice during this period.
25. See also Jackson and Giustozzi (2012).
26. Analysis of ISAF public statements suggests that they were targeting not only specific individuals but also others perhaps only tangentially connected to them, with no clear indication of what degree of proof or evidence was guiding these decisions. See Strick van Linschoten and Kuehn (2011).
27. Interview with a Taliban interlocutor and former official, January 2019.
28. There are, however, substitute mechanisms which can defuse tension in individual cases but few that would apply in the case of armed forces, see Benson and Siddiqui (2014).
29. There are, of course, many sources and different opinions on this. See Islamic Supreme Council of America (2019); see also Bonner (2006).
30. Islamic Emirate of Afghanistan (2007).
31. Interview with a Taliban commander from Charkh district, Logar, November 2018.
32. Interview with a mullah from Marja district, Helmand, December 2018.
33. Ustad Mohammad Yasir speaking in a DVD distributed by the Taliban in 2008, quoted in International Crisis Group (2008: 24).
34. Commonly referenced in interviews, as well as secondary sources. See Dorronsoro (2009), Gopal (2015), Giustozzi (2008), International Crisis Group (2008), Ladbury (2009), and Strick van Linschoten and Kuehn (2012a).
35. Interview with a man from Dahan-i-Ghori district, Baghlan, March 2018.
36. Interview with former Taliban spokesman, Dubai, January 2019.
37. Ibid.
38. See also Giustozzi (2008), Foxley (2007), Johnson (2018) and Broschk (2011).
39. Interview with a teacher from Charkh district, Logar, November 2018.
40. Reproduced and translated in AIHRC (2008: 15).
41. Reproduced and translated by Human Rights Watch here: https://www.hrw.org/legacy/campaigns/afghanistan/2006/education/letter8.htm. Retrieved 02/01, 2019.

42. See Strick van Linschoten and Kuehn (2012b).

43. Based on a reading of Taliban poetry sources through the internet and personal contacts, as well as poems reproduced in Johnson (2018) and Strick van Linschoten and Kuehn (2012b).

44. Translated and reproduced in Strick van Linschoten and Kuehn (2012b: 139).

45. Interview with a teacher from Chardara district of Kunduz, November 2017.

46. Data taken from International Telecommunication Union, World Telecommunication/ICT Development Report and database, via the World Bank: https://data.worldbank.org/indicator/IT.CEL. SETS?locations=AF&year=2017. Retrieved 2 October 2019.

47. Ibid.

48. This is an admittedly abbreviated account of the Taliban's extensive media products, which also included early attempts to set up local radio stations. For a more extensive overview, see Broschk (2011), International Crisis Group (2008) and Johnson (2018).

49. Interview with former Taliban spokesman, Dubai, January 2019. See also International Crisis Group (2008).

50. Interview with former Taliban spokesman, Dubai, January 2019. See also International Crisis Group (2008).

51. For more on Dadullah, see Strick van Linschoten and Kuehn (2014).

52. One of the most memorable incidents was the January 2016 Taliban suicide attack on a vehicle carrying seven employees of Tolo News, Afghanistan's first twenty-four-hour news channel, and others. In the preceding months, the Taliban had threatened to target the television channel after it reported allegations of summary executions, rape, kidnappings and other abuses by Taliban fighters during the first battle for Kunduz. This, of course, is not the only attack on media the Taliban claimed credit for in recent memory.

53. For a fuller account of Taliban attacks on the press, see Human Rights Watch (2015).

54. Conversation with a local journalist, Helmand, December 2018.

55. Interview with a teacher from Chardara district, Kunduz, November 2017.

56. Interview with a teacher from Tala wa Barfak district, Baghlan, March 2018.

57. Interview with a former teacher from Chardara district, Kunduz, November 2017.

58. Interview with a teacher from Chardara district, Kunduz, November 2017; interview with a nurse from Chardara district, Kunduz, November 2017.

59. Some accounts suggest that this was a relatively common practice in some areas as early as 2008. See Thruelsen (2010).
60. Islamic Emirate of Afghanistan (2018b).
61. Phone interview with a government official, Kunduz City, August 20, 2020.
62. Ibid.
63. Mampilly's work is again helpful in demonstrating how this functions. He finds a correlation between insurgent governance and pre-existing levels of state penetration and service provision, suggesting that insurgencies do, to some degree, adapt their governance to pre-existing conditions and expectations (Mampilly, 2011).
64. Interview with a former member of the leadership shura, March 2018.
65. See Carter and Clark (2010), Giustozzi (2012) and Giustozzi et al. (2012).
66. Interview with a former member of the leadership shura in Kabul, March 2018.
67. Author interviews. See also Giustozzi (2008), Jackson and Giustozzi (2012) and Jackson and Amiri (2019).
68. Author interviews. See also Jackson and Amiri (2019).
69. Taliban sources say that, by 2003, they had established governing commissions responsible for military affairs, culture, finance and political affairs in exile in Pakistan. These sources include three individuals directly involved with the creation of these commissions and two secondary sources with close knowledge of these events. However, interviews inside Afghanistan cast doubt that this level of planning and organisation had existed so early. If these commissions had existed earlier than 2006, it was likely in name only, as there is no evidence that the Taliban had been organised enough to focus on anything but immediate military tactics.
70. Interview with a former member of the leadership *shura*, May 2018.
71. Interview with a former Taliban official, March 2018.
72. The surge was a stopgap measure with a defined end date, and President Obama had announced in 2012 that US combat operations would conclude in 2014 (although the full withdrawal of US troops was repeatedly delayed by Obama and later reversed by his successor, President Donald Trump) (Roberts, 2016; Landler and Gordon, 2017).
73. See Le Duc and Sabri (1996).
74. Interview with a professor from Saydabad district, Wardak, October 2017.
75. WhatsApp interview with Zabiullah Mujahed, October 2017. In fact, we know that states and rebels tend to co-operate—even where doing so may benefit the other side—if they feel there is a significant advan-

tage in such actions, and where both sides recognise that they are unlikely to win militarily (see Schievels and Colley, 2020).

76. Interview with a teacher from Charkh district, Logar, October 2017.

77. Group interview with Logar teachers, October 2017; interview with a teacher from Charkh district, Logar, October 2017.

78. For a comparative study of corruption in health and education, see Echavez (2016).

79. Interview with NGO director in Kunduz, November 2017.

80. Interview with a doctor from Musa Qala district, Helmand, December 2017; interview with a government healthcare official, Kunduz, November 2017; interview with a government health official working in Chardara district, Kunduz, November 2017; interview with a government official assigned to Chardara district, Kunduz, November 2017; interview with a regional director of a healthcare NGO, Kabul, November 2017; interview with a nurse from Chardara district, Kunduz, November 2017.

81. A Financial Commission existed at the leadership level, and beneath it are various branches dedicated to specific activities or sectors, such as electricity, mines, customs and stones. In parallel, there are separate commissions for Minerals and Energy and for Agricultural and Government Lands. While they would appear to have overlapping mandates, interviews indicate that they covered separate geographic areas and benefitted from different revenue streams. There were also related branches or departments under the military commission, which also yield revenue, such as the seizure of property (ghanayam) department. The Finance Commission had dedicated finance officials at the provincial and local level, as well as several branches or divisions devoted to specific means of taxation and revenue streams (i.e., narcotics, customs).

82. Various interviews with Taliban fighters, Helmand, December 2017 and Nangarhar, March 2018.

83. Interview with a man from Khwajasabzposh district, Faryab, February 2019.

84. For specific examples, see Ruttig (2010) and Giustozzi (2008).

4. NAVIGATING FOREVER WAR

1. For a detailed study of restrictions on the use of force, airstrikes and civilian deaths during this period, see Crawford (2020).

2. Zartman also argued in 2015 that the conditions for 'ripeness' in Afghanistan did not exist (Zartman, 2015).

3. Group interview with elders from Tala wa Barfak, Baghlan, March 2017.
4. Interview with a teacher from Nawa district, Helmand, December 2018.
5. Interview with a teacher from Charkh district, Logar, October 2017.
6. Interview with a man from Nawa district, Helmand, October 2018.
7. Interview with a man from Gurziwan district, Faryab, February 2019.
8. Ibid.
9. Ibid.
10. Interview with an elder from Almar district, Faryab, February 2019.
11. Interview with an elder from Charkh district, Logar, February 2018.
12. Interview with an NGO worker deployed in Helmand, November 2017.
13. Ibid.
14. See Jackson and Weigand (2020).
15. Interview with an elder from Pashtunkot district, Faryab, February 2019.
16. Comment from an NGO worker from Sarobi district of Kabul, part of a small-group discussion with several NGO workers, December 2017.
17. Interview with an elder from Almar district, Faryab, February 2019.
18. Interview with an elder from Charkh district, Logar, February 2018.
19. Ibid.
20. Interview with a teacher from Nad Ali district, Helmand, December 2017.
21. Phone interview with Taliban spokesperson Zabiullah Mujahed, January 2019.
22. Interviews with an NGO and elders from Nawa district, Ghazni, November 2017.
23. Aid has, of course, long been used by foreign governments to further their political objectives in Afghanistan. See Atmar (2001) and Baitenmann (1990).
24. See also Fishstein and Wilder (2011).
25. See Jackson and Giustozzi (2012).
26. Quoted in Jackson and Giustozzi (2012: 15).
27. These dynamics have also been widely documented by others, including Norwegian Refugee Council (2018) and Collinson and Duffield (2013).
28. Quoted in Jackson and Giustozzi (2012: 7).
29. Interview with a Taliban fighter from Saydabad district, Wardak, November 2018.

30. From a private translation of a copy of the memorandum obtained via a Taliban media WhatsApp group. See also Stanikzai (2018).
31. Note that opium cultivation did not entirely disappear under the Taliban regime, and that the so-called Taliban ban on opium was more complex and ultimately less of a 'ban' than is commonly portrayed. The Taliban leadership instead issued an Islamic sanction of opium production and yielded revenue from its transport and export. See Mansfield (2016) and Ghiasy et al. (2015).
32. Summary of an example quoted in US House of Representatives (2010: 35).
33. Some reports suggest they do more than just tax the trade, and that they began in recent years to open, buy or seize drug processing labs (Giustozzi, 2018). Claims of Taliban involvement in opium cultivation and trafficking have often been poorly sourced, disputed, deeply politicised and difficult to verify (see Mansfield, 2018). Much of the credible literature suggests that the relationship between the Taliban and the narcotics trade is primarily one in which they profit off the work of others.
34. Interview with a UN agency senior officials, Kabul, October 2018.
35. Interview with a healthcare NGO director, Kunduz, November 2017; interview with a government health official, Logar, November 2017; interview with a doctor from Chardara district, Kunduz, November 2017; interview with a doctor from Charkh district, Logar, November 2017; interviews with Nangarhar residents, March 2018.
36. Interviews with health workers, Helmand, May 2018; interview with a former Taliban official from Garmsir district, Helmand, December 2017; interview with an aid worker in Kabul, May 2018.
37. Interview with an NGO worker in Kunduz, November 201; interview with a Ministry of Public Health official, Kunduz, November 2017; interview with a Ministry of Public Health official, Logar, November 2017; group interview with NGO workers in Helmand, May 2018.
38. This is educated guesswork, as such information has been incredibly difficult to obtain. This is based on research specifically into taxation carried out with Rahmatullah Amiri on aid agencies working nationally, and with civilians and Taliban locally in Ghazni, Helmand, Kunar and Kunduz.
39. Interview with a Ministry of Public Health official, Logar, November 2017; group interview with NGO workers in Helmand, May 2018. See also Jackson (2018a).
40. Interview with provincial director of the Ministry of Public Health, Kunduz, November 2017; interview with a teacher from Chardara district, Kunduz, November 2017. See also Aikins (2016).

41. Interview with nurse from Chardara district, Kunduz, November 2017; interview with a teacher from Chardara district, Kunduz, November 2017.
42. Interview with a Ministry of Public Health worker, Kunduz, November 2017.
43. This is based on the research into Taliban taxation and aid interference carried out with Rahmatullah Amiri in early 2020.
44. For a more in-depth discussion of the Taliban's evolving attitudes towards healthcare, see Jackson and Amiri (2019).
45. Interview with a healthcare NGO director, Kunduz, November 2017.
46. For a more detailed comparison between health and education hiring interference, see Jackson and Amiri (2019).
47. Interview with a professor from Maidan Shah, Wardak, July 2017.
48. Interview with a doctor at a private clinic in Kunduz City, Kunduz, November 2017.
49. US House of Representatives (2010: 34–5).
50. Comment from an Afghan NGO worker, part of a small group discussion with several NGO workers in Kabul, December 2017.
51. Ibid.
52. Conversation with a senior telecommunications company employee in Kabul, December 2017; interview with a telecommunications company employee in Dubai, January 2019; conversation with a media company executive in Kabul, February 2019.
53. Interview with a senior telecommunications company employee in Kabul, December 2017.
54. Interview with a senior telecommunications company employee in Kabul, December 2017; interview with a telecommunications company employee in Dubai, January 2019.
55. Interview with a senior telecommunications company employee in Kabul, December 2017.
56. See Ariana News (2020).
57. Interview with a Taliban fighter from Charkh district, Logar, October 2017; interview with a Taliban commander from Charkh district of Logar, July 2017; interview with a former Taliban official, Kabul, July 2017; interview with a government health official in Pul-e-Alam, Logar, November 2017; interview with a doctor from Charkh district, Logar, November 2017; interview with a landowner from Aqtash district, Kunduz, October 2017; interview with a Taliban fighter from Charkh district, Logar, July 2017; interview with a government health official, Kunduz, November 2017.
58. Group interview with NGO officials in Kabul, December 2017.

59. Interview with NGO workers and elders from Ghazni, November 2017.
60. Interview with the director of an NGO working in Uruzgan, December 2017.
61. WhatsApp interview with Taliban spokesperson Zabiullah Mujahed, October 2017.
62. Interview with a teacher from Charkh district, Logar, July 2017.
63. Interview with a midwife from Nad Ali district, Helmand, May 2018.
64. Interview with a teacher from Chardara district, Kunduz, November 2017.
65. Ibid.
66. Conversation with farmers from Nawa district, Helmand, May 2018.
67. Interview with a Taliban official from Garmsir district, Helmand, December 2018.
68. Interview with two students from Nad Ali district, Helmand, May 2018.
69. Interview with a woman from Shirintagab district, Faryab, February 2019.
70. Interview with a man from Khas Uruzgan district, Uruzgan, November 2017.
71. Group interview with teachers from Nad Ali district, Helmand, May 2018.
72. Interview with a professor from Saydabad district, Wardak, July 2017.
73. Interview with a doctor from Musa Qala district, Helmand, December 2017.
74. Mansfield finds a similar dynamic in his research in Helmand and Nangarhar, recounting that taxation was typically based on what farmers could afford. He concludes that taxes were also adjusted based on 'the bargaining of individuals' (Mansfield, 2017: 42).
75. Interview with a woman from Baraki Barak district, Logar, February 2018.
76. Interview with an elder from Charkh district, Logar, December 2018.
77. Interview with a journalist from Aqtash district, Kunduz, October 2017.
78. Interview with a man from Khas Uruzgan district, Uruzgan, November 2017.
79. Interview with an aid worker in Kabul, May 2018.
80. Interview with a Taliban commander, Tala wa Barfak district, Baghlan, March 2018.

5. THE ART OF THE DEAL

1. Drawing also on assertions made both by Kalyvas (2006) and Mampilly (2011) that the relationship between civilians and insurgents is a product of coercion and exchange.
2. Quoted in Jackson and Giustozzi (2012: 15).
3. Terminology adapted from Kalyvas (2006).
4. Interview with the district governor, Nad Ali, Helmand.
5. See Gibbons-Neff and Cooper (2018) for a fuller description of the logic behind this strategy.
6. Quoted in Jackson and Amiri (2019: 18).
7. Interview with a journalist from Aqtash district, Kunduz, October 2017.
8. Afghanistan is not alone in this respect. This echoes findings from work on Tajikistan and Uganda on the ways sustained violence erodes social capital (Cassar et al., 2003; Rohner et al., 2013).
9. See: https://twitter.com/AuliyaAtrafi/status/1069213495407845378. Retrieved 22 October 2018.
10. Interview with a member of the Taliban political commission in Doha, October 2019.
11. See also Jackson and Amiri (2019).
12. This is not unique to Afghanistan. Certainly in other instances, the tension between family ties and the claims of an insurgency has dampened insurgent participation or coherence (see Goodwin, 1997).
13. Interview with a teacher from Charkh district, Logar.
14. For more on Taliban ideology and its evolution, see Gopal and Strick van Linschoten (2017).
15. Mampilly explores this point more broadly regarding insurgencies, without reference to the Taliban (see Mampilly, 2015).
16. See Fearon (1995).
17. Interview with a woman from Baraki Barak district, Logar.
18. Interview with a man from Pashtunkot district, Faryab.
19. Interview with a student from Nad Ali district of Helmand, December 2017.

CONCLUSION

1. See, for example, Strick van Linschoten and Kuehn (2012a, 2014).
2. Interview with an elder from Saydabad district, Wardak, December 2018.
3. Interview with a teacher in Nad Ali, Helmand, May 2018.
4. Interview with Taliban fighter, Nad Ali, Helmand, October 2019.

239

5. And, indeed, Kalyvas does argue this, see Kalyvas (2006).
6. See Connable and Libicki (2010).

BIBLIOGRAPHY

Abrahms, Max. (2012). The political effectiveness of terrorism revisited. *Comparative Political Studies*, 45(3), 366–93.

Afghanistan Independent Human Rights Commission (AIHRC). (2008). *Insurgent Abuses Against Afghan Civilians*. Kabul: AIHRC.

Afghanistan Justice Project. (2005). *Casting Shadows: War Crimes and Crimes Against Humanity: 1978–2001*. Afghanistan Justice Project.

Agence France-Presse (2010). Af-Pak policy review: Obama admits Afghan gains not sustainable. *Agence France-Presse*.

Agence France-Presse (2012). Tribesmen rise up against Afghan Taliban. *Agence France-Presse*.

Agha, Mohammad Akbar. (2014). *I Am Akbar Agha* (Kindle edition). Berlin: First Draft Publishing.

Aikins, Matthieu (2016). Doctors with enemies: Did Afghan forces target the M.S.F. Hospital? *New York Times Magazine*.

Al Jazeera (2007). Interview: Mullah Dadullah. *Al Jazeera*.

Al Jazeera (2021). US downsizes its troops in Afghanistan to 2,500. *Al Jazeera*.

Amnesty International. (1995). *Afghanistan: International Responsibility for a Human Rights Disaster*. London: Amnesty International.

Amnesty International. (1999). *Women in Afghanistan: Pawns in Men's Power Struggles*. London: Amnesty International.

Anonymous. (2018). *A Woman in Berlin*. London: Hachette UK.

Arendt, Hannah. (1970). *On Violence*. Orlando, FL: Harcourt Brace Jovanovich.

Ariana News (2020). MTN to quit Afghanistan, along with other Middle Eastern countries. *Ariana News*.

Arjona, Ana. (2015). Civilian resistance to rebel governance. In Ana Arjona, Nelson Kasfir, & Zachariah Cherian Mampilly (Eds.), *Civilian Resistance to Rebel Governance* (pp. 180–202). Cambridge: Cambridge University Press.

BIBLIOGRAPHY

Arjona, Ana. (2016). *Rebelocracy: Social Order in the Colombian Civil War*. Cambridge: Cambridge University Press.

Arjona, Ana. (2017). Civilian cooperation and non-cooperation with non-state armed groups: The centrality of obedience and resistance. *Small Wars & Insurgencies*, *28*(4–5), 755–78.

Asal, Victor, Flanigan, Shawn, & Szekely, Ora. (2020). Doing good while killing: Why some insurgent groups provide community services. *Terrorism and Political Violence*.

Asey, Tamim. (2019). The price of inequality: The dangerous rural–urban divide in Afghanistan. *Global Security Review*. Retrieved 21 January 2020 from https://globalsecurityreview.com/inequality-dangerous-rural-urban -divide-afghanistan/

Asia Foundation. (2006). *Afghanistan in 2006: A Survey of the Afghan People*. Kabul: Asia Foundation.

Asia Foundation. (2018). *Afghanistan in 2018: A Survey of the Afghan People*. Kabul: Asia Foundation.

Askew, Marc, & Helbardt, Sascha. (2012). Becoming Patani warriors: Individuals and the insurgent collective in southern Thailand. *Studies in Conflict & Terrorism*, *35*(11), 779–809.

Associated Press. (2016). A timeline of US troops in Afghanistan since 2001. *Associated Press*.

Atmar, Mohammad Hanif. (2001). *Politicisation of Humanitarian Aid and Its Consequences for Afghans*. Proceedings from Politics & Humanitarian Aid; Debates, Dilemmas & Dissension Conference, London.

Aydin, Aysegul, & Emrence, Cem. (2015). *Zones of Rebellion: Kurdish Insurgents and the Turkish State*. Ithaca, NY: Cornell University Press.

Azami, Dawood (2013). The 'dissenting' clerics killed in Afghanistan. *BBC*.

Bacon, Elizabeth E. (1951). The inquiry into the history of Hazara Mongols of Afghanistan. *Southwestern Journal of Anthropology*, 7, 230–47.

Baines, Erin, & Paddon, Emily. (2012). 'This is how we survived': Civilian agency and humanitarian protection. *Security Dialogue*, *43*(3), 231–47.

Baitenmann, Helga. (1990). NGOs and the Afghan War: The politicisation of humanitarian aid. *Third World Quarterly*, *12*(1), 62–85.

Barfield, Thomas. (2010). *Afghanistan: A Cultural and Political History*. Princeton, NJ: Princeton University Press.

Barfield, Thomas. (2011). Afghanistan's ethnic puzzle: Decentralizing power before the US withdrawal. *Foreign Affairs*, *90*(5), 54–65.

Barter, Sean J. (2012). Unarmed forces: Civilian strategy in violent conflict. *Peace and Change*, *37*(4), 544–71.

Barter, Sean J. (2015). Zones of control & civilian strategy in the Aceh conflict. *Civil Wars*, *17*(3), 340–56.

BIBLIOGRAPHY

Bazerman, Max H., Baron, Jonathan, & Shonk, Katherine. (2001). *You Can't Enlarge the Pie: Six Barriers to Effective Government*. New York: Basic Books.

Benson, Bruce L., & Siddiqui, Zafar R. (2014). *Pashtunwali*—Law for the lawless, defense for the stateless. *International Review of Law and Economics*, *37*, 108–20.

Berdal, Mats. (2019). NATO's Landscape of the mind: Stabilisation and state-building in Afghanistan. *Ethnopolitics, July*, 1–18.

Bhatia, Michael, Goodhand, Jonathan, Atmar, Haneef, Pain, Adam, & Suleman, Mohammed. (2003). *Profits and Poverty: Aid, Livelihoods and Conflict in Afghanistan*. London: Overseas Development Institute.

Bleuer, Christian (2014). The study and understudy of Afghanistan's ethnic groups: What we know—and don't know. Retrieved 11 October 2019 from https://www.afghanistan-analysts.org/the-study-and-understudy -of-afghanistans-ethnic-groups/

Bolt, Neville. (2012). *The Violent Image: Insurgent Propaganda and the New Revolutionaries*. London: Hurst.

Bonner, Michael David. (2006). *Jihad in Islamic History*. Princeton, NJ: Princeton University Press.

Borchgrevink, Kaja. (2007). *Religious Actors and Civil Society in Post-2001 Afghanistan*. Oslo: International Peace Research Institute (PRIO).

Boyle, Michael J. (2009). Bargaining, fear, and denial: Explaining violence against civilians in Iraq 2004–2007. *Terrorism and Political Violence, 21*(2), 261–87.

Brick, Jennifer. (2008). *The Political Economy of Customary Village Organizations in Rural Afghanistan*. Proceedings from the Annual Meeting of the Central Eurasian Studies Society, Washington, DC.

Brick Murtazashvili, Jennifer. (2016). *Informal Order and the State in Afghanistan*. Cambridge: Cambridge University Press.

Broschk, Florian. (2011). *Inciting the Believers to Fight: A Closer Look at the Rhetoric of the Afghan Jihad*. Kabul: Afghanistan Analysts Network.

Brown, Vahid, & Rassler, Don. (2013). *Fountainhead of Jihad: The Haqqani Nexus, 1973–2012* (Kindle edition). Oxford: Oxford University Press.

Byman, Daniel. (2007). *Understanding Proto-Insurgencies*. Washington, DC: RAND Corporation.

Cacioppo, John T., & Gardner, Wendi L. (1999). Emotion. *Annual Review of Psychology*, *50*, 191–214.

Callen, Michael, Isaqzadeh, Mohammad, Long, James D., & Sprenger, Charles. (2014). Violence and risk preference: Experimental evidence from Afghanistan. *The American Economic Review, 104*(1), 123–48.

Cameron, Lisa, & Shah, Manisha. (2015). Risk-taking behavior in the wake of natural disasters. *Journal of Human Resources, 50*(2), 484–515.

CARE. (2009). *Knowledge on Fire: Attacks on Education in Afghanistan*. Kabul: CARE.

Carmil, Devora, & Breznitz, Shlomo. (1991). Personal trauma and world view—Are extremely stressful experiences related to political attitudes, religious beliefs, and future orientation? *Journal of Traumatic Stress*, *4*(3), 393–405.

Carter, Stephen, & Clark, Kate. (2010). *No Shortcut to Stability: Justice, Politics and Insurgency in Afghanistan*. London: Chatham House.

Cassar, Alexandra, Grosjean, Pauline, & Whitt, Sam. (2013). Legacies of violence: Trust and market development. *Journal of Economic Growth*, *18*(3), 285–318.

Christia, Fotini. (2012). *Alliance Formation in Civil Wars*. Cambridge: Cambridge University Press.

Christia, Fotini, & Semple, Michael. (2009). Flipping the Taliban: How to win in Afghanistan. *Foreign Affairs, July/August*, 34–45.

Cialdini, Robert. (1993). *Influence: The Psychology of Persuasion*. New York: Morrow.

Clark, Kate. (2011). *The Layha: Calling the Taleban to Account, Appendix 1. The Taleban Codes of Conduct in English*. Kabul: Afghanistan Analysts Network.

CNN. (2009). Transcript of Obama speech on Afghanistan. *CNN*.

Coleman, James. (1988). Social capital in the creation of human capital. *American Journal of Sociology*, *94*, 95–120.

Coll, Steve. (2018). *Directorate S: The C.I.A. and America's Secret Wars in Afghanistan and Pakistan*. New York: Penguin Press.

Collier, Paul, & Hoeffler, Anke. (2004). Greed and grievance in civil war. *Oxford Economic Papers, 56*, 563–95.

Collinson, Sarah, & Duffield, Mark. (2013). *Paradoxes of Presence: Risk Management and Aid Culture in Challenging Environments*. London: Overseas Development Institute.

Connable, Ben, & Libicki, Martin C. (2010). *How Insurgencies End*. Washington, DC: RAND Corporation.

Cooper, Helene. (2017). U.S. says it has 11,000 troops in Afghanistan, more than formerly disclosed. *New York Times*.

Cordesman, Anthony. (2012). *The US Cost of the Afghan War 2002–2013: Cost in Military Operating Expenditures and Aid, and Prospects for 'Transition'*. Washington, DC: Center for Strategic and International Studies.

Cordesman, Anthony. (2017). *The Afghan War: Key Developments and Metrics*. Washington, DC: Center for Strategic and International Studies.

Crawford, Neta C. (2020). *Afghanistan's Rising Civilian Death Toll Due to Airstrikes, 2017–2020*. Providence, RI: Brown University.

Crombe, Xavier with Hofman, Michiel. (2012) Afghanistan. Regaining leverage. In Claire Magone, Michaël Neuman, & Fabrice Weissman (Eds.),

BIBLIOGRAPHY

Humanitarian Negotiations Revealed: The MSF Experience (pp. 49–68). London: Hurst.

Dahl, Robert A. (1957). The concept of power. *Behavioural Science*, *6*, 273–89.

de la Calle, Luis. (2017). Compliance vs. constraints: A theory of rebel targeting in civil war. *Journal of Peace Research*, *54*(3), 427–41.

De Luca, Giacomo, & Verpoorten, Marijke. (2015). Civil war, social capital and resilience in Uganda. *Oxford Economic Papers*, *67*(3), 661-686.

Deutsch, Morton. (1973). *The Resolution of Conflict*. New Haven, CT: Yale University Press.

Dohmen, Thomas, Falk, Armin, Huffman, David, Sunde, Uwe, Schupp, Jürgen, & Wagner, Gert G. (2011). Individual risk attitudes: Measurement, determinants and behavioral consequences. *Journal of the European Economic Association*, *9*(3), 522–50.

Donnell, John C. (1967). *Viet Cong Recruitment: How and Why Men Join*. Washington, DC: RAND Corporation.

Dorronsoro, Gilles. (2005). *Revolution Unending: Afghanistan, 1979 to the Present*. London: Hurst.

Dorronsoro, Gilles. (2009). *The Taliban's Winning Strategy in Afghanistan*. Washington, DC: Carnegie Endowment for International Peace.

Dupree, Louis. (1956). The changing character of south–central Afghanistan villages. *Human Organization 14*(4), 26–9.

Dupree, Louis. (1980). *Afghanistan*. Princeton, NJ: Princeton University Press.

Echavez, Chona. (2016). *The Political Economy of Education and Health Service Delivery in Afghanistan*. Kabul: Afghanistan Research and Evaluation Unit.

Eckel, Catherine C., & Grossman, Philip J. (2002). Sex differences and statistical stereotyping in attitudes toward financial risk. *Evolution and Human Behavior*, *23*(4), 281–95.

Edwards, David B. (2002). *Before Taliban: Genealogies of the Afghan Jihad*. Berkeley, CA: University of California Press.

Englehart, Neil A. (2010). A tale of two Afghanistans: Comparative governance and insurgency in the north and south. *Asian Survey*, *50*(4), 735–58.

Faley, Thomas, & Tedeschi, James T. (1971). Status and reactions to threats. *Journal of Personality and Social Psychology*, *17*, 192–9.

Fall, Bernard B. (1994). *Street Without Joy: The French Debacle in Indochina* (Kindle edition). Mechanicsburg, PA: Stackpole Books.

Fall, Bernard B. (2000). *Last Reflections on a War* (Kindle edition). Mechanicsburg, PA: Stackpole Books.

Fanon, Frantz. (1967). *The Wretched of the Earth*. Harmondsworth, UK: Penguin.

Farrell, Theo, & Giustozzi, Antonio. (2013). The Taliban at war: Inside the Helmand insurgency, 2004–2012. *International Affairs*, *89*(3), 845–71.

Farrell, Theo, & Semple, Michael. (2017). *Ready for Peace? The Afghan Taliban after a Decade of War*. London: Royal United Services Institute for Defence and Security Studies.

Farwell, James P. (2012). *Persuasion and Power: The Art of Strategic Communication*. Washington, DC: Georgetown University Press.

Fearon, James D. (1995). Rationalist explanations for war. *International Organization*, *49*(Summer), 379–414.

Fein, Helen. (1993). Discriminating genocide from war crimes: Vietnam and Afghanistan re-examined. *Denver Journal of International Law and Policy*, *22*, 29–62.

Felbab-Brown, Vanda. (2017). Afghanistan's opium production is through the roof—here's why Washington shouldn't overreact. *Brookings Institute* (blog), 21 November.

Fisher, Roger, & Ury, William. (1991). *Getting to Yes*. New York: Random House.

Fishstein, Paul, & Wilder, Andrew. (2011). *Winning Hearts and Minds? Examining the Relationship Between Aid and Security in Afghanistan*. Medford, MA: Tufts University.

Forsberg, Carl. (2009). *The Taliban's Campaign for Kandahar*. Washington, DC: Institute for the Study of War.

Förster, Till. (2015). Dialogue direct: Rebel governance and civil order in northern Côte d'Ivoire. In Ana Arjona, Nelson Kasfir, & Zachariah Cherian Mampilly (Eds.), *Rebel Governance in Civil Wars* (pp. 203–25). New York: Cambridge University Press.

Foucault, Michel. (2015). *The Punitive Society: Lectures at the Collège de France, 1972–1973*. New York: Palgrave Macmillan.

Foxley, Tim. (2007). *The Taliban's Propaganda Activities: How Well Is the Afghan Insurgency Communicating and What Is It Saying?* Stockholm: Stockholm International Peace Research Institute.

Gall, Carlotta (2006). Taliban rebels still menacing Afghan south. *New York Times*.

Gambetta, Diego (Ed.). (2005). *Making Sense of Suicide Missions*. Oxford: Oxford University Press.

Gaston, Erica. (2009). *Losing the People: The Costs and Consequences of Civilian Suffering in Afghanistan*. Washington, DC: Center for Civilians in Conflict.

Gates, Scott. (2017). Membership matters: Coerced recruits and rebel allegiance. *Journal of Peace Research*, *54*(5), 674–86.

Gebauer, Matthias. (2007). Taliban leader Mullah Dadullah: The star of Afghanistan's jihad. *Der Spiegel*.

BIBLIOGRAPHY

Ghani, Ashraf. (1978). Islam and state-building in a tribal society—Afghanistan: 1880–1901. *Modern Asian Studies, 12*(2), 269–84.

Ghiasy, Richard, Zhou, Jiayi, & Hallgren, Henrik. (2015). *Afghanistan's Private Sector: Status and Ways Forward.* Stockholm: Stockholm International Peace Research Institute.

Gibbons-Neff, Thomas, & Cooper, Helene. (2018). Newest U.S. Strategy in Afghanistan Mirrors Past Plans for Retreat. *New York Times.*

Gibbons-Neff, Thomas, & Mashal, Mujib. (2018). U.S. to withdraw about 7,000 troops from Afghanistan, officials say. *New York Times.*

Gibbons-Neff, Thomas, & Mashal, Mujib (2019). U.S. heightens attacks on Taliban in push toward peace in Afghanistan. *New York Times.*

Giustozzi, Antonio. (2008). *Quran, Kalashnikov, and Laptop: The Neo-Taliban Insurgency in Afghanistan.* New York: Columbia University Press.

Giustozzi, Antonio. (2010). *Nation-Building Is Not for All: The Politics of Education in Afghanistan.* Kabul: Afghanistan Analysts Network.

Giustozzi, Antonio. (2012). *Taliban Networks in Afghanistan.* Newport, RI: US Naval War College.

Giustozzi, Antonio. (2017). *Afghanistan: Taliban's Intelligence and the Intimidation Campaign.* Oslo: Landinfo.

Giustozzi, Antonio. (2018). Two campaigns for the labs: Heroin, Taliban and the US. Retrieved 8 March 2019 from https://www.crpaweb.org/single-post/2018/08/12/briefing-paper-two-campaigns-for-the-labs-heroin-taliban-and-the-us-antonio-giustozzi

Giustozzi, Antonio. (2019). *The Taliban at War.* London: Hurst.

Giustozzi, Antonio, & Baczko, Adam. (2014). The politics of the Taliban's shadow judiciary, 2003–2013. *Central Asian Affairs, 1*(2), 199–224.

Giustozzi, Antonio, & Franco, Claudio. (2012). *The Battle for Schools: The Taliban and State Education.* Kabul: Afghanistan Analysts Network.

Giustozzi, Antonio, & Franco, Claudio. (2016). Revolution in the counter-revolution: Efforts to centralize the Taliban's military leadership. *Central Asian Affairs, 3*(3), 249–86.

Giustozzi, Antonio, Franco, Claudio, & Baczko, Adam. (2012). *Shadow Justice: How the Taliban Run Their Judiciary?* Kabul: Integrity Watch Afghanistan.

Giustozzi, Antonio, & Ibrahimi, Niamatullah. (2012). *Thirty Years of Conflict: Drivers of Anti-Government Mobilisation in Afghanistan, 1978–2011.* Kabul: Afghanistan Research and Evaluation Unit.

Giustozzi, Antonio, & Ullah, Noor. (2007). The inverted cycle: Kabul and the strongmen's competition for control over Kandahar, 2001–2006. *Central Asian Survey, 26*(2), 167–84.

Glatzer, Bernt. (1998). Is Afghanistan on the brink of ethnic and tribal disintegration? In William Maley (Ed.), *Fundamentalism Reborn? Afghanistan and the Taliban* (pp. 167–81). New York: New York University.

Global Partnership for Education. (2016). *Education Sector Analysis, Afghanistan, Volume I*. Washington, DC: Global Partnership for Education.

Goodwin, Jeff. (1997). The libidinal constitution of a high-risk social movement: Affectual ties and solidarity in the Huk Rebellion, 1946 to 1954. *American Sociological Review*, 62(1), 53–69.

Goodwin, Jeff. (2001). *No Other Way Out: States and Revolutionary Movements, 1945–1991*. Cambridge: Cambridge University Press.

Goodwin, Jonathan, & Skocpol, Theda. (1989). Explaining revolutions in the contemporary third world. *Politics and Society*, 17(4), 489–509.

Gopal, Anand. (2010). *The Battle for Afghanistan: Militancy and Conflict in Kandahar*. Washington, DC: New America Foundation.

Gopal, Anand. (2015). *No Good Men Among the Living: America, the Taliban, and the War Through Afghan Eyes* (Reprint edition). New York: Metropolitan Books.

Gopal, Anand, & Strick van Linschoten, Alex. (2017). *Ideology in the Afghan Taliban*. Kabul: Afghanistan Analysts Network.

Gouldner, Alvin W. (1960). The norm of reciprocity: A preliminary statement. *American Sociological Review*, 25, 161–78.

Guevara, Ernesto. (2018). *Guerrilla Warfare* (Kindle edition). Dead Authors Society.

Gutiérrez Sanín, Francisco, & Giustozzi, Antonio. (2010). Networks and armies: Structuring rebellion in Colombia and Afghanistan. *Studies in Conflict & Terrorism*, 33(9), 836–53.

Gutiérrez Sanín, Francisco, & Wood, Elisabeth Jean. (2014). Ideology in civil war: Instrumental adoption and beyond. *Journal of Peace Research*, 51(2), 213–26.

Hagan, Kevin R. (2009). *The Six Pillars of Influence: How Insurgent Organizations Manipulate Governments, Populations, and Their Operatives*. Master of Science in Information Systems and Operations. US Naval Postgraduate School, Monterey, California.

Halperin, Erin, & Schwartz, Drew. (2010). Emotions in conflict resolution and post-conflict reconciliation. *Les Cahiers Internationaux de Psychologie Sociale*, 87(3), 423–42.

Hansen, Stig. (2013). *Al-Shabaab in Somalia: The History and Ideology of a Militant Islamist Group*. Oxford: Oxford University Press.

Haque, Tobias Akhtar, Do Rosario Francisco, Maria Manuela, & Kerali, Henry G. R. (2019). *Financing Peace: Fiscal Challenges and Implications for a Post-Settlement Afghanistan*. Washington, DC: World Bank.

Harper, Mary. (2019). *Everything You Have Told Me Is True: The Many Faces of Al Shabaab*. London: Hurst.

Hatch Dupree, Nancy. (1998). Afghan women under the Taliban. In William

Maley (Ed.), *Fundamentalism Reborn? Afghanistan and the Taliban* (pp. 145–66). New York: New York University Press.

Hatch Dupree, Nancy. (2002). Cultural heritage and national identity in Afghanistan. *Third World Quarterly*, *23*(5), 977–89.

Hirose, Kentaro, Imai, Kosuke, & Lyall, Jason. (2017). Can civilian attitudes predict insurgent violence? Ideology and insurgent tactical choice in civil war. *Journal of Peace Research*, *51*(1), 47–63.

Hoffman, Frank G., & Crowther, G. Alexander. (2015). Strategic assessment and adaptation: The surges in Iraq and Afghanistan. In Richard D. Hooker & Joseph J. Collins (Eds.), *Lessons Encountered: Learning From the Long War* (pp. 89–164). Washington, DC: National Defense University Press.

Hoffmann, Kasper, & Verweijen, Judith. (2018). Rebel rule: A governmentality perspective. *African Affairs*, *118*(471), 352–74.

Hoover Green, Amelia. (2016). The commander's dilemma: Creating and controlling armed group violence. *Journal of Peace Research*, *53*(5), 619–32.

Horai, Joann, and Tedeschi, James T. (1969) 'Effects of Credibility and Magnitude of Punishment on Compliance to Threats.' *Journal of Personality and Social Psychology*, 12, 164-69.

Hovil, Lucy, & Werker, Erik. (2005). Portrait of a failed rebellion: An account of rational, sub-optimal violence in western Uganda. *Rationality and Society*, *17*(1), 5–34.

Hultman, Lisa. (2007). Battle losses and rebel violence: Raising the costs for fighting. *Terrorism and Political Violence*, *19*(2), 205–22.

Human Rights Watch. (1998). *Afghanistan: Massacre in Mazar-i-Sharif*. New York: Human Rights Watch.

Human Rights Watch. (2006). *Lessons in Terror: Attacks on Education in Afghanistan*. New York: Human Rights Watch.

Human Rights Watch. (2007). *The Human Cost: Consequences of Insurgent Attacks in Afghanistan*. New York: Human Rights Watch.

Human Rights Watch. (2015). *'Stop Reporting or We'll Kill Your Family' Threats to Media Freedom in Afghanistan*. New York: Human Rights Watch.

Independent Joint Anti-Corruption Monitoring and Evaluation Committee. (2017). *Ministry-Wide Vulnerability to Corruption Assessment of the Ministry of Education*. Kabul: Independent Joint Anti-Corruption Monitoring and Evaluation Committee.

International Committee of the Red Cross. (2009). *Views From Afghanistan: Opinion Survey, 2009*. Geneva: Ipsos/ICRC.

International Crisis Group. (2006). *Countering Afghanistan's Insurgency: No Quick Fixes*. Brussels: International Crisis Group.

International Crisis Group. (2008). *Taliban Propaganda: Winning the War of Words?* Brussels: International Crisis Group.

BIBLIOGRAPHY

ISAF. (2012a). *State of the Taliban* (internal report). Kabul: ISAF.

ISAF. (2012b). ISAF monthly data: Trends through August 2012. PowerPoint. Kabul: ISAF.

ISAF. (undated). *ISAF Commander's Counterinsurgency Guidance.* Kabul: ISAF.

Islamic Emirate of Afghanistan. (2006). *Jihadi Code of Conduct (Layha).*

Islamic Emirate of Afghanistan. (2007). *Message of Felicitation of Amir-ul-Momineen.*

Islamic Emirate of Afghanistan. (2016). *Invitation by Islamic Emirate to Workers of Invaders and Kabul Administration.*

Islamic Emirate of Afghanistan. (2018a). *New Generation and Our Collective Responsibility.*

Islamic Emirate of Afghanistan. (2018b). *Statement of Islamic Emirate Regarding Amnesty for Kabul Administration Employees Seeking Surrender.*

Islamic Supreme Council of America (2019). Jihad: A misunderstood concept from Islam—what jihad is, and is not. Retrieved 1 August 2018 from http://islamicsupremecouncil.org/understanding-islam/legal-rulings/5-jihad-a-misunderstood-concept-from-islam.html?start=9

Jackson, Ashley. (2010). *Quick Impact, Quick Collapse: The Dangers of Militarized Aid in Afghanistan.* Oxford: Oxfam.

Jackson, Ashley. (2016). *Seeing Like the Networked State: Subnational Governance in Afghanistan.* London: Secure Livelihoods Research Consortium.

Jackson, Ashley. (2018a). *Life Under the Taliban Shadow Government.* London: Overseas Development Institute.

Jackson, Ashley (2018b). The Taliban's Fight for Hearts and Minds. *Foreign Policy.* September/October issue.

Jackson, Ashley, & Amiri, Rahmatullah. (2019). *Insurgent Bureaucracy: How the Taliban Makes Policy.* Washington, DC: US Institute of Peace.

Jackson, Ashley, & Giustozzi, Antonio. (2012). Talking to the other side: Humanitarian engagement with the Taliban in Afghanistan. London: Overseas Development Institute.

Jackson, Ashley, & Minoia, Giulia. (2019). Access networks in Afghanistan. *Asian Survey,* 58(6).

Jackson, Ashley, & Weigand, Florian. (2020). Rebel rule of law: Taliban courts in the west and north-west of Afghanistan. London: Overseas Development Institute.

Jaffe, Greg. (2011). Gates says U.S. 'well-positioned' for some troop reductions in Afghanistan in July. *Washington Post.*

Jalali, Ahmad Ali, & Grau, Lester W. (1995). *The Other Side of the Mountain: Mujahideen Tactics in the Soviet–Afghan War.* Fort Leavenworth, KS: Foreign Military Studies Office.

Jennings, Colin, & Sanchez-Pages, Santiago. (2017). Social capital, conflict and welfare. *Journal of Development Economics,* 124, 157–67.

Jo, Hyeran. (2015). *Compliant Rebels: Rebel Groups and International Law in World Politics*. Cambridge: Cambridge University Press.

Johnson, Eric J., & Goldstein, Daniel. (2003). Do defaults save lives? *Science*, *302*, 1338–9.

Johnson, Thomas H. (2007). Financing Afghan terrorism: Thugs, drugs, and creative movements of money. In Jeanne K. Giraldo & Harold A. Trinkunas (Eds.), *Terrorism Financing and State Responses: A Comparative Perspective* (pp. 93–114). Stanford, CA: Stanford University Press.

Johnson, Thomas H. (2018). *Taliban Narratives: The Use and Power of Stories in the Afghanistan Conflict* (Kindle edition). Oxford: Oxford University Press.

Johnson, Thomas H., & Waheed, Ahmad. (2011). Analyzing Taliban *taranas* (chants): An effective Afghan propaganda artifact. *Small Wars & Insurgencies*, *22*(1), 3–31.

Jones, Seth G. (2017). *Waging Insurgent Warfare: From the Vietcong to the Islamic State*. Oxford: Oxford University Press.

Jose, Betcy, & Medie, Peace A. (2015). Understanding why and how civilians resort to self-protection in armed conflict. *International Studies Review*, *17*(4), 1–21.

Joseph, Dan, & Maruf, Harun. (2018). *Inside Al-Shabaab: The Secret History of Al-Qaeda's Most Powerful Ally*. Bloomington, IN: Indiana University Press.

Joshi, Madhav, & Quinn, Jason Michael. (2017). Who kills whom? The micro-dynamics of civilian targeting in civil War. *Social Science Research*, *63*, 227–41.

Kahneman, Daniel, & Tversky, Amos. (1979). Prospect theory: An analysis of decisions under risk. *Econometrica*, *47*, 263–91.

Kalyvas, Stathis N. (2006). *The Logic of Violence in Civil War*. Cambridge: Cambridge University Press.

Kalyvas, Stathis N., & Balcells, Laia. (2010). International system and technologies of rebellion: How the end of the Cold War shaped internal conflict. *American Political Science Review*, *104*(3), 415–29.

Kalyvas, Stathis N., & Kocher, Matthew A. (2007). How 'free' is free riding in civil wars?: Violence, insurgency, and the collective action problem. *World Politics*, *59*(2), 177–216.

Kantor, Paula, & Pain, Adam. (2012). Social relationships and rural livelihood security in Afghanistan. *Journal of South Asian Development*, *7*(2), 161–82.

Kaplan, Oliver. (2017). *Resisting War: How Communities Protect Themselves*. Cambridge: Cambridge University Press.

Kasfir, Nelson. (2005). Guerrillas and civilian participation: The National Resistance Army in Uganda, 1981–86. *Journal of Modern African Studies*, *43*(2), 271–96.

Kasfir, Nelson. (2015). Rebel governance—constructing a field of Inquiry: Definitions, scope, patterns, order, causes. In Ana Arjona, Nelson Kasfir, &

Zachariah Cherian Mampilly (Eds.), *Rebel Governance in Civil War* (pp. 21–46). New York: Cambridge University Press.

Keen, David. (2000). Incentives and disincentives for violence. In Mats Berdal & David Malone (Eds.). *Greed and Grievance: Economic Agendas in Civil Wars* (pp. 19–43). Boulder, CO: Lynne Rienner.

Keen, David. (2012). Greed and grievance in civil war. *International Affairs*, *88*(4), 757–77.

Kendall, Elisabeth. (2016). Al-Qaeda and the Islamic State in Yemen: A battle for local audiences. In Simon Staffell & Akil N. Awan (Eds.), *Jihadism Transformed: Al-Qaeda and Islamic State's Battle of Ideas*. London: Hurst.

Khalidi, Noor Ahmad. (1991). Afghanistan: Demographic consequences of war, 1978–1987. *Central Asian Survey*, *10*(3), 101–26.

Kilcullen, David. (2011). *The Accidental Guerrilla*. New York: Oxford University Press.

Kilcullen, David. (2013). *Out of the Mountains—The Coming Age of the Urban Guerrilla*. New York: Oxford University Press.

Kim, Young-Il, and Lee, Jungmin. (2014). The long-run impact of a traumatic experience on risk aversion. *Journal of Economic Behavior & Organization*, *108*(C), 174–186.

Kipnis, David, Schmidt, Stuart M., & Wilkinson, Ian F. (1980). Intraorganizational influence tactics: Explorations in getting one's way. *Journal of Applied Psychology*, *65*(4), 440–52.

Knight, Jack, & Ensminger, Jean. (1998). Conflict over changing social norms: bargaining, ideology, and enforcement. In Mary C. Brinton & Victor Nee (Eds.), *The New Institutionalism in Sociology* (pp. 105–26). New York: Russell Sage Foundation.

Knowlton, Brian. (2001). Rumsfeld rejects plan to allow Mullah Omar 'to live in dignity': Taliban fighters agree to surrender Kandahar. *New York Times*.

Kochai, Jamil Jan. (2019). *99 Nights in Logar*. New York: Penguin Publishing Group.

Kolenda, Christopher D., Reid, Rachel, Rogers, Chris, and Retzius, Marte. (2016). *The Strategic Costs of Civilian Harm: Applying Lessons from Afghanistan to Current and Future Conflicts*. London: Open Society Institute.

Kotter, John. (1979). *Power in Management*. New York: AMACOM.

Krause, Jana. (2016). Non-violence and civilian agency in communal war: Evidence from Jos, Nigeria. *African Affairs*, *116*(463), 261–83.

Kydd, Andrew H., & Walter, Barbara F. (2002). Sabotaging the peace: The politics of extremist violence. *International Organization*, *56*(2), 263–96.

Laber, Jeri, & Rubin, Barnett R. (1988). *'A Nation is Dying': Afghanistan Under the Soviets, 1979–87*. Chicago, IL: Northwestern University Press.

Ladbury, Sarah. (2009). *Testing Hypotheses on Radicalisation in Afghanistan: Why*

BIBLIOGRAPHY

Do Men Join the Taliban and Hizb-i Islami?: How Much Do Local Communities Support Them. Kabul: Cooperation for Peace and Unity.

Lamer, Wiebke, & Foster, Erin. (2011). *Afghan Ethnic Groups: A Brief Investigation*. Brussels: NATO Civil–Military Fusion Center.

Landler, Mark, & Gordon, Michael R. (2017). As U.S. adds troops in Afghanistan, Trump's strategy remains undefined. *New York Times*.

Lawrence, T. E. (1920). Evolution of a revolt. *Army Quarterly*, *1*(1).

Le Duc, Carol, & Sabri, Homa. (1996). *Room to Manoeuvre: Study on Women's Programming in Afghanistan*. Islamabad: UNDP.

Leary, Kimberlyn, Pillemer, Julianna, & Wheeler, Michael. (2013). Negotiating with emotion. *Harvard Business Review*, *January/February*. Retrieved 25 September 2018 from https://hbr.org/2013/01/negotiating-with-emotion

Ledgerwood, Alison, Chaiken, Shelly, Gruenfeld, Deborah H., & Judd, Charles, M. (2006). Changing minds: Persuasion in negotiations and conflict situations. In Peter T. Coleman, Morton Deutsch, & Eric C. Marcus (Eds.), *The Handbook of Conflict Resolution: Theory and Practice* (pp. 455–85). San Francisco, CA: Jossey-Bass.

Ledwidge, Frank. (2017). *Rebel Law: Insurgents, Courts and Justice in Modern Conflict*. London: Hurst.

Leites, Nathan, & Wolf, Charles. (1970). *Rebellion and Authority: An Analytic Essay on Insurgent Conflicts*. Washington, DC: RAND Corporation.

Lewicki, Roy J., Barry, Bruce, & Saunders, David M. (2010). *Negotiation*. New York: McGraw-Hill.

Lidow, Nicholai Hart. (2011). *Violent Order: Rebel Organization and Liberia's Civil War*. Stanford University, Stanford, California.

Lindner, Evelin G. (2006). *Making Enemies: Humiliation and International Conflict*. Westport, CT: Greenwood Press and Praeger Publishers.

Lindskold, Svenn, Bonoma, Thomas, & Tedeschi, James T. (1969). Relative costs and reactions to threats. *Psychonomic Science*, *15*, 205–7.

Logan, Lara. (2018). Kabul under siege while America's longest war rages on. *60 Minutes*.

Lopez, C. Todd (2020). DOD Anticipates Significant Troop Reduction in Afghanistan. *US Department of Defense, Defense News*.

Lubold, Gordon, & Youssef, Nancy A. (2017). U.S. has more troops in Afghanistan than publicly disclosed. *Wall Street Journal*.

Ludhianvi, Mufti Rasheed. (2015). *Obedience to the Amir: An Early Text on the Afghan Taliban Movement* (Kindle edition). Berlin: First Draft Publishing.

Lyall, Jason (2015). Bombing to lose? Airpower, civilian casualties, and the dynamics of violence in counterinsurgency wars. Retrieved 9 January 2018 from https://www.du.edu/korbel/sie/media/documents/research_seminar_papers/lyall-airstrikes-apr2015.pdf

BIBLIOGRAPHY

Lyall, Jason, Blair, Graeme, & Imai, Kosuke. (2013). Explaining support for combatants during wartime: A survey experiment in Afghanistan. *American Political Science Review, 107*(4), 679–705.

Malejacq, Romain. (2019). *Warlord Survival: The Delusion of State Building in Afghanistan*. Ithaca, NY: Cornell University Press.

Maley, William. (2002). *The Afghanistan Wars*. New York: Palgrave.

Mampilly, Zachariah Cherian. (2011). *Rebel Rulers: Insurgent Governance and Civilian Life During War*. Cornell, NY: Cornell University Press.

Mampilly, Zachariah Cherian. (2015). Performing the nation–state: Rebel governance and symbolic Processes. In Ana Arjona, Nelson Kasfir, & Zachariah Cherian Mampilly (Eds.), *Rebel Governance in Civil War* (pp. 74–97). New York: Cambridge University Press.

Mansfield, David. (2016). *A State Built on Sand: How Opium Undermined Afghanistan*. Oxford: Oxford University Press.

Mansfield, David. (2017). *Understanding Control and Influence: What Opium Poppy and Tax Reveal about the Writ of the Afghan State*. Kabul: Afghanistan Research and Evaluation Unit.

Mansfield, David. (2018). *Bombing Heroin Labs in Afghanistan: The Latest Act in the Theatre of Counternarcotics*. London: London School of Economics International Drug Policy Unit.

Martin, Mike. (2014). *An Intimate War: An Oral History of the Helmand Conflict, 1978–2012* (Kindle edition). Oxford: Oxford University Press.

Mason, David T. (1989). Nonelite response to state-sanctioned terror. *Western Political Quarterly, 42*(4), 476–92.

Mason, David T. (1996). Insurgency, counterinsurgency, and the rational peasant. *Public Choice, 86*(1–2), 63–83.

Mason, David T., and Fett, Patrick J. (1996). How civil wars end: A rational choice approach. *Journal of Conflict Resolution, 40*(4), 546–68.

Mao Tse-Tung. (2011). *Selected Military Writings of Mao Tse-Tung*. Seattle, WA: Praetorian Press.

McDoom, Omar Shahabudin. (2012). The psychology of threat in intergroup conflict: Emotions, rationality, and opportunity in the Rwandan genocide. *International Security, 37*(2), 119–55.

Metelits, Claire. (2009). *Inside Insurgency: Violence, Civilians, and Revolutionary Group Behavior*. New York: New York University Press.

Metz, Steven. (2012). Psychology of participation in insurgency. *Small Wars Journal, January*, online. Retrieved 28 February 2019 from http://smallwarsjournal.com/print/12195

Meyer, Christina. (1991). *Underground Voices: Insurgent Propaganda in El Salvador, Nicaragua, and Peru*. Santa Monica, CA: RAND Corporation.

Mitchell, David F. (2017). NGO presence and activity in Afghanistan, 2000–2014: A provincial-level dataset. *Stability: International Journal of Security and*

Development, 6(1). Retrieved 5 April 2019 from https://www.stabilityjournal.org/articles/10.5334/sta.497/

Mitton, Kieran. (2015). *Rebels in a Rotten State: Understanding Atrocity in the Sierra Leone Civil War*. Oxford: Oxford University Press.

Molina, Ezequiel, Trako, Iva, Hosseini Matin, Anahita, Masood, Eema, & Viollaz, Mariana. (2018). *The Learning Crisis in Afghanistan: Results of the SABER Service Delivery Survey, 2017*. Washington, DC: World Bank.

Moya, Andres. (2018). Violence, psychological trauma, and risk attitudes: Evidence from victims of violence in Colombia. *Journal of Development Economics*, 131(C), 15–27.

Nagl, John A. (2006). Foreword. In David Galula (Ed.), *Counterinsurgency Warfare: Theory and Practice* (Kindle edition). Westport, CT: Praeger Security International.

Neale, Margaret A., & Bazerman, Max H. (1992). Negotiator cognition and rationality: A behavioral decision theory perspective. *Organizational Behavior and Human Decision Processes*, 51(2), 157–75.

Newell, Richard S. (1972). *The Politics of Afghanistan*. Ithaca, NY: Cornell University Press.

Nikolaev, Alexander G. (2007). *International Negotiations: Theory, Practice, and the Connection with Domestic Politics*. Lanham, MD: Lexington Books.

Nojumi, Neamatollah, Mazurana, Dyan, & Stites, Elizabeth. (2008). *After the Taliban: Life and Security in Rural Afghanistan*. Ithaca, NY: Rowman & Littlefield Publishers.

Nordstrom, Carolyn. (1997). *A Different Kind of War Story*. Philadelphia, PA: University of Pennsylvania Press.

Norton-Taylor, Richard and Walsh, Declan. (2006). Alarm grows over missions as three more soldiers die. *Guardian*.

Norwegian Refugee Council. (2018). *Principles Under Pressure: The Impact of Counterterrorism Measures and Preventing/Countering Violent Extremism on Principled Humanitarian Action*. Oslo: Norwegian Refugee Council.

Open Society Foundations and The Liaison Office. (2011). *The Cost of Kill/ Capture: Impact of the Night Raid Surge on Afghan Civilians*. Kabul: Open Society Foundations and The Liaison Office.

Ortmann, Andreas, Fitzgerald, John, & Boeing, Carl. (2000). Trust, reciprocity and social history: A re-examination. *Experimental Economics*, 3, 81–100.

Pain, Adam. (2012). *Livelihoods, Basic Services and Social Protection in Afghanistan*. London: Secure Livelihoods Research Consortium.

Pain, Adam. (2016). *Using Village Context Analysis in Afghanistan: Methods and Wider Implications*. London: Secure Livelihoods Research Consortium.

Pain, Adam, & Kantor, Paula. (2010). *Understanding and Addressing Context in Rural Afghanistan: How Villages Differ and Why*. Kabul: Afghanistan Research and Evaluation Unit.

Pajhwok. (2017). Taliban collecting tax from Farah landowners. *Pajhwok*. Retrieved 6 April 2018 from https://www.pajhwok.com/en/2017/04/18/taliban-collecting-tax-farah-landowners

Pajhwok. (2016). Insurgents impose tax on Helmand land owners: Public reps. *Pajhwok*. Retrieved 6 April 2018 from https://www.pajhwok.com/en/2016/01/05/insurgents-impose-tax-helmand-land-owners-public-reps

Parkinson, Sarah Elizabeth. (2013). Organizing rebellion: Rethinking high-risk mobilization and social networks in war. *American Political Science Review, 107*(3), 418–32.

Petersen, Roger D. (2002). *Understanding Ethnic Violence: Fear, Hatred, and Resentment in Twentieth-Century Eastern Europe*. Cambridge: Cambridge University Press.

Peterson, Scott. (2017). How Taliban are evolving to compete in Afghanistan. *Christian Science Monitor*.

Petraeus, David, & Serchuk, Vance. (2019). The U.S. abandoned Iraq. Don't repeat history in Afghanistan. *Wall Street Journal*.

Pillutla, Madan M., Malhotra, Deepak, & Murnighan, J. Keith. (2003). Attributions of trust and the calculus of reciprocity. *Journal of Experimental Social Psychology, 39*, 448–55.

Podder, Sukanya. (2017). Understanding the legitimacy of armed groups: A relational perspective. *Small Wars & Insurgencies, 28*(4–5), 686–708.

Putnam, Robert D. (2001). *Bowling Alone: The Collapse and Revival of American Community*. New York: Simon and Schuster.

Raleigh, Clionadh. (2012). Violence against civilians: A disaggregated analysis. *International Interactions, 38*(4), 462–81.

Rashid, Ahmed. (2001). *Taliban: The Story of Afghan Warlords*. London: Pan Books.

Ratelle, Jean-François, & Souleimanov, Emil Aslan. (2017). Retaliation in rebellion: The missing link to explaining insurgent violence in Dagestan. *Terrorism and Political Violence, 29*(4), 573–92.

Reno, Will. (2015). Predatory rebellions and governance: The National Patriotic Front of Liberia, 1989–1992. In Ana Arjona, Nelson Kasfir, & Zachariah Cherian Mampilly (Eds.), *Rebel Governance in Civil War* (pp. 265–85). New York: Cambridge University Press.

Reuters. (2003). Taliban concedes killing UN Worker. *Reuters*.

Revkin, Mara, & Ahram, Ariel I. (2017). Exit, voice, and loyalty under the Islamic State. In Lauren Baker (Ed.), *Islam in a Changing Middle East: Adaptation Strategies of Islamist Movements* (pp. 26–30). Washington, DC: Project on Middle East Political Science, George Washington University.

Ritov, Ilana, & Baron, Jonathan. (1990). Reluctance to vaccinate: Omission bias and ambiguity. *Journal of Behavioral Decision Making, 3*(4), 263–77.

BIBLIOGRAPHY

Roberts, Dan. (2016). Obama delays US troop withdrawal from 'precarious' Afghanistan. *The Guardian*.

Roggio, Bill, & Gutowski, Alexandra. (2019). Mapping Taliban control in Afghanistan. Retrieved 1 December 2019 from https://www.longwarjournal.org/mapping-taliban-control-in-afghanistan

Rohner, Dominic, Thoenig, Mathias, & Zilibotti, Fabrizio. (2013). Seeds of distrust: Conflict in Uganda. *Journal of Economic Growth*, *18*(3), 217–52.

Roy, Olivier. (1990). *Islam and Resistance in Afghanistan*. Cambridge: Cambridge University Press.

Rubin, Barnett. (2002). *The Fragmentation of Afghanistan: State Formation and Collapse in the International System*. New Haven, CT: Yale University Press.

Ruttig, Thomas. (2009). *The Other Side, Dimensions of the Afghan Insurgency: Causes, Actors and Approaches to 'Talks'*. Kabul: Afghanistan Analysts Network.

Ruttig, Thomas. (2010). *How Tribal Are the Taleban? Afghanistan's Largest Insurgent Movement Between Its Tribal Roots and Islamist Ideology*. Kabul: Afghanistan Analysts Network.

Ruttig, Thomas. (2011). *Afghanistan's Not-So-Hermetic Rural-Urban Divide*. Kabul: Afghanistan Analysts Network.

Saikal, Amin. (1998). The Rabbani Government, 1992–1996. In *Fundamentalism Reborn? Afghanistan and the Taliban* (pp. 29–42). New York: New York University Press.

Salehyan, Idean, Siroky, David, & Wood, Reed M. (2014). External rebel sponsorship and civilian abuse: A principal-agent analysis of wartime atrocities. *International Organization*, *68*(3), 631–66.

Samuelson, William F., & Zeckhauser, Richard. (1988). Status quo bias in decision making. *Journal of Risk and Uncertainty*, *1*, 7–59.

Sanaullah. (2020). Effectiveness of civilians' survival strategies: Insights from the Taliban's insurgency (2007–09) in Swat Valley, Pakistan. *Global Change, Peace & Security 32*, 3, 275–96.

Schacter, Daniel L., Gilbert, Daniel T., Wegner, Daniel M., & Hood, Bruce. (2011). *Psychology: European Edition*. London: Palgrave Macmillan.

Schafer, Jessica. (2001). Guerrillas and violence in the war in Mozambique: De-socialization or Re-socialization. *African Affairs*, 100(399), 215–37.

Schievels, Jelte Johannes, & Colley, Thomas. (2020). Explaining rebel–state collaboration in insurgency: Keep your friends close but your enemies closer. *Small Wars & Insurgencies*, October, 1–33.

Schlichte, Klaus, & Schneckener, Ulrich. (2015). Armed groups and the politics of legitimacy. *Civil Wars*, *17*(4), 409–24.

Schmeidl, Susanne, & Maley, William. (2006). The case of the Afghan refugee population: Finding durable solutions in contested transitions. In Howard Adelman (Ed.), *Protracted Displacement in Asia: No Place to Call Home* (pp. 131–79). London: Ashgate Gower.

Schmitt, Eric, & Rohde, David. (2004). THE REACH OF WAR: AFGHANISTAN; Taliban fighters increase attacks, with troubling toll among G.I.'s and Afghans. *New York Times*.

Scott, James C. (1990). *Domination and the Arts of Resistance: Hidden Transcripts*. New Haven, CT: Yale University Press.

Sebenius, James K., & Lax, David A. (1991). Thinking coalitionally: Party arithmetic, process opportunism, and strategic sequencing. In H. P. Young (Ed.), *Negotiation Analysis* (pp. 153–91). Ann Arbor, MI: University of Michigan Press.

Semple, Kirk, & Lehren, Andrew W. (2008). 500: Deadly U.S. milestone in Afghan War. *New York Times*.

Sexton, Renard. (2016). Aid as a tool against insurgency: Evidence from contested and controlled territory in Afghanistan. *American Political Science Review*, *110*(4), 731–49.

Shah, Taimoor, & Gall, Carlotta. (2007). Key Taliban leader is killed in Afghanistan in joint operation. *New York Times*.

Shahrani, M. Nazif, & Canfield, Robert L. (1984). *Revolutions and Rebellions in Afghanistan: Anthropological Perspectives*. Berkeley, CA: University of California.

Shapiro, Daniel. (2004). Emotions in negotiation: Peril or promise. *Marquette Law Review*, *87*(4), 737–45.

Sharan, Timor. (2013). *The Network Politics of International Statebuilding: Intervention and Statehood in Post-2001 Afghanistan*. University of Exeter, Exeter.

Sharifi, Shoaib, & Adamou, Louise. (2018). Taliban threaten 70% of Afghanistan, BBC Finds. *BBC*.

Sherman, Jake, & DiDomenico, Victoria. (2009). *The Public Cost of Private Security in Afghanistan*. New York: Center on International Cooperation, New York University.

Shuja, Ahmad. (2011). How one op-ed explains American ignorance about Afghanistan. *UN Dispatch*.

Shultz, Richard. (1978). The limits of terrorism in insurgency warfare: The case of the Viet Cong. *Polity*, *11*(1), 67–91.

Slim, Hugo. (2008). *Killing Civilians: Method, Madness and Morality in War*. New York: Columbia University Press.

Smith, Josh. (2015). Afghans struggle to get injured off the front lines. *Stars and Stripes*.

Special Inspector General for Afghanistan Reconstruction. (SIGAR). (2012). *Quarterly Report to US Congress, April 30, 2012*. Washington, DC: SIGAR.

Special Inspector General for Afghanistan Reconstruction (SIGAR). (2017). *Reconstructing the Afghan National Defense and Security Forces: Lessons from the U.S. Experience in Afghanistan*. Washington, DC: SIGAR.

BIBLIOGRAPHY

Special Inspector General for Afghanistan Reconstruction. (SIGAR). (2018). *Private Sector Development and Economic Growth: Lessons from the U.S. Experience in Afghanistan.* Washington, DC: SIGAR.

Special Inspector General for Afghanistan Reconstruction. (SIGAR). (2019). *Quarterly Report to US Congress, January 30, 2019.* Washington, DC: SIGAR.

Stanikzai, Zainullah. (2018). Mullah Manan's killing to weaken insurgency in Helmand. *Pajhwok.*

Staniland, Paul. (2014). *Networks of Rebellion: Explaining Insurgent Cohesion and Collapse.* Cornell, NY: Cornell University Press.

Stern, Jessica. (2003). *Terror in the Name of God: Why Religious Militants Kill.* New York: Harper Collins.

Strick van Linschoten, Alex. (2016). *Mullah Wars: The Afghan Taliban Between Village and State, 1979–2001.* PhD. King's College London, London.

Strick van Linschoten, Alex, & Kuehn, Felix. (2011). *A Knock on the Door: 22 Months of ISAF Press Releases.* Kabul: Afghanistan Analysts Network.

Strick van Linschoten, Alex, & Kuehn, Felix. (2012a). *Lessons Learnt 'Islamic, Independent, Perfect and Strong': Parsing the Taliban's Strategic Intentions, 2001–2011.* Swindon: Arts and Humanities Research Council.

Strick van Linschoten, Alex, & Kuehn, Felix. (2012b). *The Poetry of the Taliban.* New York: Hachette.

Strick van Linschoten, Alex, & Kuehn, Felix. (2014). *An Enemy We Created: The Myth of the Taliban–Al Qaeda Merger in Afghanistan* (Reprint edition). Oxford: Oxford University Press.

Strick van Linschoten, Alex, & Kuehn, Felix. (2018). *The Taliban Reader: War, Islam and Politics in their Own Words.* Oxford: Oxford University Press.

Suarez, Carla. (2017). 'Living between two lions': Civilian protection strategies during armed violence in the eastern Democratic Republic of the Congo. *Journal of Peacebuilding and Development, 12*(3), 54–67.

Suhrke, Astri. (1990). Afghanistan: Retribalization of the war. *Journal of Peace Research, 27*(3), 241–6.

Suhrke, Astri. (2008). A contradictory mission? NATO from stabilization to combat in Afghanistan. *International Peacekeeping, 15*(2), 214–36.

Tedeschi, Richard G., & Calhoun, L. G. (2004). Posttraumatic growth: Conceptual foundations and empirical evidence. *Psychological Inquiry, 15*(1), 1–18.

Terpstra, Niels, & Frerks, Georg. (2017). Rebel governance and legitimacy: Understanding the impact of rebel legitimation on civilian compliance with the LTTE Rule. *Civil Wars, 19*(3), 279–307.

Thompson, Robert. (1966). *Defeating Communist Insurgency: The Lessons of Malaya and Vietnam.* New York: F. A. Praeger.

Thruelsen, Peter Dahl. (2010). The Taliban in southern Afghanistan: A localised insurgency with a local objective. *Small Wars & Insurgencies*, *21*(2), 259–76.

Tomsen, Peter. (2011). *The Wars of Afghanistan: Messianic Terrorism, Tribal Conflicts, and the Failure of Great Powers*. New York: PublicAffairs.

Trofimov, Yaroslav. (2010). Risky ally in the war on polio: The Taliban. *Wall Street Journal*.

UN General Assembly. (2010). *The Situation in Afghanistan and Its Implications for International Peace and Security: Report of the Secretary–General*. New York: UN General Assembly.

UN Office on Drugs and Crime. (2007). *Afghan Opium Survey*. Kabul: UN Office on Drugs and Crime.

UNAMA. (2014). *The Stolen Lands of Afghanistan and Its People, The Legal Framework*. Kabul: UNAMA.

UNAMA Human Rights. (2009). *Afghanistan Annual Report 2008: Protection of Civilians in Armed Conflict*. Kabul: UNAMA Human Rights.

UNAMA Human Rights. (2010a). *Afghanistan Annual Report 2009: Protection of Civilians in Armed Conflict*. Kabul: UNAMA Human Rights.

UNAMA Human Rights. (2010b). *Mid-Year Report 2010: Protection of Civilians in Armed Conflict*. Kabul: UNAMA Human Rights.

UNAMA Human Rights. (2011). *Afghanistan Annual Report 2010: Protection of Civilians in Armed Conflict*. Kabul: UNAMA Human Rights.

UNAMA Human Rights. (2012). *Afghanistan Annual Report 2011: Protection of Civilians in Armed Conflict*. Kabul: UNAMA Human Rights.

UNAMA Human Rights. (2013). *Afghanistan Annual Report 2012: Protection of Civilians in Armed Conflict*. Kabul: UNAMA Human Rights.

UNAMA Human Rights. (2014). *Afghanistan Annual Report 2013: Protection of Civilians in Armed Conflict*. Kabul: UNAMA Human Rights.

UNAMA Human Rights. (2017). *Afghanistan Annual Report 2016: Protection of Civilians in Armed Conflict*. Kabul: UNAMA Human Rights.

UNAMA Human Rights. (2018). *Afghanistan Annual Report 2017: Protection of Civilians in Armed Conflit*. Kabul: UNAMA Human Rights.

UNAMA Human Rights. (2019). *Afghanistan Annual Report 2018: Protection of Civilians in Armed Conflict*. Kabul: UNAMA Human Rights.

UNHCR. (1995). Statistical Yearbook Country Datasheet—Afghanistan 1995. Retrieved 3 May 2019 from http://www.unhcr.org/cgi-bin/texis/vtx/search?page=search&docid=44e5c7402&query =afghanistan %201995

UNHCR. (2005). *Searching for a Solution: 25 Years of UNHCR–Pakistan Cooperation*. Geneva: UNHCR.

US Army. (2009). *Handbook no. 09-27: Commander's Guide to Money as a Weapons System*. Washington, DC: Department of the Army.

US Army. (2014). *FM 3-24 MCWP 3-33.5 Insurgencies and Countering Insurgencies*. Washington, DC: Headquarters, Department of the Army.

BIBLIOGRAPHY

US Department of the Army. (2006). *Counterinsurgency (FM 3-24 MCWP 3-33.5)*. Washington, DC: Department of the Army.

US Government Accountability Office. (2012). *Afghanistan: Improvements Needed to Strengthen Management of U.S. Civilian Presence*. Washington, DC: Government Accountability Office.

US House of Representatives. (2010). *Warlord, Inc.: Extortion and Corruption Along the U.S. Supply Chain in Afghanistan*. Washington, DC: US House of Representatives.

USAID. (2004). *Afghanistan Reborn: Building Afghan Democracy*. Washington, DC: USAID.

USFOR-A Public Affairs. (2015). 2014 was a year of transition and drawdown for USFOR-A (Press release). *US Army*.

Valentino, Benjamin, Huth, Paul, & Balch-Lindsay, Dylan. (2004). Draining the sea: Mass killing and guerrilla warfare. *International Organization*, *58*(Spring), 375–407.

Voors, Maarten J., Nillesen, Eleonora E. M., Verwimp, Philip, Bulte, Erwin H., Lensink, Robert, & Van Soest, Daan P. (2012). Violent conflict and behavior: A field experiment in Burundi. *The American Economic Review, 102*(2), 941–64.

Weinstein, Jeremy M. (2006). *Inside Rebellion: The Politics of Insurgent Violence*. Cambridge: Cambridge University Press.

Weiss, Joshua N. (2015). From Aristotle to Sadat: A short strategic persuasion framework for negotiators. *Negotiation*, *31*(3), 211–22.

Wellman, Phillip Walter. (2018). The US has dropped more munitions in 2018 in Afghanistan than it has in any year in over a decade. *Stars and Stripes*.

Wily, Liz A. (2013). *Land, People and the State in Afghanistan 2002–2012*. Kabul: Afghanistan Research and Evaluation Unit.

Wolfe, Rebecca J., & Mcginn, Kathleen L. (2005). Perceived relative power and its influence on negotiations. *Group Decision and Negotiation*, *14*, 3–20.

Wood, Elisabeth Jean. (2003). *Insurgent Collective Action and Civil War in El Salvador*. New York: Cambridge University Press.

Wood, Reed M. (2010). *Competing for Control: Conflict Power Dynamics, Civilian Loyalties and Violence in Civil War*. Doctor of Philosophy in the Department of Political Science. University of North Carolina at Chapel Hill, Chapel Hill, North Carolina.

Wright, Julia E., & Bachmann, Michael. (2015). Inciting criminal violence: An examination of Al Qaida's persuasive devices in the digital world. *Journal of Terrorism Research*, *6*(2), 70–82.

Yousafzai, Sami. (2009). The Taliban's oral history of the Afghanistan War. *Newsweek*.

Zaeef, Abdul Salam. (2010). *My Life With the Taliban*. London: Hurst.

BIBLIOGRAPHY

Zartman, I. William. (1989). *Ripe for Resolution: Conflict and Intervention in Africa*. Oxford: Oxford University Press.

Zartman, I. William. (2000). Ripeness: The hurting stalemate and beyond. *International Conflict Resolution After the Cold War, 2*, 225–50.

Zartman, I. William. (2001). The timing of peace initiatives: Hurting stalemates and ripe moments. *Ethnopolitics, 1*(1), 8–18.

Zartman, I. William. (2015). Mediation: Ripeness and its challenges in the Middle East. *International Negotiation* 20(3), 479–93.

Zartman, I. William and Berman, Maureen. (1982). *The Practical Negotiator*. New Haven: Yale University Press.

INDEX

Aceh conflict, 216–17
Afghan forces, 1, 78, 119, 122, 154,
    158–9, 230n8
  responsibility for security, 74–5
  Taliban demobilisation efforts, 95
Afghan media, 12–13
  Taliban media attack (Jan 2016),
    232n52
Afghan police, 80, 93
Afghan War, 4, 9, 27, 70, 85
Afghanistan Independent Human
  Rights Commission (AIHRC), 89,
  101
Afghanistan
  aid ecosystem, 162–6
  black-market economy, 67
  Bonn Conference (Dec 2001), 67
  conflict experiences, 62–81
  education sector assessment (2017),
    135
  ethnic groups in, 53–6
  Gross Domestic Product (GDP),
    166
  insecurity, growth of (Jun 2003–Jun
    2006), 71f
  intelligence agencies, 167
  International intervention and
    nascent insurgency (2001–9),
    67–74

mobile phone and internet usage,
  117–18
mujahedeen government and civil
  war (1989–94), 64–5
opium cultivation and taxation,
  167, 198, 236n31, 236n33
opium economy, 166, 167
post-2001 years, 63, 64, 162
Provincial Reconstruction Teams
  (PRTs), 71, 72, 228–9n19
public healthcare, 134–6, 165,
  173–6
Russian occupation and civil war
  (1979–89), 57, 63–4
social, cultural and political history,
  10
Soviet forces withdrawal, 64
Soviet Union invasion of (Dec
  1979), 62, 63–4
Taliban schools attacks, 101–2, 104
telecommunications companies,
  172
Afghanistan (*continued*)
under Taliban rule (1994–2001),
  65–7, 128
'urban-rural divide', 56–7,
  227–8n3
US airstrikes, 19, 78, 90, 91f, 148
US troop surge, 74–8, 75f